On Core Mathematics

Grade 4

HOUGHTON MIFFLIN HARCOURT

Cover photo credit: Enio Berwanger/SambaPhoto/Getty Images

Printed in the U.S.A.

ISBN 978-0-547-57518-6

15 16 17 18 19 20 21 1409 19 18 17 16 15 14

4500481749 ^ B C D E F G

Table of Contents

Operations and Algebraic Thinking

Number and Operations in Base Ten

▶ **Use place value understanding and properties of operations to perform multi-digit arithmetic.**

Number and Operations – Fractions

Measurement and Data

▶ **Solve problems involving measurement and conversion of measurements from a larger unit to a smaller unit.**

▶ **Represent and interpret data.**

▶ **Geometric measurement: understand concepts of angle and measure angles.**

Geometry

▶ **Draw and identify lines and angles, and classify shapes by properties of their lines and angles.**

Name ______________________________

Lesson 1

COMMON CORE STANDARD CC.4.OA.1

Lesson Objective: Relate multiplication equations and comparison statements.

Algebra • Multiplication Comparisons

Tara has 3 times as many soccer medals as Greg. Greg has 4 soccer medals. How many soccer medals does Tara have?

Step 1 Draw a model.

Greg ○○○○

Tara ○○○○ ○○○○ ○○○○

Step 2 Use the model to write an equation.

$n =$ __3__ $\times$ __4__ **Think:** n is how many soccer medals Tara has.

Step 3 Solve the equation.

$n =$ __12__

So, Tara has __12__ soccer medals.

Draw a model and write an equation.

1. 4 times as many as 7 is 28.

____

2. 16 is 8 times as many as 2.

____

3. 3 times as many as 6 is 18.

____

4. 10 is 2 times as many as 5.

____

Name ______________________________

Lesson 1

CC.4.OA.1

Multiplication Comparisons

Write a comparison sentence.

1. $6 \times 3 = 18$

6 times as many as 3 is 18.

2. $63 = 7 \times 9$

_____ is _____ times as many as _____.

3. $5 \times 4 = 20$

_____ times as many as _____ is _____.

4. $48 = 8 \times 6$

_____ is _____ times as many as _____.

Write an equation.

5. 2 times as many as 8 is 16.

____

6. 42 is 6 times as many as 7.

____

7. 3 times as many as 5 is 15.

____

8. 36 is 9 times as many as 4.

____

9. 72 is 8 times as many as 9.

____

10. 5 times as many as 6 is 30.

____

Problem Solving REAL WORLD

11. Alan is 14 years old. This is twice as old as his brother James is. How old is James?

____

12. There are 27 campers. This is nine times as many as the number of counselors. How many counselors are there?

____

Name ______________________

Lesson 2

COMMON CORE STANDARD CC.4.OA.2

Lesson Objective: Solve problems involving multiplicative comparison and additive comparison.

Algebra • Comparison Problems

Jamie has 3 times as many baseball cards as Rick. Together, they have 20 baseball cards. How many cards does Jamie have?

Step 1 Draw a box with the letter n in it to show that Rick has an unknown number of cards. Jamie has 3 times as many cards as Rick, so draw three identical boxes to represent Jamie's cards.

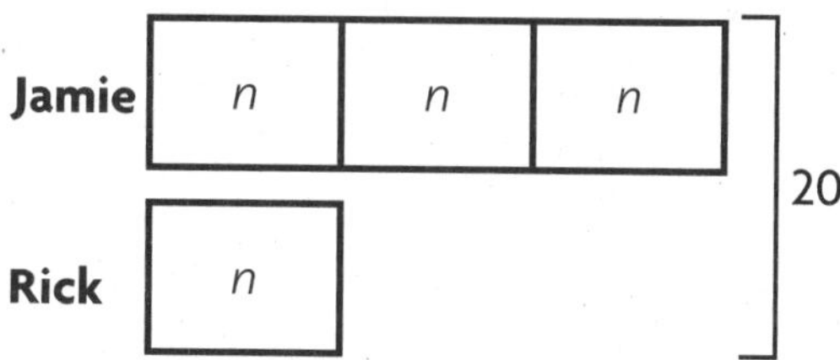

Step 2 Use the model to write an equation.

Think: There are 4 equal bars. The number in each bar is represented by n.

There are a total of 20 cards. So, __4__ $\times n =$ __20__.

Step 3 Solve the equation to find the value of n.

Think: 4 times what number is 20?

Since $4 \times$ __5__ $= 20$, the value of n is __5__.

Rick has __5__ cards.

Step 4 Find how many cards Jamie has.

Think: Jamie has 3 times as many cards as Rick.

So, Jamie has $3 \times$ __5__ $=$ __15__ baseball cards.

Draw a model. Write an equation and solve.

1. Maddie has 2 times as many stickers on her notebook as Meg. Together, they have 15 stickers. How many stickers are on Maddie's notebook?

____

2. How many more stickers are on Maddie's notebook than on Meg's notebook?

____

Name ______________________

Comparison Problems

Lesson 2

CC.4.OA.2

Draw a model. Write an equation and solve.

1. Stacey made a necklace using 4 times as many blue beads as red beads. She used a total of 40 beads. How many blue beads did Stacey use?

   Think: Stacey used a total of 40 beads. Let *n* represent the number of red beads.

   blue | *n* | *n* | *n* | *n* |
   red | *n* |
   40

   $5 \times n = 40$; $5 \times 8 = 40$;
   $4 \times 8 = 32$ blue beads

2. At the zoo, there were 3 times as many monkeys as lions. Tom counted a total of 24 monkeys and lions. How many monkeys were there?

   ____

3. Fred's frog jumped 7 times as far as Al's frog. The two frogs jumped a total of 56 inches. How far did Fred's frog jump?

   ____

4. Sheila has 5 times as many markers as Dave. Together, they have 18 markers. How many markers does Sheila have?

   ____

Problem Solving REAL WORLD

5. Rafael counted a total of 40 white cars and yellow cars. There were 9 times as many white cars as yellow cars. How many white cars did Rafael count?

   ____

6. Sue scored a total of 35 points in two games. She scored 6 times as many points in the second game as in the first. How many more points did she score in the second game?

   ____

Name ______________________

COMMON CORE STANDARD CC.4.OA.3

Lesson Objective: Use the *draw a diagram* strategy to solve multistep problems.

Problem Solving • Multistep Multiplication Problems

Use the strategy *draw a diagram* to solve a multistep multiplication problem.

Amy planted 8 rows with 18 tulips in each row. In each of the 4 middle rows, there are 4 red tulips. All of the other tulips are yellow. How many of the tulips are yellow tulips?

Read the Problem	Solve the Problem
What do I need to find? I need to find the total number of <u>yellow</u> tulips.	I drew a diagram for each color of tulip. 18 tulips; 4 rows; 8 rows; R R R R; R R R R; R R R R; R R R R; 4 tulips
What information do I need to use? There are <u>8</u> rows of tulips with <u>18</u> tulips in each row. There are <u>4</u> rows of tulips with <u>4</u> red tulips in each row.	Next, I found the number in each section. **All Tulips** $8 \times 18 = 144$ **Red Tulips** $4 \times 4 = 16$
How will I use the information? I can <u>multiply</u> to find the total number of tulips and the number of red tulips. Then I can <u>subtract</u> to find the number of yellow tulips.	Last, I subtracted the number of red tulips from the total number of tulips. <u>144</u> − <u>16</u> = <u>128</u> So, there are <u>128</u> yellow tulips.

1. A car dealer has 8 rows of cars with 16 cars in each row. In each of the first 3 rows, 6 are used cars. The rest of the cars are new cars. How many new cars does the dealer have?

   ____

2. An orchard has 4 rows of apple trees with 12 trees in each row. There are also 6 rows of pear trees with 15 trees in each row. How many apple and pear trees are in the orchard?

   ____

Name ______________________

Problem Solving • Multistep Multiplication Problems

Solve each problem.

1. A community park has 6 tables with a chessboard painted on top. Each board has 8 rows of 8 squares. When a game is set up, 4 rows of 8 squares on each board are covered with chess pieces. If a game is set up on each table, how many total squares are NOT covered by chess pieces?

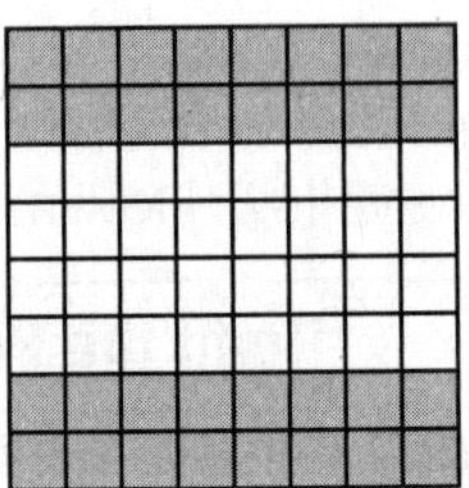

$4 \times 8 = 32$
$32 \times 6 = \square$

192 squares

2. Jonah and his friends go apple picking. Jonah fills 5 baskets. Each basket holds 15 apples. If 4 of Jonah's friends pick the same amount as Jonah, how many apples do Jonah and his friends pick in all? Draw a diagram to solve the problem.

____

3. There are 6 rows of 16 chairs set up for the third-grade play. In the first 4 rows, 2 chairs on each end are reserved for teachers. The rest of the chairs are for students. How many chairs are there for students?

____

Name ____________________

Lesson 4

COMMON CORE STANDARD CC.4.OA.3

Lesson Objective: Represent and solve multistep problems using equations.

Algebra • Solve Multistep Problems Using Equations

The **Order of Operations** is a special set of rules which gives the order in which calculations are done in an expression. First, multiply and divide from left to right. Then, add and subtract from left to right.

Use the order of operations to find the value of *n*.

$6 \times 26 + 3 \times 45 - 11 = n$

Step 1 Circle the first multiplication expression in the equation.

$\bigcirc(6 \times 26) + 3 \times 45 - 11 = n$

Step 2 Multiply 6×26.

$\underline{156} + 3 \times 45 - 11 = n$

Step 3 Circle the next multiplication expression in the equation.

$156 + \bigcirc(3 \times 45) - 11 = n$

Step 4 Multiply 3×45.

$156 + \underline{135} - 11 = n$

Step 5 There are no more multiplication or division expressions. Circle the first addition expression in the equation.

$\bigcirc(156 + 135) - 11 = n$

Step 6 Add $156 + 135$.

$\underline{291} - 11 = n$

Step 7 Subtract $291 - 11$.

$\underline{280} = n$

Find the value of *n*.

1. $5 \times 43 + 9 \times 24 + 25 = n$

______ $= n$

2. $7 \times 29 + 4 \times 46 - 56 = n$

______ $= n$

Name ______________________________

Solve Multistep Problems Using Equations

Find the value of *n*.

1. $4 \times 27 + 5 \times 34 - 94 = n$

   $108 + 5 \times 34 - 94 = n$

   $108 + 170 - 94 = n$

   $278 - 94 = n$

   $184 = n$

2. $7 \times 38 + 3 \times 45 - 56 = n$

   ______ $= n$

3. $6 \times 21 + 7 \times 29 - 83 = n$

   ______ $= n$

4. $9 \times 19 + 2 \times 57 - 75 = n$

   ______ $= n$

5. $5 \times 62 + 6 \times 33 - 68 = n$

   ______ $= n$

6. $8 \times 19 + 4 \times 49 - 39 = n$

   ______ $= n$

Problem Solving REAL WORLD

7. A bakery has 4 trays with 16 muffins on each tray. The bakery has 3 trays of cupcakes with 24 cupcakes on each tray. If 15 cupcakes are sold, how many muffins and cupcakes are left?

   ____

   ____

8. Katy bought 5 packages of stickers with 25 stickers in each package. She also bought 3 boxes of markers with 12 markers in each box. If she receives 8 stickers from a friend, how many stickers and markers does Katy have now?

   ____

   ____

Name ______________________

Lesson 5

COMMON CORE STANDARD CC.4.OA.3

Lesson Objective: Use the strategy *draw a diagram* to solve multistep multiplication problems.

Problem Solving • Multiply 2-Digit Numbers

A library ordered 17 cases with 24 books in each case. In 12 of the cases, 18 books were fiction books. The rest of the books were nonfiction. How many nonfiction books did the library order?

Read the Problem	Solve the Problem
What do I need to find? I need to find <u>how many nonfiction books</u> were ordered.	• First, find the total number of books ordered. <u>17</u> × <u>24</u> = <u>408</u> books ordered • Next, find the number of fiction books. <u>12</u> × <u>18</u> = <u>216</u> fiction books
What information do I need to use? <u>17</u> cases of <u>24</u> books each were ordered. In <u>12</u> cases, <u>18</u> books were fiction books.	• Last, draw a bar model. I need to subtract. 408 books ordered 216 fiction books ?
How will I use the information? I can find the <u>total number of books ordered</u> and the <u>number of fiction books ordered</u>. Then I can draw a bar model to compare the <u>total number of books</u> to the <u>number of fiction books</u>.	408 − 216 = <u>192</u> So, the library ordered <u>192</u> nonfiction books.

1. A grocer ordered 32 cases with 28 small cans of fruit in each case. The grocer also ordered 24 cases with 18 large cans of fruit in each case. How many more small cans of fruit did the grocer order?

____

____

2. Rebecca rode her bike 16 miles each day for 30 days. Michael rode his bike 25 miles for 28 days. Who rode farther? How much farther?

____

____

Name ______________________________

Problem Solving • Multiply 2-Digit Numbers

Lesson 5
CC.4.OA.3

Solve each problem. Use a bar model to help.

1. Mason counted an average of 18 birds at his bird feeder each day for 20 days. Gloria counted an average of 21 birds at her bird feeder each day for 16 days. How many more birds did Mason count at his feeder than Gloria counted at hers?

Birds counted by Mason: 18 × 20 = 360

Birds counted by Gloria: 21 × 16 = 336

Draw a bar model to compare.

Subtract. 360 − 336 = 24

360 birds counted by Mason

336 birds counted by Gloria

?

So, Mason counted __24__ more birds.

2. The 24 students in Ms. Lee's class each collected an average of 18 cans for recycling. The 21 students in Mr. Galvez's class each collected an average of 25 cans for recycling. How many more cans were collected by Mr. Galvez's class than Ms. Lee's class?

____

3. At East School, each of the 45 classrooms has an average of 22 students. At West School, each of the 42 classrooms has an average of 23 students. How many more students are at East School than at West School?

____

4. A zoo gift shop orders 18 boxes of 75 key rings each and 15 boxes of 80 refrigerator magnets each. How many more key rings than refrigerator magnets does the gift shop order?

____

Name ______________________

Lesson 6

COMMON CORE STANDARD CC.4.OA.3

Lesson Objective: Use remainders to solve division problems.

Interpret the Remainder

When you solve a division problem with a remainder, the way you interpret the remainder depends on the situation and the question.

Way 1: Write the remainder as a fraction. Callie has a board that is 60 inches long. She wants to cut 8 shelves of equal length from the board and use the entire board. How long will each shelf be? Divide. 60 ÷ 8 __7 r4__ The remainder, 4 inches, can be divided into 8 equal parts. $\frac{4}{8}$ ← remainder / ← divisor Write the remainder as a fraction. Each shelf will be $7\frac{4}{8}$ inches long.	**Way 2: Drop the remainder.** Callie has 60 beads. She wants to make 8 identical bracelets and use as many beads as possible on each bracelet. How many beads will be on each bracelet? Divide. 60 ÷ 8 __7 r4__ The remainder is the number of beads left over. Those beads will not be used. Drop the remainder. Callie will use __7__ beads on each bracelet.
Way 3: Add 1 to the quotient. Callie has 60 beads. She wants to put 8 beads in each container. How many containers will she need? Divide. 60 ÷ 8 __7 r4__ The answer shows that Callie can fill 7 containers but will have 4 beads left over. She will need 1 more container for the 4 leftover beads. Add 1 to the quotient. Callie will need __8__ containers.	**Way 4: Use only the remainder.** Callie has 60 stickers. She wants to give an equal number of stickers to 8 friends. She will give the leftover stickers to her sister. How many stickers will Callie give to her sister? Divide. 60 ÷ 8 __7 r4__ The remainder is the number of stickers left over. Use the remainder as the answer. Callie will give her sister __4__ stickers.

1. There are 35 students going to the zoo. Each van can hold 6 students. How many vans are needed?

   ____

2. Sue has 55 inches of ribbon. She wants to cut the ribbon into 6 equal pieces. How long will each piece be?

   ____

Name ____________________

Interpret the Remainder

Lesson 6
CC.4.OA.3

Interpret the remainder to solve.

1. Hakeem has 100 tomato plants. He wants to plant them in rows of 8. How many full rows will he have?

Think: $100 \div 8$ is 12 with a remainder of 4. The question asks "how many full rows," so use only the quotient.

12 full rows

2. A teacher has 27 students in her class. She asks the students to form as many groups of 4 as possible. How many students will not be in a group?

____

3. A sporting goods company can ship 6 footballs in each carton. How many cartons are needed to ship 75 footballs?

____

4. A carpenter has a board that is 10 feet long. He wants to make 6 table legs that are all the same length. What is the longest each leg can be?

____

5. Allie wants to arrange her flower garden in 8 equal rows. She buys 60 plants. What is the greatest number of plants she can put in each row?

____

Problem Solving

6. Joanna has 70 beads. She uses 8 beads for each bracelet. She makes as many bracelets as possible. How many beads will Joanna have left over?

____

7. A teacher wants to give 3 markers to each of her 25 students. Markers come in packages of 8. How many packages of markers will the teacher need?

____

Name ___________________________

COMMON CORE STANDARD CC.4.OA.3

Lesson Objective: Solve problems by using the strategy *draw a diagram.*

Problem Solving • Multistep Division Problems

There are 72 third graders and 84 fourth graders going on a field trip. An equal number of students will ride on each of 4 buses. How many students will ride on each bus?

Read the Problem	Solve the Problem
What do I need to find? I need to find the number of students who will ride on each bus.	I can model the number of students in all using a bar diagram. | 72 | 84 | 156
What information do I need to use? There are 72 third graders and 84 fourth graders. There will be 4 buses.	I can model the number of buses and divide to find the number of students on each bus. | 39 | 39 | 39 | 39 | 156
How will I use the information? I will make a bar diagram for each step. I will add 72 and 84 to find the total number of students. I will divide by 4 to find how many students will ride on each bus.	So, 39 students will ride on each bus.

1. Miranda has 180 beads for making jewelry. She buys 240 more beads. She wants to store the beads in a case with 6 sections. She wants to put the same number of beads in each section. How many beads should Miranda put in each section?

____

2. All 203 students at Polk School eat lunch at the same time. One day 19 students were absent. If 8 students sit at each table in the lunchroom, how many tables were used that day at lunch?

____

Name ________________________

Lesson 7
CC.4.OA.3

Problem Solving • Multistep Division Problems

Solve. Draw a diagram to help you.

1. There are 3 trays of eggs. Each tray holds 30 eggs. How many people can be served if each person eats 2 eggs?

Think: What do I need to find? How can I draw a diagram to help?

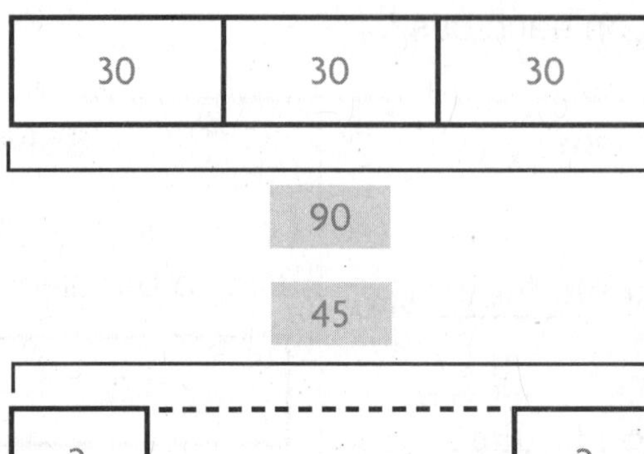

90

Multiply to find the total number of eggs.

Divide to find how many people can be served 2 eggs.

45 people can be served.

2. There are 8 pencils in a package. How many packages will be needed for 28 children if each child gets 4 pencils?

____

3. There are 3 boxes of tangerines. Each box has 93 tangerines. The tangerines will be divided equally among 9 classrooms. How many tangerines will each classroom get?

____

4. Misty has 84 photos from her vacation and 48 photos from a class outing. She wants to put all the photos in an album with 4 photos on each page. How many pages does she need?

____

Name ______________________

COMMON CORE STANDARD CC.4.OA.4

Lesson Objective: Find all the factors of a number by using models.

Model Factors

Use tiles to find all the factors of 25. Record the arrays and write the factors shown.

Step 1 Record the array and list the factors. **Think:** Every whole number greater than 1 has at least two factors, that number and 1.	$1 \times 25 = 25$ Factors: 1 , 25
Step 2 Make an array to see if 2 is a factor of 25. **Think:** An array has the same number of tiles in every row and the same number of tiles in every column.	 You cannot use all 25 tiles to make an array that has 2 rows. There is 1 tile left. So, 2 is not a factor of 25.

Step 3 Continue making arrays, counting by 1, to find all the other factors of 25.

Is 3 a factor?

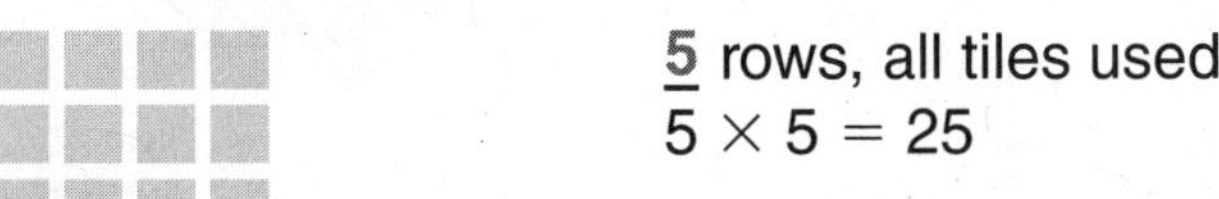

3 rows, 1 tile left

No, 3 is not a factor of 25.

Is 4 a factor?

4 rows, 1 tile left

No, 4 is not a factor of 25.

Is 5 a factor?

5 rows, all tiles used.

$5 \times 5 = 25$

There are the same number of tiles in each row and column. **Yes, 5 is a factor of 25.**

If you continue to make arrays up to 24, you will find there are no additional factors of 25.

So, the factors of 25 are **1, 5, and 25.**

Two factors that make a product are sometimes called a factor pair. What are the factor pairs for 25? **1 and 25, 5 and 5**

Use tiles to find all the factors of the product. Record the arrays and write the factors shown.

1. 35

____

2. 36

____

Name ____________________

Model Factors

Use tiles to find all the factors of the product.
Record the arrays on grid paper and write the factors shown.

1. 15

   $1 \times 15 = 15$

   $3 \times 5 = 15$

   1, 3, 5, 15

2. 30
3. 45
4. 19
5. 40
6. 36
7. 22
8. 4
9. 26
10. 49
11. 32
12. 23

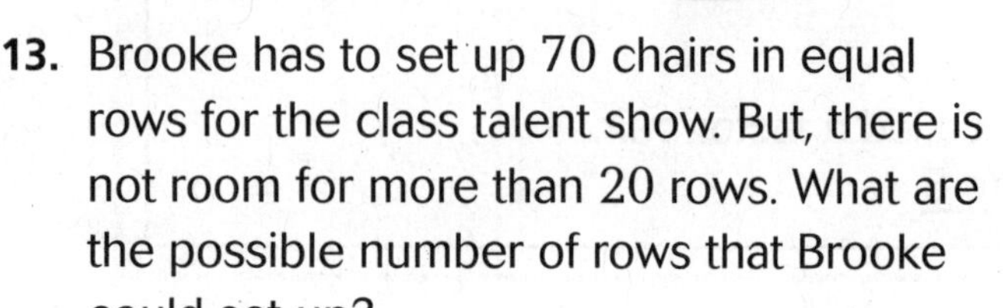

13. Brooke has to set up 70 chairs in equal rows for the class talent show. But, there is not room for more than 20 rows. What are the possible number of rows that Brooke could set up?

14. Eduardo thinks of a number between 1 and 20 that has exactly 5 factors. What number is he thinking of?

Name ____________________

Lesson 9

COMMON CORE STANDARD CC.4.OA.4

Lesson Objective: Determine whether a number is a factor of a given number.

Factors and Divisibility

A number is divisible by another number if the quotient is a counting number and the remainder is 0.
You can decide if a number is divisible by 2, 3, 5, 6, or 9 by using divisibility rules instead of dividing. Divisibility rules help you decide if one number is a factor of another.

Is 39 divisible by 2, 3, 5, 6, or 9?

	Result	Conclusion	Divisibility Rules
39 ÷ 2	19 r1	39 is not divisible by 2.	The last digit, 9, is not even, so 39 is not divisible by 2.
39 ÷ 3	13 r0	39 is divisible by 3.	The sum of the digits, 3 + 9 = 12, is divisible by 3, so 39 is divisible by 3.
39 ÷ 5	7 r4	39 is not divisible by 5.	The last digit, 9, is not a 0 or 5, so 39 is not divisible by 5.
39 ÷ 6	6 r3	39 is not divisible by 6.	39 is not divisible by both 2 and 3, so it is not divisible by 6.
39 ÷ 9	4 r3	39 is not divisible by 9.	The sum of the digits, 3 + 9 = 12, is not divisible by 9, so 39 is not divisible by 9.

39 is divisible by 3.
So, 3 is a factor of 39.

Use the chart to tell whether 30 is divisible by each divisor. Explain.

		Result	Conclusion (yes/no)	Explanation
1.	30 ÷ 2			
2.	30 ÷ 3			
3.	30 ÷ 5			
4.	30 ÷ 6			
5.	30 ÷ 9			

Is 4 a factor of the number? Write *yes* or *no*.

6. 81 ____________

7. 24 ____________

8. 56 ____________

Name ______________________

Lesson 9

CC.4.OA.4

Factors and Divisibility

Is 6 a factor of the number? Write *yes* or *no*.

1. 36

   Think: $6 \times 6 = 36$

   yes

2. 56 ______

3. 42 ______

4. 66 ______

Is 5 a factor of the number? Write *yes* or *no*.

5. 38 ______

6. 45 ______

7. 60 ______

8. 39 ______

List all the factor pairs in the table.

9.

Factors of 12	
___ × ___ = ___	___, ___
___ × ___ = ___	___, ___
___ × ___ = ___	___, ___

10.

Factors of 25	
___ × ___ = ___	___, ___
___ × ___ = ___	___, ___

11. List all the factor pairs for 48. Make a table to help.

____

____

Problem Solving 

12. Bryson buys a bag of 64 plastic miniature dinosaurs. Could he distribute them equally into six storage containers and not have any left over? **Explain**.

____

13. Lori wants to distribute 35 peaches equally into baskets. She will use more than 1 but fewer than 10 baskets. How many baskets does Lori need?

____

Name ______________________

COMMON CORE STANDARD CC.4.OA.4

Lesson Objective: Solve problems by using the strategy *make a list.*

Problem Solving • Common Factors

Susan sorts a collection of beads. There are 35 blue, 49 red, and 21 pink beads. She arranges all the beads into rows. Each row will have the same number of beads, and all the beads in a row will be the same color. How many beads can she put in each row?

Read the Problem	Solve the Problem
What do I need to find? I need to find the number of beads in each row, if each row is equal and has only one color.	
What information do I need to use? Susan has 35 blue, 49 red, and 21 pink beads.	
How will I use the information? I can make a list to find all of the factors of 35, 49, and 21. Then I can use the list to find the common factors.	The common factors are 7 and 1. So, Susan can put 1 or 7 beads in each row.

Factors of 35	Factors of 49	Factors of 21
1	1	1
5	7	3
7	49	7
35		21

1. Allyson has 60 purple buttons, 36 black buttons, and 24 green buttons. She wants to put all of the buttons in bins. She wants each bin to have only one color and all bins to have the same number of buttons. How many buttons can Allyson put in one bin?

____

2. Ricardo has a marble collection with 54 blue marbles, 24 red marbles, and 18 yellow marbles. He arranges the marbles into equal rows. The marbles in each row will be the same color. How many marbles can he put in one row?

____

Name ______________________________

Problem Solving • Common Factors

Lesson 10
CC.4.OA.4

Solve each problem.

1. Grace is preparing grab bags for her store's open house. She has 24 candles, 16 pens, and 40 figurines. Each grab bag will have the same number of items, and all the items in a bag will be the same. How many items can Grace put in each bag?

Find the common factors of 24, 16, and 40.

1, 2, 4, or 8 items

---

2. Simon is making wreaths to sell. He has 60 bows, 36 silk roses, and 48 silk carnations. He wants to put the same number of items on each wreath. All the items on a wreath will be the same type. How many items can Simon put on each wreath?

____

---

3. Justin has 20 pencils, 25 erasers, and 40 paper clips. He organizes them into groups with the same number of items in each group. All the items in a group will be the same type. How many items can he put in each group?

____

---

4. A food bank has 50 cans of vegetables, 30 loaves of bread, and 100 bottles of water. The volunteers will put the items into boxes. Each box will have the same number of food items and all the items in the box will be the same type. How many items can they put in each box?

____

---

5. A debate competition has participants from three different schools: 15 from James Elementary, 18 from George Washington School, and 12 from the MLK Jr. Academy. All teams must have the same number of students. Each team can have only students from the same school. How many students can be on each team?

____

Name ______________________________

Lesson 11

COMMON CORE STANDARD CC.4.OA.4

Lesson Objective: Understand the relationship between factors and multiples, and determine whether a number is a multiple of a given number.

Factors and Multiples

You know that $1 \times 10 = \underline{10}$ and $2 \times 5 = \underline{10}$.

So, 1, 2, 5, and 10 are all **factors** of $\underline{10}$.

You can skip count to find **multiples** of a number:

Count by 1s: 1, 2, 3, 4, 5, 6, 7, 8, 9, **10,** . . .

Count by 2s: 2, 4, 6, 8, **10,** 12, . . .

Count by 5s: 5, **10,** 15, 20, 25, . . .

Count by 10s: **10,** 20, 30, 40, . . .

Note that **10** is a multiple of 1, 2, 5, and 10. A number is a multiple of all of its factors.

A **common multiple** is a multiple of two or more numbers. So, 10 is a common multiple of 1, 2, 5, and 10.

1. Multiply to list the next five multiples of 3.

3, ____, ____, ____, ____, ____

2. Multiply to list the next five multiples of 7.

7, ____, ____, ____, ____, ____

Is the number a factor of 8? Write *yes* or *no*.

3. 2 ______ **4.** 8 ______ **5.** 15 ______ **6.** 20 ______

Is the number a multiple of 4? Write *yes* or *no*.

7. 2 ______ **8.** 12 ______ **9.** 16 ______ **10.** 18 ______

Name ______________________________

Factors and Multiples

Lesson 11
CC.4.OA.4

Is the number a multiple of 8? Write *yes* or *no*.

1. 4

Think: Since $4 \times 2 = 8$, 4 is a *factor* of 8, not a multiple of 8.

no

2. 8 ______

3. 20 ______

4. 40 ______

List the next nine multiples of each number. Find the common multiples.

5. Multiples of 4: 4, ______________________

Multiples of 7: 7, ______________________

Common multiples: ______________________

6. Multiples of 3: 3, ______________________

Multiples of 9: 9, ______________________

Common multiples: ______________________

7. Multiples of 6: 6, ______________________

Multiples of 8: 8, ______________________

Common multiples: ______________________

Tell whether 24 is a factor or multiple of the number. Write *factor, multiple,* or *neither*.

8. 6 ______________

9. 36 ______________

10. 48 ______________

Problem Solving REAL WORLD

11. Ken paid $12 for two magazines. The cost of each magazine was a multiple of $3. What are the possible prices of the magazines?

____

12. Jodie bought some shirts for $6 each. Marge bought some shirts for $8 each. The girls spent the same amount of money on shirts. What is the least amount they could have spent?

____

Name ____________________

Lesson 12

COMMON CORE STANDARD CC.4.OA.4

Lesson Objective: Determine whether a number is prime or composite.

Prime and Composite Numbers

A **prime number** is a whole number greater than 1 that has exactly two factors, 1 and the number itself.

A **composite number** is a whole number greater than 1 that has more than two factors.

You can use division to find the factors of a number and tell whether the number is prime or composite.

Tell whether 55 is *prime* or *composite*.

Use division to find all the numbers that divide into 55 without a remainder. Those numbers are the factors of 55.

$55 \div 1 = 55$, so 1 and 55 are factors.

$55 \div 5 = 11$, so 5 and 11 are factors.

The factors of 55 are 1, 5, 11, and 55.

Because 55 has more than two factors, 55 is a composite number.

Tell whether 61 is *prime* or *composite*.

Use division to find all the numbers that divide into 61 without a remainder. Those numbers are the factors of 61.

$61 \div 1 = 61$, so 1 and 61 are factors.

There are no other numbers that divide into 61 evenly without a remainder.

The factors of 61 are 1 and 61.

Because 61 has exactly two factors, 61 is a prime number.

Tell whether the number is *prime* or *composite*.

1. 44 ____________

   Think: Is 44 divisible by any number other than 1 and 44?

2. 53 ____________

   Think: Does 53 have other factors besides 1 and itself?

3. 12 ____________

4. 50 ____________

5. 24 ____________

6. 67 ____________

7. 83 ____________

8. 27 ____________

9. 34 ____________

10. 78 ____________

Name ____________________

Lesson 12

CC.4.OA.4

Prime and Composite Numbers

Tell whether the number is *prime* or *composite*.

1. 47

   Think: Does 47 have other factors besides 1 and itself?

   prime

2. 68 ____________

3. 52 ____________

4. 63 ____________

5. 75 ____________

6. 31 ____________

7. 77 ____________

8. 59 ____________

9. 87 ____________

10. 72 ____________

11. 49 ____________

12. 73 ____________

Problem Solving

13. Kai wrote the number 85 on the board. Is 85 prime or composite? **Explain.**

14. Lisa says that 43 is a 2-digit odd number that is composite. Is she correct? **Explain.**

Name ______________________

COMMON CORE STANDARD CC.4.OA.5

Lesson Objective: Generate a number pattern and describe features of the pattern.

Algebra • Number Patterns

A pattern is an ordered set of numbers or objects, called terms. The numbers below form a pattern. The first term in the pattern is 2.

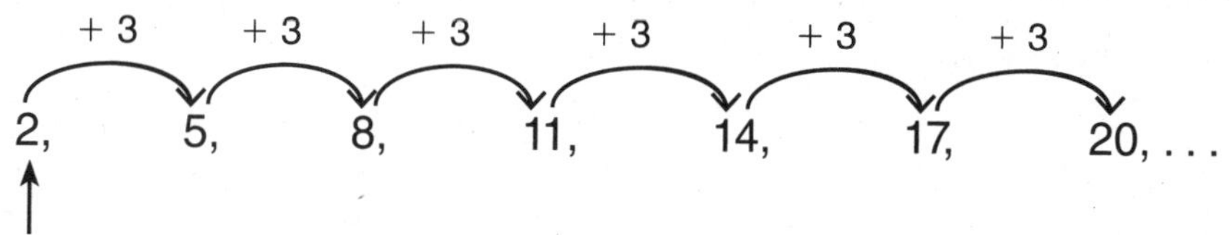

First term

A rule is used to describe a pattern. The rule for this pattern is ***add 3.***

You can describe other patterns in the numbers. Notice that the terms in the pattern shown alternate between even and odd numbers.

For some patterns, the rule may have two operations.

− 2, × 2, − 2, × 2, − 2, × 2

8, 6, 12, 10, 20, 18, 36, . . .

The rule for this pattern is ***subtract 2, multiply by 2.*** The first term is 8. Notice that all of the terms in this pattern are even numbers.

Use the rule to write the numbers in the pattern.

1. Rule: Add 7. First term: 12

12, ____, ____, ____, ____, . . .

2. Rule: Multiply by 3, subtract 1. First term: 2

2, ____, ____, ____, ____, . . .

Use the rule to write the numbers in the pattern.
Describe another pattern in the numbers.

3. Rule: Subtract 5. First term: 50

50, ____, ____, ____, ____, . . .

____

____

4. Rule: Multiply by 2, add 1. First term: 4

4, ____, ____, ____, ____, . . .

____

____

Name ____________________

Number Patterns

Use the rule to write the first twelve numbers in the pattern. Describe another pattern in the numbers.

1. Rule: Add 8. First term: 5

Think: Add 8.

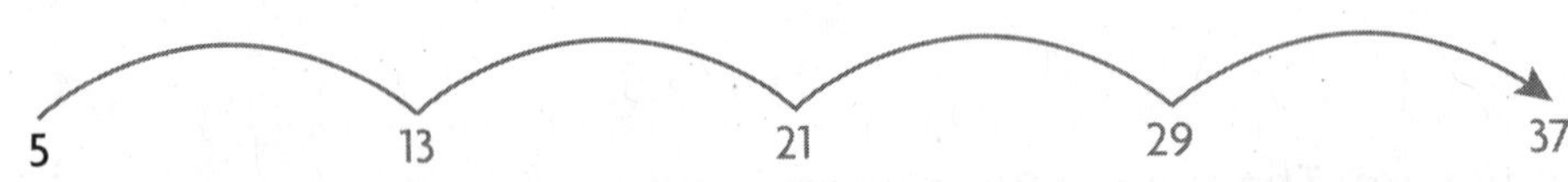

5, 13, 21, 29, 37, 45, 53, 61, 69, 77, 85, 93

All the terms are odd numbers.

2. Rule: Subtract 7. First term: 95

3. Rule: Add 15, subtract 10. First term: 4

4. Rule: Add 1, multiply by 2. First term: 2

Problem Solving REAL WORLD

5. Barb is making a bead necklace. She strings 1 white bead, then 3 blue beads, then 1 white bead, and so on. Write the numbers for the first eight beads that are white. What is a rule for the pattern?

6. An artist is arranging tiles in rows to decorate a wall. Each new row has 2 fewer tiles than the row below it. If the first row has 23 tiles, how many tiles will be in the seventh row?

Name ______________________________

Lesson 14

COMMON CORE STANDARD CC.4.OA.5

Lesson Objective: Use the strategy *act it out* to solve problems.

Problem Solving • Shape Patterns

Use the strategy *act it out* to solve pattern problems.

What might be the next three figures in the pattern below?

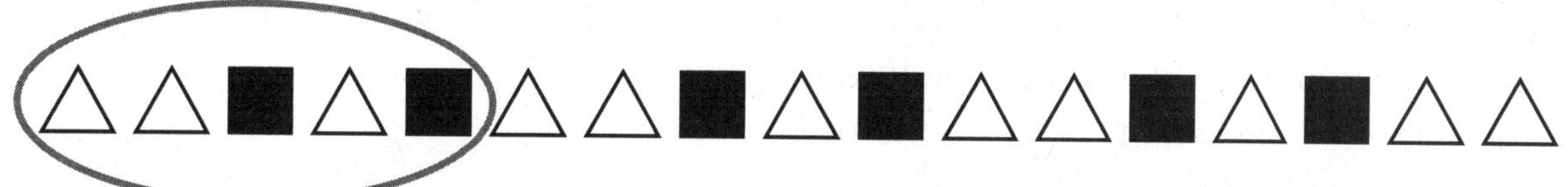

Read the Problem		
What do I need to find? I need to find the next three **figures** in the pattern.	**What information do I need to use?** I need to look for **a group of figures** that repeat.	**How will I use the information?** I will use pattern blocks to model the **pattern** and act out the problem.

Solve the Problem

Look for a group of figures that repeat and circle that group.

The repeating group is **triangle**, **triangle**, **square**, **triangle**, **square**.

I used **triangles** and **squares** to model and continue the pattern by repeating the figures in the group.

These are the next three figures in the pattern: 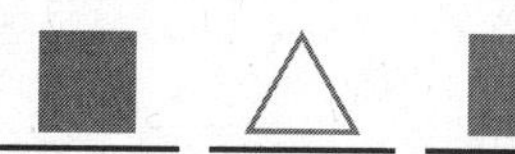

1. Describe the pattern shown at right. Draw what might be the next figure in the pattern.

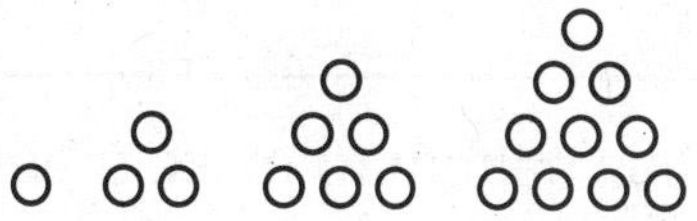

____

____

____

____

2. Use the pattern. How many circles will be in the sixth figure?

____

Name ______________________________

Problem Solving • Shape Patterns

Solve each problem.

1. Marta is using this pattern to decorate a picture frame. Describe the pattern. Draw what might be the next three figures in the pattern.

Possible answer: the pattern repeats: one triangle followed by two squares.

2. Describe the pattern. Draw what might be the next three figures in the pattern. How many circles are in the sixth figure in the pattern?

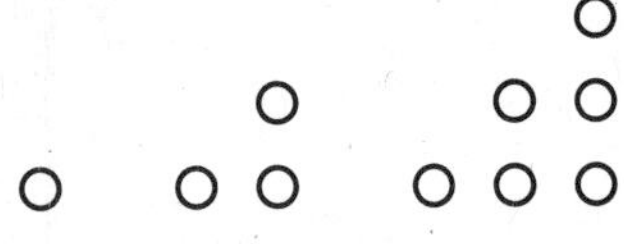

____

____

3. Larry stencils this pattern to make a border at the top of his bedroom walls. Describe the pattern. Draw what might be the missing figure in the pattern.

      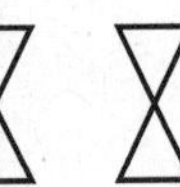    

____

____

Name ______________________

Lesson 15

COMMON CORE STANDARD CC.4.NBT.1

Lesson Objective: Model the 10-to-1 relationship among place-value positions in the base-ten number system.

Model Place Value Relationships

A hundred grid can help you understand place-value relationships.

- One small square has been shaded to represent 1.
- Shade the rest of the first column. Count the number of small squares. There are 10 small squares. The model for 10 has 10 times as many squares as the model for 1.
- Shade the remaining 9 columns. Count the number of small squares. There are 100 small squares. The model for 100 has 10 times as many squares as the model for 10.
- If you shade ten hundred grids, you will have shaded 1,000 squares. So, the model for 1,000 has 10 times as many squares as the model for 100.

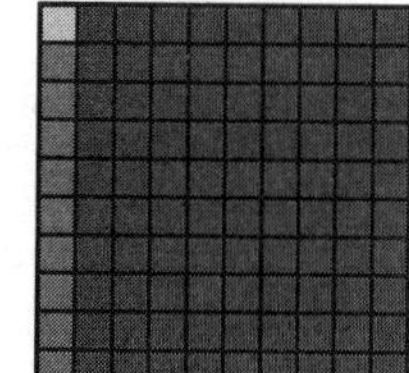

A place-value chart helps you find the value of each digit in a number.

THOUSANDS			ONES		
Hundreds	Tens	Ones	Hundreds	Tens	Ones
		8,	5	1	6

In the number 8,516:

The value of the digit 8 is 8 thousands, or 8,000.

The value of the digit 5 is 5 hundreds, or 500.

The value of the digit 1 is 1 ten, or 10.

The value of the digit 6 is 6 ones, or 6.

Find the value of the underlined digit.

1. 756 ______

2. 1,025 ______

3. 4,279 ______

4. 35,703 ______

Compare the values of the underlined digits.

5. 700 and 70

The value of 7 in ______ is ______ times the value of 7 in ______.

6. 5,000 and 500

The value of 5 in ______ is ______ times the value of 5 in ______.

Name ____________________

Lesson 15

CC.4.NBT.1

Model Place Value Relationships

Find the value of the underlined digit.

1. 6,0$\underline{3}$5 ____________
2. 43,$\underline{7}$82 ____________
3. 506,08$\underline{7}$ ____________
4. 4$\underline{9}$,254 ____________
5. 1$\underline{3}$6,422 ____________
6. 673,$\underline{5}$12 ____________
7. $\underline{8}$14,295 ____________
8. 73$\underline{6}$,144 ____________

Compare the values of the underlined digits.

9. 6,$\underline{3}$00 and 5$\underline{3}$0

   The value of 3 in ________ is _____ times the value of 3 in ________.

10. $\underline{2}$,783 and 7,$\underline{2}$83

    The value of 2 in ________ is _____ times the value of 2 in ________.

11. 3$\underline{4}$,258 and $\underline{4}$7,163

    The value of 4 in ________ is _____ times the value of 4 in ________.

12. 503,49$\underline{7}$ and 26,4$\underline{7}$5

    The value of 7 in ________ is _____ times the value of 7 in ________.

Problem Solving REAL WORLD

Use the table for 13–14.

13. What is the value of the digit 9 in the attendance at the Redskins vs. Titans game?

    ____

14. The attendance at which game has a 7 in the ten thousands place?

    ____

Football Game Attendance

Game	Attendance
Redskins vs. Titans	69,143
Ravens vs. Panthers	73,021
Patriots vs. Colts	68,756

Name ______________________

COMMON CORE STANDARD CC.4.NBT.1

Lesson Objective: Rename whole numbers by regrouping.

Rename Numbers

You can use place value to rename whole numbers.
Here are different ways to name the number 1,400.

- **As thousands and hundreds**

  Think: 1,400 = 1 thousand 4 hundreds.
  You can draw a quick picture to help.

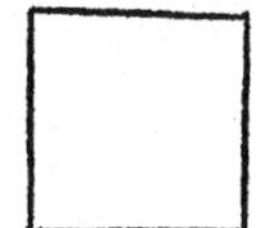

- **As hundreds**

  Think: 1,400 = 14 hundreds.
  You can draw a quick picture to help.

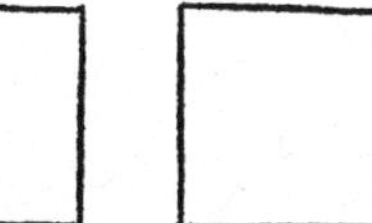

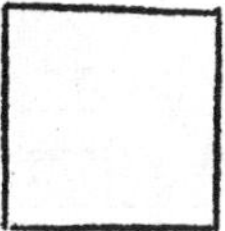

- **As tens**

  Think: 1,400 = 140 tens.

- **As ones**

  Think: 1,400 = 1,400 ones.

Rename the number. Draw a quick picture to help.

1. 180 = ______ tens

2. 1,600 = ______ hundreds

3. 6,000 = ______ thousands

4. 2,700 = 27 ______

5. 2 hundreds 6 tens = ______ tens

6. 71 thousands = ______

Name ______________________________

Lesson 16
CC.4.NBT.1

Rename Numbers

Rename the number. Use the place-value chart to help.

1. 760 hundreds = 76,000

THOUSANDS			ONES		
Hundreds	Tens	Ones	Hundreds	Tens	Ones
	7	6,	0	0	0

2. 805 tens = ___________

THOUSANDS			ONES		
Hundreds	Tens	Ones	Hundreds	Tens	Ones

3. 24 ten thousands = ___________

THOUSANDS			ONES		
Hundreds	Tens	Ones	Hundreds	Tens	Ones

Rename the number.

4. 720 = ___________ tens

5. 4 thousands 7 hundreds = 47 ___________

6. 25,600 = ___________ hundreds

7. 204 thousands = ___________

Problem Solving REAL WORLD

8. For the fair, the organizers ordered 32 rolls of tickets. Each roll of tickets has 100 tickets. How many tickets were ordered in all?

____

9. An apple orchard sells apples in bags of 10. The orchard sold a total of 2,430 apples one day. How many bags of apples was this?

____

Name ______________________________

Lesson 17

COMMON CORE STANDARD CC.4.NBT.2

Lesson Objective: Read and write whole numbers in standard form, word form, and expanded form.

Read and Write Numbers

Look at the digit 6 in the place-value chart below. It is in the hundred thousands place. So, its value is 6 hundred thousands.

In **word form**, the value of this digit is six hundred thousands.

In **standard form**, the value of the digit 6 is 600,000.

THOUSANDS			ONES		
Hundreds	Tens	Ones	Hundreds	Tens	Ones
6	5	9,	0	5	8

Read the number shown in the place-value chart. In word form, this number is written as six hundred fifty-nine thousand, fifty-eight.

You can also write the number in **expanded form**: 600,000 + 50,000 + 9,000 + 50 + 8

Note that when writing a number in words, a comma separates periods.

Read and write each number in two other forms.

1. 40,000 + 1,000 + 300 + 70 + 8

____

2. twenty-one thousand, four hundred

____

3. 391,032

____

____

Name ______________________

Lesson 17

CC.4.NBT.2

Read and Write Numbers

Read and write the number in two other forms.

1. six hundred ninety-two thousand, four

   standard form: 692,004; expanded form: 600,000 + 90,000 + 2,000 + 4

2. 314,207

   ____

3. 600,000 + 80,000 + 10

   ____

Use the number 913,256.

4. Write the name of the period that has the digits 913.

   ____

5. Write the digit in the ten thousands place.

   ____

6. Write the value of the digit 9.

   ____

Problem Solving REAL WORLD

Use the table for 7 and 8.

Population in 2008

State	Population
Alaska	686,293
South Dakota	804,194
Wyoming	532,668

7. Which state had a population of eight hundred four thousand, one hundred ninety-four?

   ____

8. What is the value of the digit 8 in Alaska's population?

   ____

Name ______________________________

Lesson 18

COMMON CORE STANDARD CC.4.NBT.2

Lesson Objective: Compare and order whole numbers based on the values of the digits in each number.

Compare and Order Numbers

Compare 31,072 and 34,318. Write <, >, or =.

Step 1 Align the numbers by place value using grid paper.

Step 2 Compare the digits in each place value. Start at the greatest place.

Are the digits in the ten thousands place the same?
Yes. Move to the thousands place.
Are the digits in the thousands place the same?
No. 1 thousand is less than 4 thousands.

start here

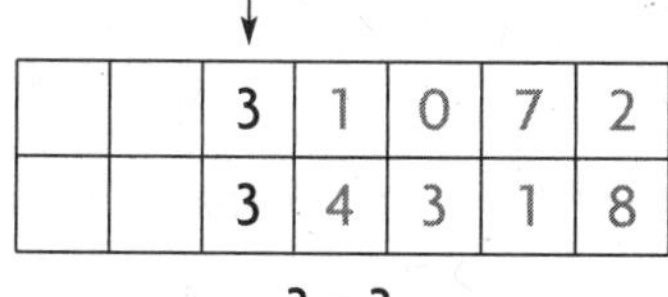

3 = 3

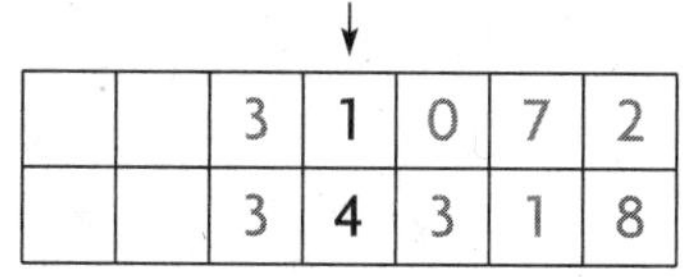

1 < 4

Step 3 Use the symbols <, >, or = to compare the numbers.

< means *is less than.* > means *is greater than.* = means *is equal to.*

There are two ways to write the comparison.

31,072 (<) 34,318 or 34,318 (>) 31,072

1. Use the grid paper to compare 21,409 and 20,891. Write <, >, or =.

21,409  20,891

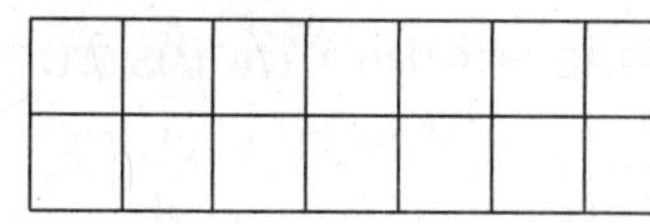

Compare. Write <, >, or =.

2. $53,621  $53,760

3. 82,550  80,711

Order from greatest to least.

4. 16,451; 16,250; 17,014

____

5. 561,028; 582,073; 549,006

____

Name ______________________________

Compare and Order Numbers

Compare. Write <, >, or =.

1. 3,273 (<) 3,279
2. $1,323 ◯ $1,400
3. 52,692 ◯ 52,692
4. $413,005 ◯ $62,910
5. 382,144 ◯ 382,144
6. 157,932 ◯ 200,013
7. 401,322 ◯ 410,322
8. 989,063 ◯ 980,639
9. 258,766 ◯ 258,596

Order from least to greatest.

10. 23,710; 23,751; 23,715

____

11. 52,701; 54,025; 5,206

____

12. 465,321; 456,321; 456,231

____

____

13. $330,820; $329,854; $303,962

____

____

Problem Solving

14. An online newspaper had 350,080 visitors in October, 350,489 visitors in November, and 305,939 visitors in December. What is the order of the months from greatest to least number of visitors?

____

____

____

15. The total land area in square miles of each of three states is shown below.
    Colorado: 103,718
    New Mexico: 121,356
    Arizona: 113,635
    What is the order of the states from least to greatest total land area?

____

____

Name ______________________________

Lesson 19

COMMON CORE STANDARD CC.4.NBT.3

Lesson Objective: Round a whole number to any place.

Round Numbers

When you round a number, you replace it with a number that is easier to work with but not as exact. You can round numbers to different place values.

Round <u>4</u>78,456 to the place value of the underlined digit.

Step 1 Identify the underlined digit.
The underlined digit, 4, is in the **hundred thousands place**.

Step 2 Look at the number to the right of the underlined digit.

If that number is 0–4, the underlined digit stays the same.

If that number is 5–9, the underlined digit is increased by 1.

The number to the right of the underlined digit is 7, so the underlined digit, 4, will be increased by one; 4 + 1 = 5.

Step 3 Change all the digits to the right of the hundred thousands place to zeros.

So, 478,456 rounded to the nearest hundred thousand is **500,000**.

1. In 2010, the population of North Dakota was 672,591 people. Use the number line to round this number to the nearest hundred thousand.

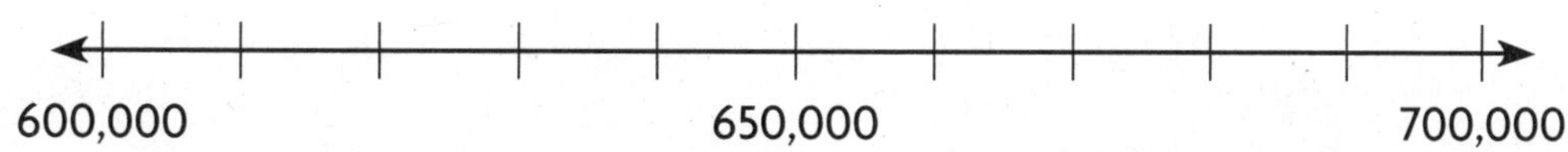

672,591 is closer to ______________ than ______________,

so it rounds to ______________.

Round to the place value of the underlined digit.

2. 3,<u>4</u>52 ______________

3. <u>1</u>80 ______________

4. $<u>7</u>2,471 ______________

5. <u>5</u>72,000 ______________

6. <u>9</u>50 ______________

7. <u>6</u>,495 ______________

8. 8<u>3</u>5,834 ______________

9. 96,<u>6</u>25 ______________

Name ______________________

Lesson 19
CC.4.NBT.3

Round Numbers

Round to the place value of the underlined digit.

1. 8$\underline{6}$2,840

8$\underline{6}$2,840 ↑ less than 5 — **860,000**

- Look at the digit to the right. If the digit to the right is *less than* 5, the digit in the rounding place stays the same.
- Change all the digits to the right of the rounding place to zero.

2. 12$\underline{3}$,499 ______________

3. $\underline{5}$52,945 ______________

4. 3$\underline{8}$9,422 ______________

5. $\underline{2}$09,767 ______________

6. 19$\underline{1}$,306 ______________

7. $\underline{6}$6,098 ______________

8. 7$\underline{3}$,590 ______________

9. $\underline{1}$49,903 ______________

10. 68$\underline{4}$,303 ______________

11. 49$\underline{9}$,553 ______________

Problem Solving REAL WORLD

Use the table for 12–13.

12. Find the height of Mt. Whitney in the table. Round the height to the nearest thousand feet.

______________ feet

13. What is the height of Mt. Bona rounded to the nearest ten thousand feet?

______________ feet

Mountain Heights

Name	State	Height (feet)
Mt. Bona	Alaska	16,500
Mt. Whitney	California	14,494

Name ____________________

Lesson 20

COMMON CORE STANDARD CC.4.NBT.4

Lesson Objective: Add whole numbers and determine whether solutions to addition problems are reasonable.

Add Whole Numbers

Find the sum. 63,821 + 34,765

Step 1 Round each addend to estimate.
60,000 + 30,000 = 90,000

Step 2 Use a place-value chart to line up the digits by place value.

Step 3 Start with the ones place. Add from right to left. Regroup as needed.

	Hundred Thousands	Ten Thousands	Thousands	Hundreds	Tens	Ones
			1			
		6	3,	8	2	1
	+	3	4,	7	6	5
		9	8,	5	8	6

The sum is 98,586. Since 98,586 is close to the estimate 90,000, the answer is reasonable.

Estimate. Then find the sum.

1. Find 238,503 + 341,978. Use the grid to help.

Estimate: ____________

2. Estimate: ____________

$$\begin{array}{r} 52{,}851 \\ +\ 65{,}601 \\ \hline \end{array}$$

3. Estimate: ____________

$$\begin{array}{r} 54{,}980 \\ +\ 24{,}611 \\ \hline \end{array}$$

4. Estimate: ____________

$$\begin{array}{r} 604{,}542 \\ +\ 87{,}106 \\ \hline \end{array}$$

5. Estimate: ____________

$$\begin{array}{r} 147{,}026 \\ +\ 106{,}792 \\ \hline \end{array}$$

6. Estimate: ____________

$$\begin{array}{r} 278{,}309 \\ +\ 422{,}182 \\ \hline \end{array}$$

7. Estimate: ____________

$$\begin{array}{r} 540{,}721 \\ +\ 375{,}899 \\ \hline \end{array}$$

Name ______________________

Add Whole Numbers

Lesson 20

CC.4.NBT.4

Estimate. Then find the sum.

1. Estimate: 90,000

```
   11
   63,824 →   60,000
 + 29,452 → + 30,000
 --------   --------
   93,276     90,000
```

2. Estimate: __________

```
   73,404
 + 27,865
```

3. Estimate: __________

```
   403,446
 + 396,755
```

4. Estimate: __________

```
   137,638
 +  52,091
```

5. Estimate: __________

```
   200,629
 +  28,542
```

6. Estimate: __________

```
   212,514
 + 396,705
```

7. Estimate: __________

```
   324,867
 +   6,233
```

8. Estimate: __________

```
   462,809
 + 256,738
```

9. Estimate: __________

```
   624,836
 + 282,189
```

Problem Solving REAL WORLD

Use the table for 10–12.

10. Beth and Cade were on one team. What was their total score?

____

11. Dillan and Elaine were on the other team. What was their total score?

____

12. Which team scored the most points?

____

Individual Game Scores	
Student	**Score**
Beth	251,567
Cade	155,935
Dillan	188,983
Elaine	220,945

Name ______________________________

Lesson 21

COMMON CORE STANDARD CC.4.NBT.4

Lesson Objective: Subtract whole numbers and determine whether solutions to subtraction problems are reasonable.

Subtract Whole Numbers

Find the difference. 5,128 − 3,956

Estimate first.
Think: 5,128 is close to 5,000. 3,956 is close to 4,000.
So, an estimate is 5,000 − 4,000 = 1,000.

Write the problem vertically. Use grid paper to align digits by place value.

Step 1 Subtract the ones.

	5,	1	2	8	
−	3,	9	5	6	
				2	

8 − 6 = 2

Step 2 Subtract the tens.

		0	12		
	5,	~~1~~	~~2~~	8	
−	3,	9	5	6	
			7	2	

There are not enough tens to subtract. Regroup 1 hundred as 10 tens.
12 tens − 5 tens = 7 tens

Step 3 Subtract the hundreds.

	4	10 ~~0~~	12		
	~~5~~,	~~1~~	~~2~~	8	
−	3,	9	5	6	
		1	7	2	

There are not enough hundreds to subtract. Regroup 1 thousand as 10 hundreds.
10 hundreds − 9 hundreds = 1 hundred

Step 4 Subtract the thousands.

	4	10 ~~0~~	12		
	~~5~~,	~~1~~	~~2~~	8	
−	3,	9	5	6	
	1	1	7	2	

4 thousands − 3 thousands = 1 thousand

The difference is **1,172**. Since 1,172 is close to the estimate of 1,000, the answer is reasonable.

Estimate. Then find the difference.

1. Estimate: ____________

  6,253
− 3,718

2. Estimate: ____________

  74,529
− 38,453

3. Estimate: ____________

  232,318
− 126,705

Name ______________________

Subtract Whole Numbers

Lesson 21
CC.4.NBT.4

Estimate. Then find the difference.

1. Estimate: 600,000

```
   9
 7 10 15 6 13
  780,573
– 229,615
  550,958
```

Think: 780,573 rounds to 800,000.
229,615 rounds to 200,000.
So an estimate is 800,000 – 200,000 = 600,000.

2. Estimate: ____________

$$\begin{array}{r} 428,731 \\ -\ 175,842 \\ \hline \end{array}$$

3. Estimate: ____________

$$\begin{array}{r} 920,026 \\ -\ 535,722 \\ \hline \end{array}$$

4. Estimate: ____________

$$\begin{array}{r} 253,495 \\ -\ 48,617 \\ \hline \end{array}$$

Subtract. Add to check.

5. 735,249 – 575,388 ____________

6. 512,724 – 96,473 ____________

7. 600,000 – 145,782 ____________

Problem Solving REAL WORLD

Use the table for 8 and 9.

8. How many more people attended the Magic's games than attended the Pacers' games?

____

9. How many fewer people attended the Pacers' games than attended the Clippers' games?

____

Season Attendance for Three NBA Teams

Team	Attendance
Indiana Pacers	582,295
Orlando Magic	715,901
Los Angeles Clippers	670,063

Name ______________________

Lesson 22

COMMON CORE STANDARD CC.4.NBT.4

Lesson Objective: Use the strategy *draw a diagram* to solve comparison problems with addition and subtraction.

Problem Solving • Comparison Problems with Addition and Subtraction

For a community recycling project, a school collects aluminum cans and plastic containers. This year the fourth grade collected 5,923 cans and 4,182 containers. This is 410 more cans and 24 more containers than the fourth grade collected last year. How many cans did the fourth grade collect last year?

Read the Problem		
What do I need to find?	**What information do I need to use?**	**How will I use the information?**
I need to find the number of **cans the fourth grade collected last year.**	The fourth grade students collected **5,923** cans this year. They collected **410** more cans this year than the fourth grade collected last year.	I can draw a **bar model** to find the number of cans the fourth grade collected last year.

Solve the Problem

I can draw a bar model and write an equation to represent the problem.

5,923

410 | 5,513

5,923 − 410 = **5,513**

So, the fourth grade collected **5,513** aluminum cans last year.

Use the information above for 1 and 2.

1. Altogether, how many aluminum cans and plastic containers did the fourth grade collect this year?

____

____

2. This year the fifth grade collected 216 fewer plastic containers than the fourth grade. How many plastic containers did the fifth grade collect?

____

____

Name ______________________

Lesson 22
CC.4.NBT.4

Problem Solving • Comparison Problems with Addition and Subtraction

Use the information in the table for 1–3.

Surface Area of the Great Lakes	
Lake	**Surface Area (in square miles)**
Lake Superior	31,700
Lake Michigan	22,278
Lake Huron	22,973
Lake Erie	9,906
Lake Ontario	7,340

1. How many square miles larger is the surface area of Lake Huron than the surface area of Lake Erie?

Think: How can a bar model help represent the problem? What equation can be written?

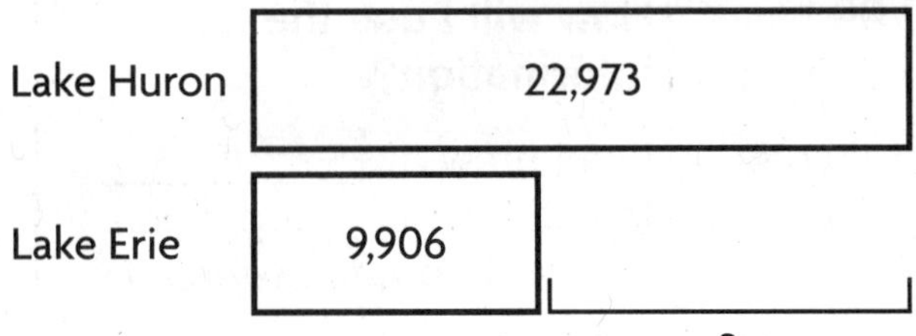

22,973 − 9,906 = **13,067** square miles

13,067 square miles

---

2. Which lake has a surface area that is 14,938 square miles greater than the surface area of Lake Ontario? Draw a model and write a number sentence to solve the problem.

____

---

3. Lake Victoria has the largest surface area of all lakes in Africa. Its surface area is 26,828 square miles. How much larger is the surface area of Lake Superior than that of Lake Victoria?

____

---

4. At 840,000 square miles, Greenland is the largest island in the world. The second-largest island is New Guinea, at 306,000 square miles. How much larger is Greenland than New Guinea?

____

Name ______________________

COMMON CORE STANDARD CC.4.NBT.5

Lesson Objective: Multiply tens, hundreds, and thousands by whole numbers through 10.

Multiply Tens, Hundreds, and Thousands

You can use a pattern to multiply with tens, hundreds, and thousands.

Count the number of zeros in the factors.

4 × 6 = 24 ← basic fact

4 × 6<u>0</u> = 24<u>0</u> ← When you multiply by tens, the last digit in the product is 0.

4 × 6<u>00</u> = 2,4<u>00</u> ← When you multiply by hundreds, the last two digits in the product are 0.

4 × 6,<u>000</u> = 24,<u>000</u> ← When you multiply by thousands, the last three digits in the product are 0.

When the basic fact has a zero in the product, there will be an extra zero in the final product:

5 × 4 = 2**0**, so 5 × 4,<u>000</u> = 2**0**,<u>000</u>

Complete the pattern.

1. 9 × 2 = 18

   9 × 20 = ______

   9 × 200 = ______

   9 × 2,000 = ______

2. 8 × 4 = 32

   8 × 40 = ______

   8 × 400 = ______

   8 × 4,000 = ______

3. 6 × 6 = 36

   6 × 60 = ______

   6 × 600 = ______

   6 × 6,000 = ______

4. 4 × 7 = 28

   4 × 70 = ______

   4 × 700 = ______

   4 × 7,000 = ______

Find the product.

5. 7 × 300 = 7 × ______ hundreds

   = ______ hundreds

   = ______

6. 5 × 8,000 = 5 × ______ thousands

   = ______ thousands

   = ______

Name ______________________

Multiply Tens, Hundreds, and Thousands

Lesson 23
CC.4.NBT.5

Find the product.

1. $4 \times 7{,}000 =$ **28,000**

Think: $4 \times 7 = 28$
So, $4 \times 7{,}000 = 28{,}000$

2. $9 \times 60 =$ ____________

3. $8 \times 200 =$ ____________

4. $5 \times 6{,}000 =$ ____________

5. $7 \times 800 =$ ____________

6. $8 \times 90 =$ ____________

7. $6 \times 3{,}000 =$ ____________

8. $3 \times 8{,}000 =$ ____________

9. $5 \times 500 =$ ____________

10. $9 \times 4{,}000 =$ ____________

11. $7 \times 7{,}000 =$ ____________

12. $3 \times 40 =$ ____________

13. $4 \times 5{,}000 =$ ____________

14. $2 \times 9{,}000 =$ ____________

Problem Solving REAL WORLD

15. A bank teller has 7 rolls of coins. Each roll has 40 coins. How many coins does the bank teller have?

____

16. Theo buys 5 packages of paper. There are 500 sheets of paper in each package. How many sheets of paper does Theo buy?

____

Name ______________________________

Lesson 24

COMMON CORE STANDARD CC.4.NBT.5

Lesson Objective: Estimate products by rounding and determine if exact answers to multiplication problems are reasonable.

Estimate Products

You can use rounding to estimate products.

Round the greater factor. Then use mental math to estimate the product.

6 × 95

Step 1 Round 95 to the nearest hundred. — 95 rounds to **100.**

Step 2 Use patterns and mental math.

$6 \times 1 = 6$

$6 \times 10 = 60$

$6 \times 100 = \mathbf{600}$

Find two numbers the exact answer is between.

7 × 759

Step 1 Estimate by rounding to the lesser hundred.

7 × 759 ↓ 7 × **700 = 4,900**

Think: $7 \times 7 = 49$
$7 \times 70 = 490$
$7 \times 700 = 4,900$

Step 2 Estimate by rounding to the greater hundred.

7 × 759 ↓ 7 × **800 = 5,600**

Think: $7 \times 8 = 56$
$7 \times 80 = 560$
$7 \times 800 = 5,600$

So, the product is between 4,900 and 5,600.

Estimate the product by rounding.

1. 6 × 316 ______________

2. 5 × 29 ______________

3. 4 × 703 ______________

Estimate the product by finding two numbers the exact answer is between.

4. 3 × 558 ______________

5. 7 × 252 ______________

6. 8 × 361 ______________

Name ______________________

Estimate Products

Lesson 24
CC.4.NBT.5

Estimate the product by rounding.

1. 4×472

   4×472
   ↓
   $4 \times \mathbf{500}$
   2,000

2. $2 \times 6{,}254$

3. 9×54

4. $5 \times 5{,}503$

5. 3×832

6. 6×98

7. $8 \times 3{,}250$

8. 7×777

Find two numbers the exact answer is between.

9. 3×567

10. $6 \times 7{,}381$

11. 4×94

12. 8×684

Problem Solving REAL WORLD

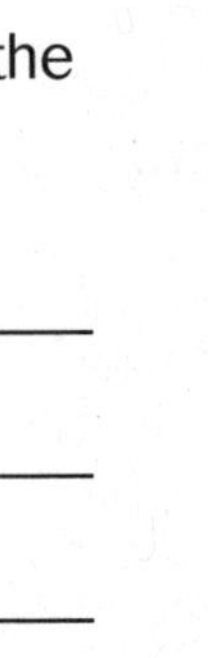

13. Isaac drinks 8 glasses of water each day. He says he will drink 2,920 glasses of water in a year that has 365 days. Is the exact answer reasonable? **Explain.**

14. Most Americans throw away about 1,365 pounds of trash each year. Is it reasonable to estimate that Americans throw away over 10,000 pounds of trash in 5 years? **Explain.**

Name ______________________________

Lesson 25

COMMON CORE STANDARD CC.4.NBT.5

Lesson Objective: Use the Distributive Property to multiply a 2-digit number by a 1-digit number.

Multiply Using the Distributive Property

You can use rectangular models to multiply 2-digit numbers by 1-digit numbers.

Find 9×14.

Step 1 Draw a 9 by 14 rectangle on grid paper.

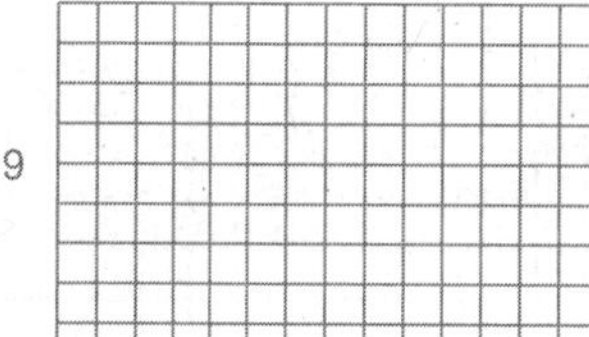

Step 2 Use the Distributive Property and products you know to break apart the model into two smaller rectangles.
Think: 14 = 10 + 4.

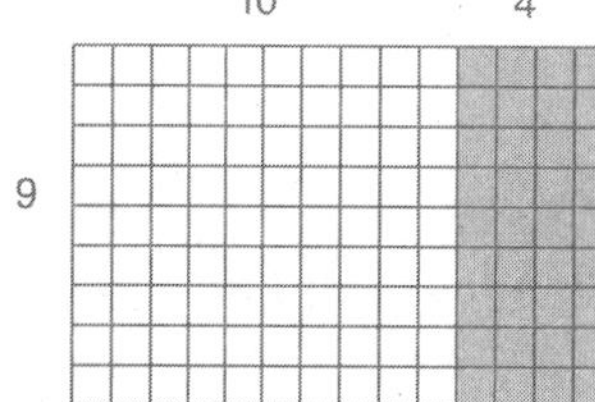

Step 3 Find the product each smaller rectangle represents.

$9 \times 10 = \mathbf{90}$

$9 \times 4 = \mathbf{36}$

Step 4 Find the sum of the products. $90 + 36 = \mathbf{126}$

So, $9 \times 14 = 126$.

Model the product on the grid. Record the product.

1. 3×13

____

2. 6×16

____

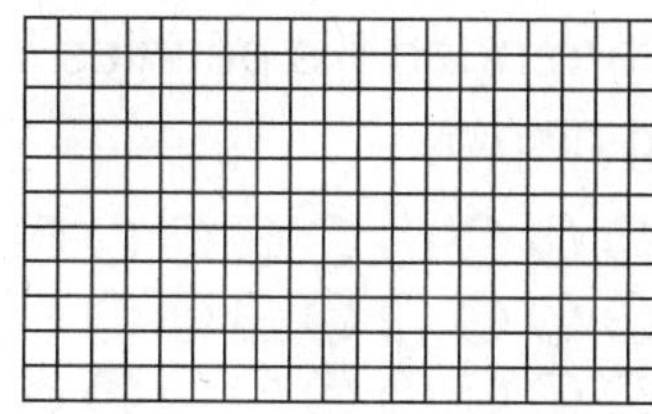

3. 5×17

____

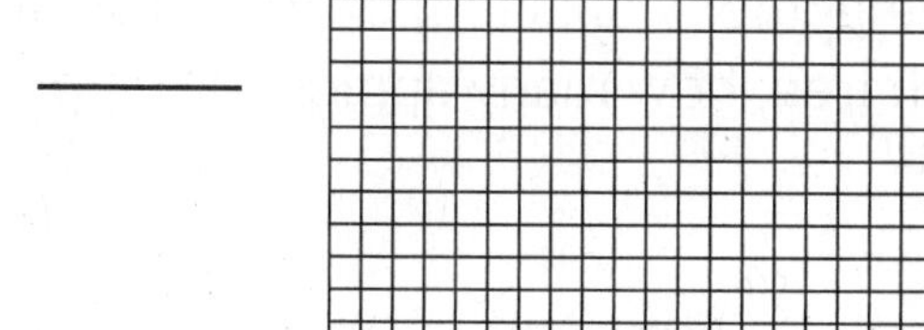

4. 4×14

____

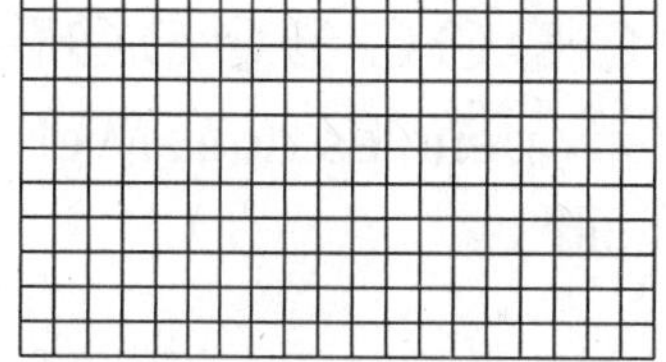

Name ______________________

Lesson 25
CC.4.NBT.5

Multiply Using the Distributive Property

Model the product on the grid. Record the product.

1. $4 \times 19 =$ 76

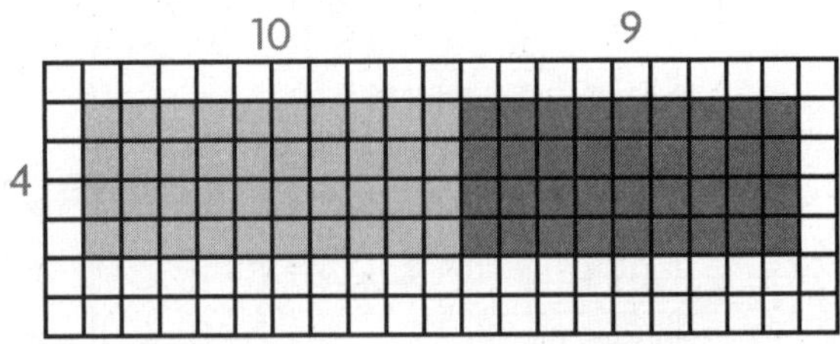

$4 \times 10 = 40$ and $4 \times 9 = 36$

$40 + 36 = 76$

2. $5 \times 13 =$ ______

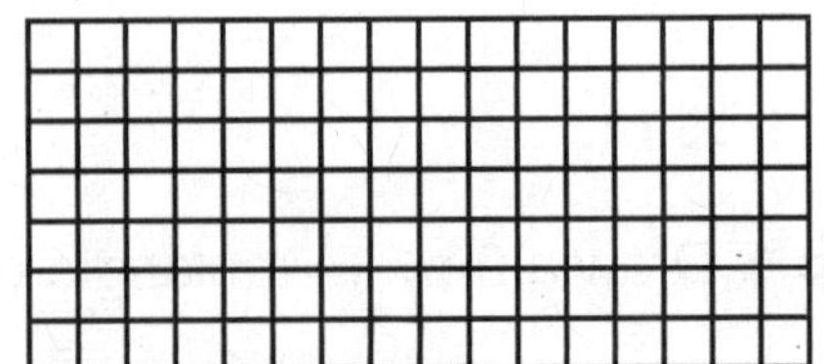

Find the product.

3. $4 \times 14 =$ ______

4. $3 \times 17 =$ ______

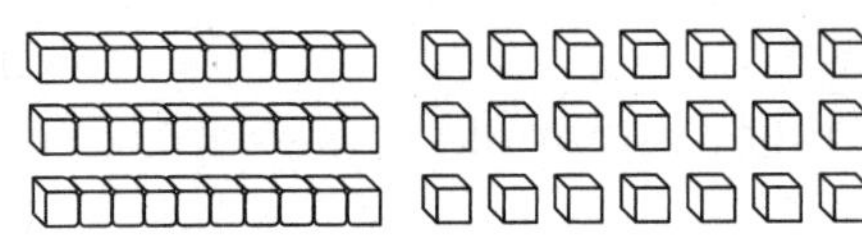

5. $6 \times 15 =$ ______

Problem Solving

6. Michael arranged his pennies in the following display.

How many pennies does Michael have in all?

____

7. A farmer has an apple orchard with the trees arranged as shown below.

If the farmer wants to pick one apple from each tree, how many apples will he pick?

____

Name ______________________________

Lesson 26

COMMON CORE STANDARD CC.4.NBT.5

Lesson Objective: Use expanded form to multiply a multidigit number by a 1-digit number.

Multiply Using Expanded Form

You can use expanded form or a model to find products.

Multiply. 3×26

Think and Write

Step 1 Write 26 in expanded form.

$26 = 20 + 6$

$3 \times 26 = 3 \times (20 + 6)$

Step 2 Use the Distributive Property.

$3 \times 26 = (3 \times 20) + (\underline{3} \times \underline{6})$

Step 3 Multiply the tens. Multiply the ones.

$3 \times 26 = (3 \times 20) + (3 \times 6)$

$= \underline{60} + \underline{18}$

Step 4 Add the partial products.

$$\begin{array}{r} 60 \\ +18 \\ \hline 78 \end{array}$$

So, $3 \times 26 = \underline{78}$.

Use a Model

Step 1 Show 3 groups of 26.

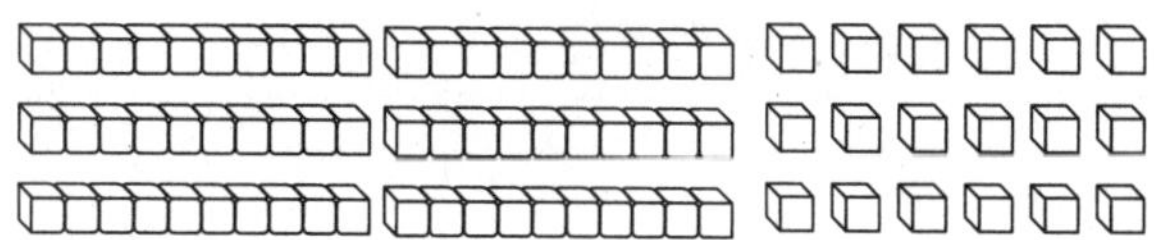

Step 2 Break the model into tens and ones.

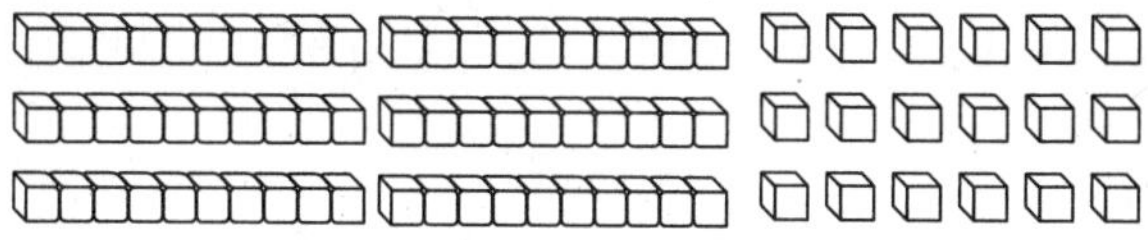

(3 × 2 tens)	(3 × 6 ones)
(3 × 20)	(3 × 6)
60	18

Step 3 Add to find the total product.

$\underline{60} + \underline{18} = \underline{78}$

Record the product. Use expanded form to help.

1. $6 \times 14 =$ ________

____

____

2. $4 \times 52 =$ ________

____

____

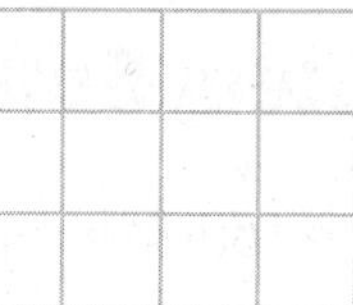

3. $5 \times 162 =$ ________

____

____

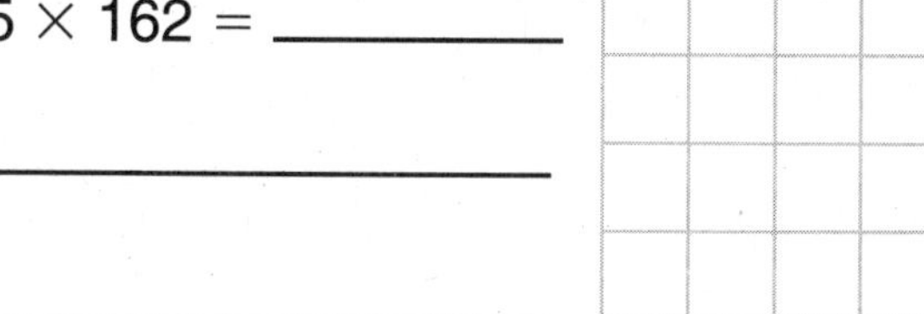

4. $3 \times 279 =$ ________

____

____

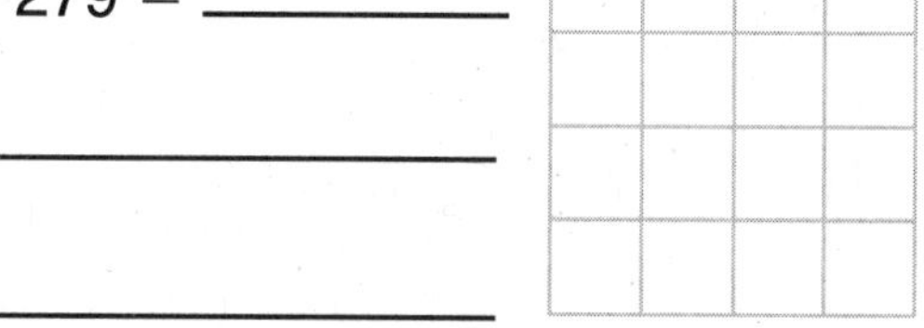

Name ____________________

Multiply Using Expanded Form

Record the product. Use expanded form to help.

1. $7 \times 14 =$ **98**

   $7 \times 14 = 7 \times (10 + 4)$

   $= (7 \times 10) + (7 \times 4)$

   $= 70 + 28$

   $= 98$

2. $8 \times 43 =$ ____________

3. $6 \times 532 =$ ____________

4. $5 \times 923 =$ ____________

5. $4 \times 2{,}371 =$ ____________

6. $7 \times 1{,}829 =$ ____________

Problem Solving REAL WORLD

7. The fourth-grade students at Riverside School are going on a field trip. There are 68 students on each of the 4 buses. How many students are going on the field trip?

   ____

8. There are 5,280 feet in one mile. Hannah likes to walk 5 miles each week for exercise. How many feet does Hannah walk each week?

   ____

Name ______________________

Lesson 27

COMMON CORE STANDARD CC.4.NBT.5

Lesson Objective: Use place value and partial products to multiply a multidigit number by a 1-digit number.

Multiply Using Partial Products

Use partial products to multiply.

Multiply. 7 × $332

Step 1 Estimate the product. 332 rounds to 300; 7 × $300 = $2,100.

Step 2 Multiply the 3 hundreds, or 300, by 7.

$$\begin{array}{r} \$\mathbf{3}32 \\ \times\ \ \mathbf{7} \\ \hline \end{array} \quad \text{or} \quad \begin{array}{r} \$300 \\ \times\ \ 7 \\ \hline \$2,100 \end{array}$$

Step 3 Multiply the 3 tens, or 30, by 7.

$$\begin{array}{r} \$3\mathbf{3}2 \\ \times\ \ \mathbf{7} \\ \hline \end{array} \quad \text{or} \quad \begin{array}{r} \$30 \\ \times\ \ 7 \\ \hline \$210 \end{array}$$

Step 4 Multiply the 2 ones, or 2, by 7.

$$\begin{array}{r} \$33\mathbf{2} \\ \times\ \ \mathbf{7} \\ \hline \end{array} \quad \text{or} \quad \begin{array}{r} \$2 \\ \times\ 7 \\ \hline \$14 \end{array}$$

Step 5 Add the partial products. $2,100 + $210 + $14 = $2,324

So, 7 × $332 = $2,324. Since $2,324 is close to the estimate of $2,100, it is reasonable.

Estimate. Then record the product.

1. Estimate: ______

$$\begin{array}{r} 181 \\ \times\ \ 2 \\ \hline \end{array}$$

2. Estimate: ______

$$\begin{array}{r} 156 \\ \times\ \ 4 \\ \hline \end{array}$$

3. Estimate: ______

$$\begin{array}{r} \$210 \\ \times\ \ 5 \\ \hline \end{array}$$

4. Estimate: ______

$$\begin{array}{r} 303 \\ \times\ \ 6 \\ \hline \end{array}$$

5. Estimate: ______

$$\begin{array}{r} \$427 \\ \times\ \ 2 \\ \hline \end{array}$$

6. Estimate: ______

$$\begin{array}{r} \$367 \\ \times\ \ 5 \\ \hline \end{array}$$

Name ______________________

Lesson 27

CC.4.NBT.5

Multiply Using Partial Products

Estimate. Then record the product.

1. Estimate: 1,200

```
   243
×    6
 1,200
   240
+   18
 1,458
```

2. Estimate: ______

```
 640
×  3
```

3. Estimate: ______

```
 $149
×    5
```

4. Estimate: ______

```
 721
×  8
```

5. Estimate: ______

```
 293
×  4
```

6. Estimate: ______

```
 $416
×    6
```

7. Estimate: ______

```
 961
×  2
```

8. Estimate: ______

```
 837
×  9
```

9. Estimate: ______

```
 652
×  4
```

10. Estimate: ______

```
 307
×  3
```

11. Estimate: ______

```
 543
×  7
```

12. Estimate: ______

```
 $822
×    5
```

Problem Solving REAL WORLD

13. A maze at a county fair is made from 275 bales of hay. The maze at the state fair is made from 4 times as many bales of hay. How many bales of hay are used for the maze at the state fair?

____

14. Pedro gets 8 hours of sleep each night. How many hours does Pedro sleep in a year with 365 days?

____

Name ____________________

Multiply Using Mental Math

Lesson 28

COMMON CORE STANDARD CC.4.NBT.5

Lesson Objective: Use mental math and properties to multiply a multidigit number by a 1-digit number.

Use addition to break apart the larger factor. **Find 8 × 214.** **Think:** 214 = 200 + 14 8 × 214 = (8 × 200) + (8 × 14) = 1,600 + 112 = 1,712	Use subtraction to break apart the larger factor. **Find 6 × 298.** **Think:** 298 = 300 − 2 6 × 298 = (6 × 300) − (6 × 2) = 1,800 − 12 = 1,788
Use halving and doubling. **Find 14 × 50.** **Think:** 14 can be evenly divided by 2. 14 ÷ 2 = 7 7 × 50 = 350 2 × 350 = 700	When multiplying more than two numbers, use the Commutative Property to change the order of the factors. **Find 2 × 9 × 50.** **Think:** 2 × 50 = 100 2 × 9 × 50 = 2 × 50 × 9 = 100 × 9 = 900

Find the product. Tell which strategy you used.

1. 5 × 7 × 20

____

2. 6 × 321

____

3. 86 × 50

____

4. 9 × 399

____

Name ______________________________

Multiply Using Mental Math

Lesson 28
CC.4.NBT.5

Find the product. Tell which strategy you used.

1. 6×297 **Think:** $297 = 300 - 3$

$$\begin{aligned} 6 \times 297 &= 6 \times (300 - 3) \\ &= (6 \times 300) - (6 \times 3) \\ &= 1{,}800 - 18 \\ &= 1{,}782 \end{aligned}$$

1,782;

use subtraction

2. $8 \times 25 \times 23$

____

____

3. 8×604

____

____

4. 50×28

____

____

5. 9×199

____

____

6. $20 \times 72 \times 5$

____

____

7. 32×25

____

____

Problem Solving REAL WORLD

8. Section J in an arena has 20 rows. Each row has 15 seats. All tickets cost $18 each. If all the seats are sold, how much money will the arena collect for Section J?

____

9. At a high-school gym, the bleachers are divided into 6 equal sections. Each section can seat 395 people. How many people can be seated in the gym?

____

Name ____________________

Lesson 29

COMMON CORE STANDARD CC.4.NBT.5

Lesson Objective: Use regrouping to multiply a 2-digit number by a 1-digit number.

Multiply 2-Digit Numbers with Regrouping

Use place value to multiply with regrouping.

Multiply. 7×63

Step 1 Estimate the product.

$7 \times 60 = 420$

Step 2 Multiply the ones. Regroup 21 ones as 2 tens 1 one. Record the 1 one below the ones column and the 2 tens above the tens column.

7×3 ones $=$ **21 ones**

$$\begin{array}{r} {\scriptstyle 2} \\ 63 \\ \times\ 7 \\ \hline 1 \end{array}$$

Step 3 Multiply the tens. Then, add the regrouped tens. Record the tens.

$$\begin{array}{r} {\scriptstyle 2} \\ 63 \\ \times\ 7 \\ \hline 441 \end{array}$$

44 tens = 4 hundreds 4 tens

7×6 tens $=$ **42 tens**

Add the 2 regrouped tens.

42 tens + 2 tens = **44 tens**

So, $7 \times 63 = 441$. Since 441 is close to the estimate of 420, it is **reasonable**.

Estimate. Then record the product.

1. Estimate: ________

$$\begin{array}{r} 42 \\ \times\ 6 \\ \hline \end{array}$$

2. Estimate: ________

$$\begin{array}{r} \$98 \\ \times\ \ 6 \\ \hline \end{array}$$

3. Estimate: ________

$$\begin{array}{r} 37 \\ \times\ 8 \\ \hline \end{array}$$

4. Estimate: ________

$$\begin{array}{r} \$54 \\ \times\ \ 9 \\ \hline \end{array}$$

5. Estimate: ________

$$\begin{array}{r} 37 \\ \times\ 5 \\ \hline \end{array}$$

6. Estimate: ________

$$\begin{array}{r} 93 \\ \times\ 4 \\ \hline \end{array}$$

7. Estimate: ________

$$\begin{array}{r} 86 \\ \times\ 9 \\ \hline \end{array}$$

8. Estimate: ________

$$\begin{array}{r} 59 \\ \times\ 7 \\ \hline \end{array}$$

Name ______________________

Multiply 2-Digit Numbers with Regrouping

Estimate. Then record the product.

1. Estimate: 150

$$\begin{array}{r} \scriptstyle 1 \\ 46 \\ \times \quad 3 \\ \hline 138 \end{array}$$

2. Estimate: ______

$$\begin{array}{r} 32 \\ \times \quad 8 \\ \hline \end{array}$$

3. Estimate: ______

$$\begin{array}{r} \$55 \\ \times \quad 2 \\ \hline \end{array}$$

4. Estimate: ______

$$\begin{array}{r} 61 \\ \times \quad 8 \\ \hline \end{array}$$

5. Estimate: ______

$$\begin{array}{r} 37 \\ \times \quad 9 \\ \hline \end{array}$$

6. Estimate: ______

$$\begin{array}{r} \$18 \\ \times \quad 7 \\ \hline \end{array}$$

7. Estimate: ______

$$\begin{array}{r} 83 \\ \times \quad 5 \\ \hline \end{array}$$

8. Estimate: ______

$$\begin{array}{r} 95 \\ \times \quad 8 \\ \hline \end{array}$$

9. Estimate: ______

$$\begin{array}{r} 94 \\ \times \quad 9 \\ \hline \end{array}$$

10. Estimate: ______

$$\begin{array}{r} 57 \\ \times \quad 6 \\ \hline \end{array}$$

11. Estimate: ______

$$\begin{array}{r} 72 \\ \times \quad 3 \\ \hline \end{array}$$

12. Estimate: ______

$$\begin{array}{r} \$79 \\ \times \quad 8 \\ \hline \end{array}$$

Problem Solving REAL WORLD

13. Sharon is 54 inches tall. A tree in her backyard is 5 times as tall as she is. The floor of her treehouse is at a height that is twice as tall as she is. What is the difference, in inches, between the top of the tree and the floor of the treehouse?

____

14. Mr. Diaz's class is taking a field trip to the science museum. There are 23 students in the class, and a student admission ticket is $8. How much will the student tickets cost?

____

Name ______________________

Lesson 30

COMMON CORE STANDARD CC.4.NBT.5

Lesson Objective: Use regrouping to multiply a multidigit number by a 1-digit number.

Multiply 3-Digit and 4-Digit Numbers with Regrouping

When you multiply 3-digit and 4-digit numbers, you may need to regroup.

Estimate. Then find the product. $\begin{array}{r} \$1{,}324 \\ \times \quad 7 \\ \hline \end{array}$

Step 1 Estimate the product. $1,324 rounds to $1,000; $1,000 × 7 = **$7,000.**

Step 2 Multiply the 4 ones by 7.
Regroup the 28 ones as 2 tens 8 ones.

$\begin{array}{r} {}^{2} \\ \$1{,}324 \\ \times \quad 7 \\ \hline 8 \end{array}$

Step 3 Multiply the 2 tens by 7.
Add the regrouped tens.
Regroup the 16 tens as 1 hundred 6 tens.

$\begin{array}{r} {}^{1\,2} \\ \$1{,}324 \\ \times \quad 7 \\ \hline 68 \end{array}$

Step 4 Multiply the 3 hundreds by 7.
Add the regrouped hundred.
Regroup the 22 hundreds as 2 thousands 2 hundreds.

$\begin{array}{r} {}^{2\,1\,2} \\ \$1{,}324 \\ \times \quad 7 \\ \hline 268 \end{array}$

Step 5 Multiply the 1 thousand by 7.
Add the regrouped thousands.

$\begin{array}{r} {}^{2\,1\,2} \\ \$1{,}324 \\ \times \quad 7 \\ \hline \$9{,}268 \end{array}$

So, 7 × $1,324 = $9,268.
Since $9,268 is close to the estimate of $7,000, the answer is **reasonable**.

Estimate. Then find the product.

1. Estimate: ________ $\begin{array}{r} 3{,}184 \\ \times \quad 2 \\ \hline \end{array}$

2. Estimate: ________ $\begin{array}{r} \$828 \\ \times \quad 4 \\ \hline \end{array}$

3. Estimate: ________ $\begin{array}{r} 2{,}637 \\ \times \quad 5 \\ \hline \end{array}$

4. Estimate: ________ $\begin{array}{r} \$6{,}900 \\ \times \quad 7 \\ \hline \end{array}$

Name ____________________

Multiply 3-Digit and 4-Digit Numbers with Regrouping

Estimate. Then find the product.

1. Estimate: 4,000

$$\begin{array}{r} {}^{1\,2\,2} \\ 1{,}467 \\ \times \quad 4 \\ \hline 5{,}868 \end{array}$$

2. Estimate: ______

$$\begin{array}{r} 5{,}339 \\ \times \quad 6 \\ \hline \end{array}$$

3. Estimate: ______

$$\begin{array}{r} \$879 \\ \times \quad 8 \\ \hline \end{array}$$

4. Estimate: ______

$$\begin{array}{r} 3{,}182 \\ \times \quad 5 \\ \hline \end{array}$$

5. Estimate: ______

$$\begin{array}{r} 4{,}616 \\ \times \quad 3 \\ \hline \end{array}$$

6. Estimate: ______

$$\begin{array}{r} \$2{,}854 \\ \times \quad 9 \\ \hline \end{array}$$

7. Estimate: ______

$$\begin{array}{r} 7{,}500 \\ \times \quad 2 \\ \hline \end{array}$$

8. Estimate: ______

$$\begin{array}{r} 948 \\ \times \quad 7 \\ \hline \end{array}$$

9. Estimate: ______

$$\begin{array}{r} 1{,}752 \\ \times \quad 6 \\ \hline \end{array}$$

10. Estimate: ______

$$\begin{array}{r} 550 \\ \times \quad 9 \\ \hline \end{array}$$

11. Estimate: ______

$$\begin{array}{r} 6{,}839 \\ \times \quad 4 \\ \hline \end{array}$$

12. Estimate: ______

$$\begin{array}{r} \$9{,}614 \\ \times \quad 3 \\ \hline \end{array}$$

Problem Solving REAL WORLD

13. Lafayette County has a population of 7,022 people. Columbia County's population is 8 times as great as Lafayette County's population. What is the population of Columbia County?

____

14. A seafood company sold 9,125 pounds of fish last month. If 6 seafood companies sold the same amount of fish, how much fish did the 6 companies sell last month in all?

____

Name ___________________________

COMMON CORE STANDARD CC.4.NBT.5

Lesson Objective: Use place value and multiplication properties to multiply by tens.

Multiply by Tens

One section of seating at an arena has 40 rows. Each row has 30 seats. How many seats in all are in that section?

Multiply. 30 × 40

Step 1 Think of each factor as a multiple of 10 and as a repeated addition.

40 = 4 × 10 or 10 + 10 + 10 + 10

30 = 3 × 10 or 10 + 10 + 10

Step 2 Draw a diagram to show the multiplication.

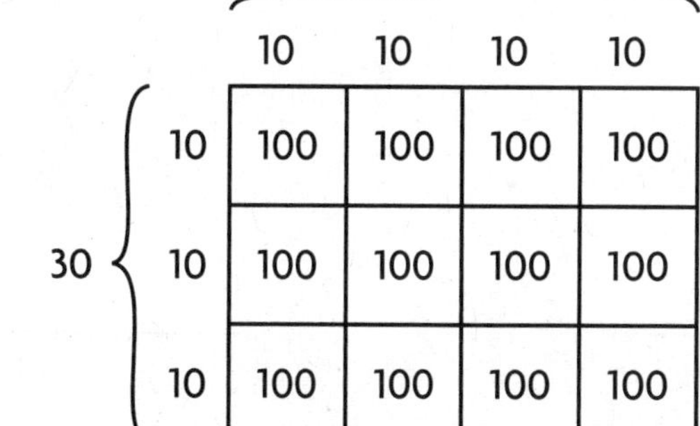

Step 3 Each small square in the diagram shows 10 × 10, or 100. Count the squares.

There are 12 squares of 100.

Step 4 Use patterns and mental math to find 12 × 100.

12 × 1 = 12

12 × 10 = 120

12 × 100 = 1,200

There are 1,200 seats in that section.

Choose a method. Then find the product.

1. 20 × 90 = ________ **2.** 40 × 40 = ________ **3.** 60 × 70 = ________

4. 50 × 30 = ________ **5.** 80 × 60 = ________ **6.** 90 × 40 = ________

Name ______________________

Multiply by Tens

Lesson 31
CC.4.NBT.5

Choose a method. Then find the product.

1. 16×60

Use the halving-and-doubling strategy.

Find half of 16: $16 \div 2 = 8$.

Multiply this number by 60: $8 \times 60 = 480$

Double this result: $2 \times 480 = 960$

960

2. 80×22 ____________

3. 30×52 ____________

4. 60×20 ____________

5. 40×35 ____________

6. 10×90 ____________

7. 31×50 ____________

Problem Solving REAL WORLD

8. Kenny bought 20 packs of baseball cards. There are 12 cards in each pack. How many cards did Kenny buy?

____

9. The Hart family drove 10 hours to their vacation spot. They drove an average of 48 miles each hour. How many miles did they drive in all?

____

Name ______________________

Lesson 32

COMMON CORE STANDARD CC.4.NBT.5

Lesson Objective: Estimate products by rounding or by using compatible numbers.

Estimate Products

You can use rounding and compatible numbers to estimate products.

Use mental math and rounding to estimate the product.

Estimate. 62 × $23

Step 1 Round each factor to the nearest ten.
62 rounds to **60**.
$23 rounds to **$20**.

Step 2 Rewrite the problem using the rounded numbers.
60 × $20

Step 3 Use mental math.
6 × $2 = **$12**
6 × $20 = **$120**
60 × $20 = **$1,200**

So, 62 × $23 is about **$1,200**.

Use mental math and compatible numbers to estimate the product.

Estimate. 24 × 78

Step 1 Use compatible numbers. 25 × 80

Step 2 Use 25 × 4 = 100 to help find 25 × 8.
25 × 8 = **200**

Step 3 Since 80 has 1 zero, write 1 zero to the right of the product.

24 × 78
↓ ↓
25 × 80 = 2,000

So, 24 × 78 is about **2,000**.

Estimate the product. Choose a method.

1. 78 × 21 ________	**2.** 59 × $46 ________	**3.** 81 × 33 ________	**4.** 67 × 21 ________
5. 88 × $42 ________	**6.** 51 × 36 ________	**7.** 73 × 73 ________	**8.** 99 × $44 ________
9. 92 × 19 ________	**10.** 26 × 37 ________	**11.** 89 × 18 ________	**12.** 58 × 59 ________

Name ______________________

Lesson 32

CC.4.NBT.5

Estimate Products

Estimate the product. Choose a method.

1. 38 × 21

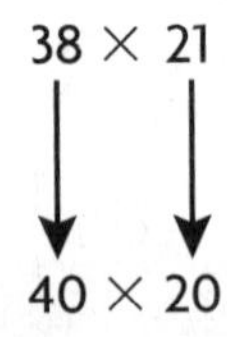

800

2. 63 × 19

______

3. 27 × $42

______

4. 73 × 67

______

5. 37 × $44

______

6. 85 × 71

______

7. 88 × 56

______

8. 97 × 13

______

9. 92 × 64

______

Problem Solving REAL WORLD

10. A dime has a diameter of about 18 millimeters. About how many millimeters long would a row of 34 dimes be?

______

11. A half-dollar has a diameter of about 31 millimeters. About how many millimeters long would a row of 56 half-dollars be?

______

Name ____________________

Lesson 33

COMMON CORE STANDARD CC.4.NBT.5

Lesson Objective: Use area models and partial products to multiply 2-digit numbers.

Area Models and Partial Products

You can use area models to multiply 2-digit numbers by 2-digit numbers.

Use the model and partial products to solve.

Draw a rectangle to find 19 × 18.

The rectangle is 19 units long and 18 units wide.

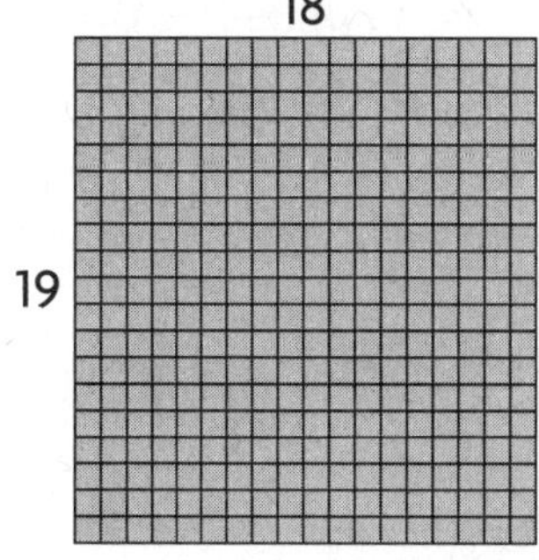

Step 1 Break apart the factors into tens and ones. Divide the area model into four smaller rectangles to show the factors.

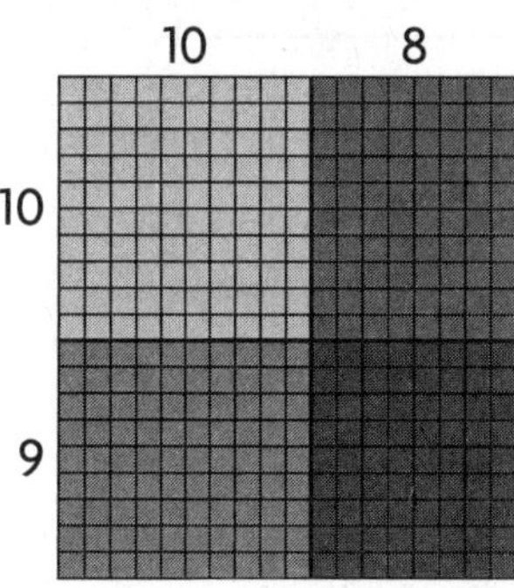

Step 2 Find the products for each of the smaller rectangles.

10 × 10 = **100** 10 × 8 = **80** 9 × 10 = **90** 9 × 8 = **72**

Step 3 Find the sum of the products. **100 + 80 + 90 + 72 = 342**

So, 19 × 18 = **342**.

Draw a model to represent the product. Then record the product.

1. 21 × 25

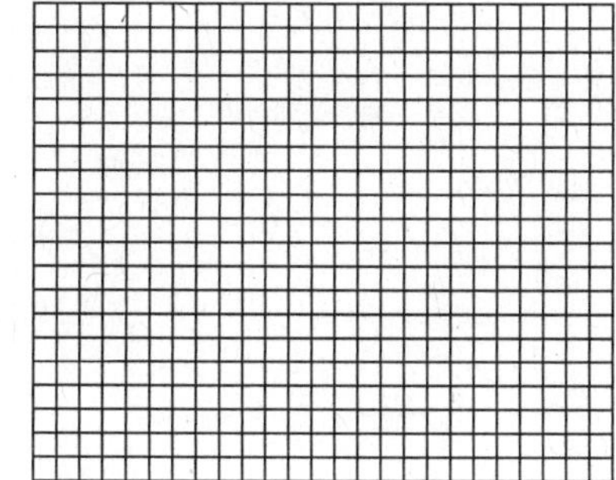

____

2. 16 × 14

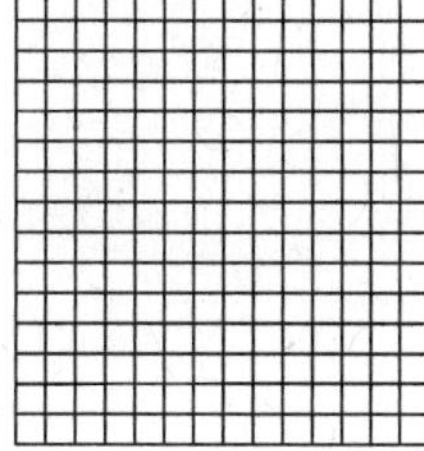

____

3. 24 × 15

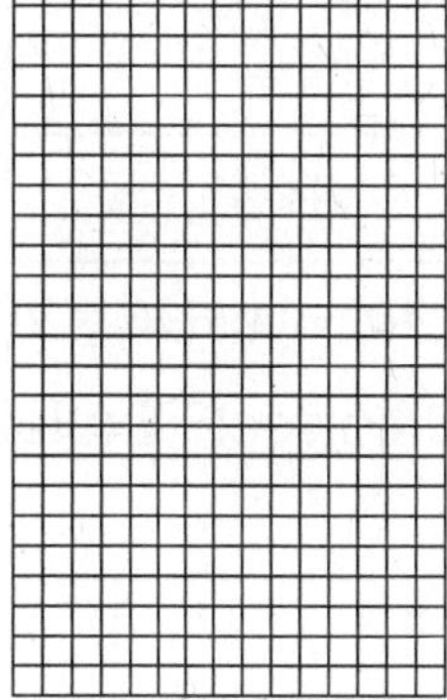

____

Name ______________________

Lesson 33
CC.4.NBT.5

Area Models and Partial Products

Draw a model to represent the product. Then record the product.

1. 13×42

	40	2
10	400	20
3	120	6

$400 + 20 + 120 + 6 =$ **546**

2. 18×34

____

3. 22×26

____

4. 15×33

____

5. 23×29

____

6. 19×36

____

Problem Solving REAL WORLD

7. Sebastian made the following model to find the product 17×24.

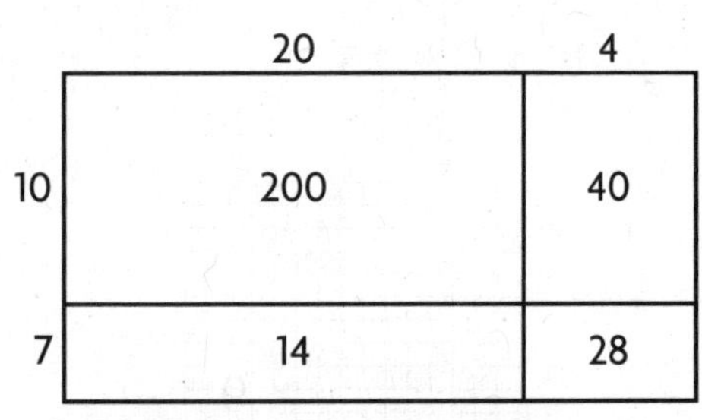

$200 + 40 + 14 + 28 = 282$

Is his model correct? **Explain.**

____

____

8. Each student in Ms. Sike's kindergarten class has a box of crayons. Each box has 36 crayons. If there are 18 students in Ms. Sike's class, how many crayons are there in all?

____

Name ______________________________

COMMON CORE STANDARD CC.4.NBT.5

Lesson Objective: Use place value and partial products to multiply 2-digit numbers.

Multiply Using Partial Products

Multiply 25 × 43. Record the product.

Think: I can use partial products to find 25 × 43.

Step 1 Multiply the tens by the tens.
20 × 4 tens = 80 tens, or 800. → 800

Step 2 Multiply the ones by the tens.
20 × 3 ones = 60 ones, or 60. → 60

Step 3 Multiply the tens by the ones.
5 × 4 tens = 20 tens, or 200. → 200

Step 4 Multiply the ones by the ones.
5 × 3 ones = 15 ones, or 15. → + 15

Step 5 Add the partial products.
800 + 60 + 200 + 15 = 1,075. → 1,075

	tens	ones
	4	3
×	2	5
8	0	0
	6	0
2	0	0
+	1	5
1,0	7	5

So, 25 × 43 = 1,075.

Record the product.

1. 25 × 62

2. 59 × 38

3. 85 × 72

4. 46 × 52

5. 76 × 23

6. 38 × 95

Name ______________________

Multiply Using Partial Products

Record the product.

1. 23 × 79
   1,400
   210
   180
   + 27
   1,817

2. 56 × 32

3. 87 × 64

4. 33 × 25

5. 94 × 12

6. 51 × 77

7. 69 × 49

8. 86 × 84

9. 98 × 42

10. 73 × 37

11. 85 × 51

Problem Solving REAL WORLD

12. Evelyn drinks 8 glasses of water a day, which is 56 glasses of water a week. How many glasses of water does she drink in a year? (1 year = 52 weeks)

____

13. Joe wants to use the Hiking Club's funds to purchase new walking sticks for each of its 19 members. The sticks cost $26 each. The club has $480. Is this enough money to buy each member a new walking stick? If not, how much more money is needed?

____

Name ______________________________

Lesson 35

COMMON CORE STANDARD CC.4.NBT.5

Lesson Objective: Use regrouping to multiply 2-digit numbers.

Multiply with Regrouping

Estimate. Then use regrouping to find 28 × 43.

Step 1 Round to estimate the product. 30 × 40 = 1,200

Step 2 Think: 28 = 2 tens 8 ones.
Multiply 43 by 8 ones.
8 × 3 = 24. Record the 4. Write the regrouped 2 above the tens place.
8 × 40 = 320. Add the regrouped tens: 320 + 20 = 340.

$$\begin{array}{r} \overset{2}{4}3 \\ \times\ 28 \\ \hline 344 \end{array} \longleftarrow 8 \times 43$$

Step 3 Multiply 43 by 2 tens.
20 × 3 = 60 and 20 × 40 = 800.
Record 860 below 344.

$$\begin{array}{r} \overset{2}{4}3 \\ \times\ 28 \\ \hline 344 \\ 860 \\ \hline 1{,}204 \end{array} \begin{array}{l} \\ \\ \\ \longleftarrow 20 \times 43 \\ \longleftarrow 344 + 860 \end{array}$$

Step 4 Add the partial products.

So, 28 × 43 = <u>1,204</u>. 1,204 is close to 1,200. The answer is **reasonable**.

Estimate. Then find the product.

1. Estimate: __________

$$\begin{array}{r} 36 \\ \times\ 12 \\ \hline \end{array}$$

2. Estimate: __________

$$\begin{array}{r} 43 \\ \times\ 29 \\ \hline \end{array}$$

3. Estimate: __________

$$\begin{array}{r} 51 \\ \times\ 47 \\ \hline \end{array}$$

Name ______________________

Lesson 35

CC.4.NBT.5

Multiply with Regrouping

Estimate. Then find the product.

1. Estimate: 2,700

$$\begin{array}{r} \overset{2}{\overset{1}{8}}7 \\ \times\ 32 \\ \hline 174 \\ +\ 2,610 \\ \hline 2,784 \end{array}$$

Think: 87 is close to 90 and 32 is close to 30.

$90 \times 30 = 2,700$

2. Estimate: ________

$$\begin{array}{r} 73 \\ \times\ 28 \\ \hline \end{array}$$

3. Estimate: ________

$$\begin{array}{r} 48 \\ \times\ 38 \\ \hline \end{array}$$

4. Estimate: ________

$$\begin{array}{r} 59 \\ \times\ 52 \\ \hline \end{array}$$

5. Estimate: ________

$$\begin{array}{r} 84 \\ \times\ 40 \\ \hline \end{array}$$

6. Estimate: ________

$$\begin{array}{r} 83 \\ \times\ 77 \\ \hline \end{array}$$

7. Estimate: ________

$$\begin{array}{r} 91 \\ \times\ 19 \\ \hline \end{array}$$

Problem Solving REAL WORLD

8. Baseballs come in cartons of 84 baseballs. A team orders 18 cartons of baseballs. How many baseballs does the team order?

____

9. There are 16 tables in the school lunch room. Each table can seat 22 students. How many students can be seated at lunch at one time?

____

Name ______________________

Lesson 36

COMMON CORE STANDARD CC.4.NBT.5

Lesson Objective: Choose a method to multiply 2-digit numbers.

Choose a Multiplication Method

Estimate. Then use regrouping to find 47 × 89.

$$\begin{array}{r} 89 \\ \times\ 47 \\ \hline \end{array}$$

Step 1 Estimate the product. 50 × 90 = 4,500

Step 2 Multiply the 9 ones by the 7 ones. Regroup the 63 ones as 6 tens 3 ones.

$$\begin{array}{r} {}^{6} \\ 89 \\ \times\ 47 \\ \hline 3 \end{array}$$

Step 3 Multiply the 8 tens, or 80, by the 7 ones, or 7. Add the regrouped tens. Regroup the 62 tens as 6 hundreds 2 tens.

$$\begin{array}{r} {}^{6} \\ 89 \\ \times\ 47 \\ \hline 623 \end{array}$$

Step 4 Multiply the 9 ones by the 4 tens, or 40. Regroup the 36 tens as 3 hundreds 6 tens.

$$\begin{array}{r} {}^{3} \\ \not{6} \\ 89 \\ \times\ 47 \\ \hline 623 \\ 60 \end{array}$$

Step 5 Multiply the 8 tens, or 80, by the 4 tens, or 40. Add the regrouped tens. Regroup the 35 hundreds as 3 thousands 5 hundreds.

$$\begin{array}{r} {}^{3} \\ \not{6} \\ 89 \\ \times\ 47 \\ \hline 623 \\ 3{,}560 \end{array}$$

Step 6 Add the partial products.

$$\begin{array}{r} {}^{3} \\ \not{6} \\ 89 \\ \times\ 47 \\ \hline 623 \\ +\ 3{,}560 \\ \hline 4{,}183 \end{array}$$

So, 47 × 89 = **4,183**. Since 4,183 is close to the estimate of 4,500, it is reasonable.

Estimate. Then choose a method to find the product.

1. Estimate: ________

$$\begin{array}{r} 76 \\ \times\ 31 \\ \hline \end{array}$$

2. Estimate: ________

$$\begin{array}{r} 24 \\ \times\ 35 \\ \hline \end{array}$$

3. Estimate: ________

$$\begin{array}{r} 14 \\ \times\ 28 \\ \hline \end{array}$$

4. Estimate: ________

$$\begin{array}{r} 64 \\ \times\ 56 \\ \hline \end{array}$$

Name ______________________________

Lesson 36
CC.4.NBT.5

Choose a Multiplication Method

Estimate. Then choose a method to find the product.

1. Estimate: 1,200

$$\begin{array}{r} 31 \\ \times \ 43 \\ \hline 93 \\ +\ 1{,}240 \\ \hline 1{,}333 \end{array}$$

2. Estimate: ______

$$\begin{array}{r} 67 \\ \times \ 85 \\ \hline \end{array}$$

3. Estimate: ______

$$\begin{array}{r} 68 \\ \times \ 38 \\ \hline \end{array}$$

4. Estimate: ______

$$\begin{array}{r} 95 \\ \times \ 17 \\ \hline \end{array}$$

5. Estimate: ______

$$\begin{array}{r} 49 \\ \times \ 54 \\ \hline \end{array}$$

6. Estimate: ______

$$\begin{array}{r} 91 \\ \times \ 26 \\ \hline \end{array}$$

7. Estimate: ______

$$\begin{array}{r} 82 \\ \times \ 19 \\ \hline \end{array}$$

8. Estimate: ______

$$\begin{array}{r} 46 \\ \times \ 27 \\ \hline \end{array}$$

9. Estimate: ______

$$\begin{array}{r} 41 \\ \times \ 33 \\ \hline \end{array}$$

10. Estimate: ______

$$\begin{array}{r} 97 \\ \times \ 13 \\ \hline \end{array}$$

11. Estimate: ______

$$\begin{array}{r} 75 \\ \times \ 69 \\ \hline \end{array}$$

Problem Solving REAL WORLD

12. A movie theatre has 26 rows of seats. There are 18 seats in each row. How many seats are there in all?

____

13. Each class at Briarwood Elementary collected at least 54 cans of food during the food drive. If there are 29 classes in the school, what was the least number of cans collected?

____

Name ______________________________

Lesson 37

COMMON CORE STANDARD CC.4.NBT.6

Lesson Objective: Use multiples to estimate quotients.

Estimate Quotients Using Multiples

Find two numbers the quotient of 142 ÷ 5 is between. Then estimate the quotient.

You can use multiples to estimate. A **multiple** of a number is the product of a number and a counting number.

Step 1 Think: What number multiplied by 5 is about 142? Since 142 is greater than 10 × 5, or 50, use counting numbers 10, 20, 30, and so on to find multiples of 5.

Step 2 Multiply 5 by multiples of 10 and make a table.

Counting Number	10	20	30	40
Multiple of 5	**50**	**100**	**150**	**200**

Step 3 Use the table to find multiples of 5 closest to 142.

20 × 5 = <u>100</u>

30 × 5 = <u>150</u>

← 142 is between <u>100</u> and <u>150</u>.

142 is closest to <u>150</u>, so 142 ÷ 5 is about <u>30</u>.

Find two numbers the quotient is between. Then estimate the quotient.

1. 136 ÷ 6

between _____ and _____

about _____

2. 95 ÷ 3

between _____ and _____

about _____

3. 124 ÷ 9

between _____ and _____

about _____

4. 238 ÷ 7

between _____ and _____

about _____

Name ______________________________

Estimate Quotients Using Multiples

Find two numbers the quotient is between. Then estimate the quotient.

1. $175 \div 6$

between 20 and 30

about 30

Think: $6 \times 20 = 120$ and $6 \times 30 = 180$.
So, $175 \div 6$ is between 20 and 30. Since 175 is closer to 180 than to 120, the quotient is about 30.

2. $53 \div 3$

____
____

3. $75 \div 4$

____
____

4. $215 \div 9$

____
____

5. $284 \div 5$

____
____

6. $191 \div 3$

____
____

7. $100 \div 7$

____
____

8. $438 \div 7$

____
____

9. $103 \div 8$

____
____

10. $255 \div 9$

____
____

Problem Solving REAL WORLD

11. Joy collected 287 aluminum cans in 6 hours. About how many cans did she collect per hour?

____

12. Paul sold 162 cups of lemonade in 5 hours. About how many cups of lemonade did he sell each hour?

____

Name ____________________

COMMON CORE STANDARD CC.4.NBT.6

Lesson Objective: Use models to divide whole numbers that do not divide evenly.

Remainders

Use counters to find the quotient and remainder.

$9\overline{)26}$

- Use 26 counters to represent the dividend, 26.
- Since you are dividing 26 by 9, draw 9 circles. Divide the 26 counters into 9 equal-sized groups.

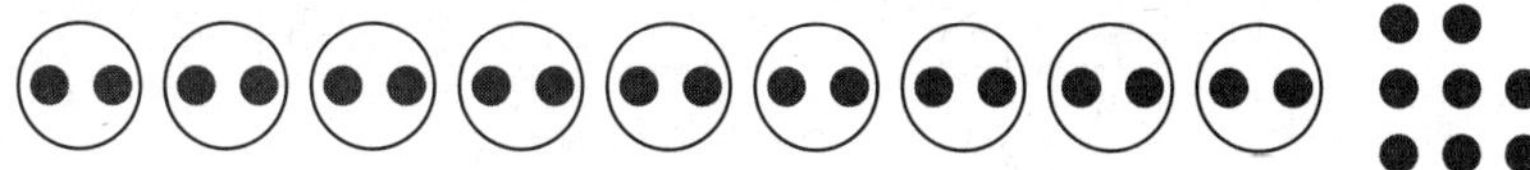

- There are 2 counters in each circle, so the quotient is **2**. There are 8 counters left over, so the remainder is **8**.

$$\begin{array}{r} \textbf{2 r8} \\ 9\overline{)26} \end{array}$$

Divide. Draw a quick picture to help.

$7\overline{)66}$

- Use 66 counters to represent the dividend, 66.
- Since you are dividing 66 by 7, draw 7 circles. Divide 66 counters into 7 equal-sized groups.

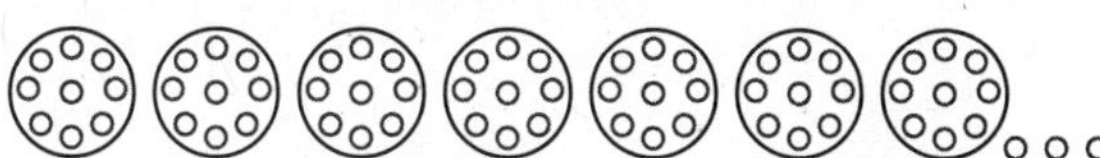

- There are 9 counters in each circle, so the quotient is **9**. There are 3 counters left over, so the remainder is **3**.

$$\begin{array}{r} \textbf{9 r3} \\ 7\overline{)66} \end{array}$$

Use counters to find the quotient and remainder.

1. $6\overline{)19}$

2. $3\overline{)14}$

Divide. Draw a quick picture to help.

3. $39 \div 4$

____

4. $29 \div 3$

____

Name ______________________

Remainders

Use counters to find the quotient and remainder.

1. $13 \div 4$ 3 r1
2. $24 \div 7$ ______
3. $39 \div 5$ ______
4. $36 \div 8$ ______
5. $6\overline{)27}$ ______
6. $25 \div 9$ ______
7. $3\overline{)17}$ ______
8. $26 \div 4$ ______

Divide. Draw a quick picture to help.

9. $14 \div 3$ ______
10. $5\overline{)29}$ ______

Problem Solving

11. What is the quotient and remainder in the division problem modeled below?

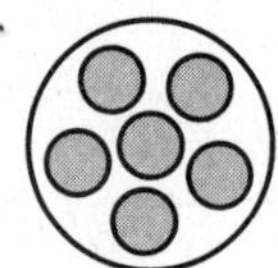
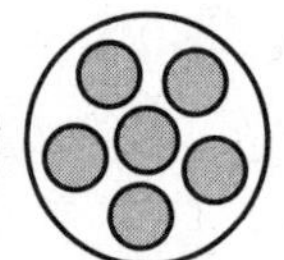
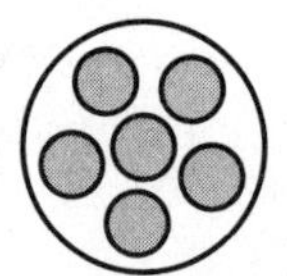

______

12. Mark drew the following model and said it represented the problem $21 \div 4$. Is Mark's model correct? If so, what is the quotient and remainder? If not, what is the correct quotient and remainder?

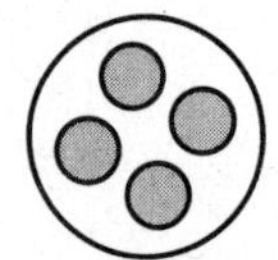
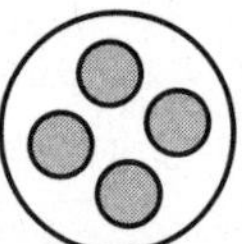
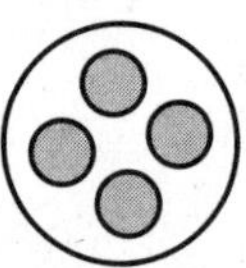
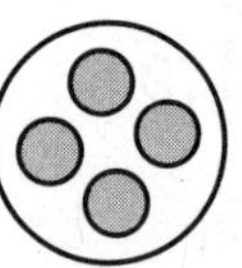
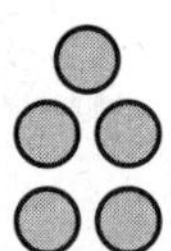

______

Name ______________________________

Lesson 39

COMMON CORE STANDARD CC.4.NBT.6

Lesson Objective: Divide tens, hundreds, and thousands by whole numbers through 10.

Divide Tens, Hundreds, and Thousands

You can use base-ten blocks, place value, and basic facts to divide.

Divide. 240 ÷ 3

Use base-ten blocks.	Use place value.
Step 1 Draw a quick picture to show 240.	**Step 1** Identify the basic fact to use. Use 24 ÷ 3.
Step 2 You cannot divide 2 hundreds into 3 equal groups. Rename 2 hundreds as tens. 240 = 24 tens	**Step 2** Use place value to rewrite 240 as tens. 240 = 24 tens
Step 3 Separate the tens into 3 equal groups to divide. There are 3 groups of 8 tens. Write the answer. 240 ÷ 3 = 80	**Step 3** Divide. 24 tens ÷ 3 = 8 tens = 80 Write the answer. 240 ÷ 3 = 80

Use basic facts and place value to find the quotient.

1. 280 ÷ 4

What division fact can you use?

____

280 = ______ tens

28 tens ÷ 4 = ______ tens

280 ÷ 4 = ______

2. 1,800 ÷ 9

What division fact can you use?

____

1,800 = ______ hundreds

18 hundreds ÷ 9 = ______ hundreds

1,800 ÷ 9 = ______

3. 560 ÷ 7 = ______

4. 180 ÷ 6 = ______

5. 1,500 ÷ 5 = ______

6. 3,200 ÷ 4 = ______

Name ______________________

Divide Tens, Hundreds, and Thousands

Lesson 39
CC.4.NBT.6

Use basic facts and place value to find the quotient.

1. 3,600 ÷ 4 = **900**

Think: 3,600 is 36 hundreds.

Use the basic fact 36 ÷ 4 = 9.

So, 36 hundreds ÷ 4 = 9 hundreds, or 900.

2. 240 ÷ 6 = ________
3. 5,400 ÷ 9 = ________
4. 300 ÷ 5 = ________
5. 4,800 ÷ 6 = ________
6. 420 ÷ 7 = ________
7. 150 ÷ 3 = ________
8. 6,300 ÷ 7 = ________
9. 1,200 ÷ 4 = ________
10. 360 ÷ 6 = ________

Find the quotient.

11. 28 ÷ 4 = ________
    280 ÷ 4 = ________
    2,800 ÷ 4 = ________
12. 18 ÷ 3 = ________
    180 ÷ 3 = ________
    1,800 ÷ 3 = ________
13. 45 ÷ 9 = ________
    450 ÷ 9 = ________
    4,500 ÷ 9 = ________

Problem Solving REAL WORLD

14. At an assembly, 180 students sit in 9 equal rows. How many students sit in each row?

    ____

15. Hilary can read 560 words in 7 minutes. How many words can Hilary read in 1 minute?

    ____

16. A company produces 7,200 gallons of bottled water each day. The company puts 8 one-gallon bottles in each carton. How many cartons are needed to hold all the one-gallon bottles produced in one day?

    ____

17. An airplane flew 2,400 miles in 4 hours. If the plane flew the same number of miles each hour, how many miles did it fly in 1 hour?

    ____

Name ______________________________

Lesson 40

COMMON CORE STANDARD CC.4.NBT.6

Lesson Objective: Use compatible numbers to estimate quotients.

Estimate Quotients Using Compatible Numbers

Compatible numbers are numbers that are easy to compute mentally. In division, one compatible number divides evenly into the other. Think of the multiples of a number to help you find compatible numbers.

Estimate. $6\overline{)216}$

Step 1 Think of these multiples of 6:

6 12 18 24 30 36 42 48 54

Find multiples that are close to the first 2 digits of the dividend. __18__ tens and __24__ tens are both close to __21__ tens. You can use either or both numbers to estimate the quotient.

Step 2 Estimate using compatible numbers.

$216 \div 6$ → **$180 \div 6 = 30$**

$216 \div 6$ → **$240 \div 6 = 40$**

So, $216 \div 6$ is between __30__ and __40__.

Step 3 Decide whether the estimate is closer to 30 or 40.

$216 - 180 = 36$ **$240 - 216 = 24$**

216 is closer to 240, so use __40__ as the estimate.

Use compatible numbers to estimate the quotient.

1. $3\overline{)252}$ ____________

2. $6\overline{)546}$ ____________

3. $4\overline{)2{,}545}$ ____________

4. $5\overline{)314}$ ____________

5. $2\overline{)1{,}578}$ ____________

6. $8\overline{)289}$ ____________

Name ______________________

Lesson 40

CC.4.NBT.6

Estimate Quotients Using Compatible Numbers

Use compatible numbers to estimate the quotient.

1. 389 ÷ 4

400 ÷ 4 = 100

2. 358 ÷ 3

______

3. 784 ÷ 8

______

4. 179 ÷ 9

______

5. 315 ÷ 8

______

6. 2,116 ÷ 7

______

7. 4,156 ÷ 7

______

8. 474 ÷ 9

______

Use compatible numbers to find two estimates that the quotient is between.

9. 1,624 ÷ 3

______

10. 2,593 ÷ 6

______

11. 1,045 ÷ 2

______

12. 1,754 ÷ 9

______

13. 2,363 ÷ 8

______

14. 1,649 ÷ 5

______

15. 5,535 ÷ 7

______

16. 3,640 ÷ 6

______

Problem Solving REAL WORLD

17. A CD store sold 3,467 CDs in 7 days. About the same number of CDs were sold each day. About how many CDs did the store sell each day?

______

18. Marcus has 731 books. He puts about the same number of books on each of 9 shelves in his a bookcase. About how many books are on each shelf?

______

Name ________________________________

Lesson 41

COMMON CORE STANDARD CC.4.NBT.6

Lesson Objective: Use the Distributive Property to find quotients.

Division and the Distributive Property

Divide. 78 ÷ 6

Use the Distributive Property and quick pictures to break apart numbers to make them easier to divide.

Step 1 Draw a quick picture to show 78.

Step 2 Think about how to break apart 78. You know 6 tens ÷ 6 = 10, so use 78 = **60 + 18**. Draw a quick picture to show 6 tens and 18 ones.

Step 3 Draw circles to show 6 tens ÷ 6 and 18 ones ÷ 6. Your drawing shows the use of the Distributive Property.
78 ÷ 6 = **(60 ÷ 6)** + **(18 ÷ 6)**

Step 4 Add the quotients to find 78 ÷ 6.

78 ÷ 6 = (60 ÷ 6) + (18 ÷ 6)
= **10** + **3**
= **13**

Use quick pictures to model the quotient.

1. 84 ÷ 4 = ____

2. 54 ÷ 3 = ____

3. 68 ÷ 2 = ____

4. 65 ÷ 5 = ____

5. 96 ÷ 8 = ____

6. 90 ÷ 6 = ____

Name ____________________

Lesson 41
CC.4.NBT.6

Division and the Distributive Property

Find the quotient.

1. 54 ÷ 3 = (30 ÷ 3) + (24 ÷ 3)

= 10 + 8

= 18

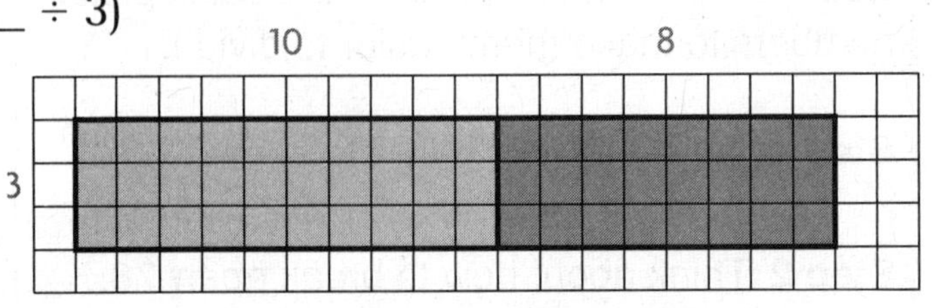

2. 81 ÷ 3 = ________

3. 232 ÷ 4 = ________

4. 305 ÷ 5 = ________

5. 246 ÷ 6 = ________

6. 69 ÷ 3 = ________

7. 477 ÷ 9 = ________

8. 224 ÷ 7 = ________

9. 72 ÷ 4 = ________

10. 315 ÷ 3 = ________

Problem Solving REAL WORLD

11. Cecily picked 219 apples. She divided the apples equally into 3 baskets. How many apples are in each basket?

____

12. Jordan has 260 basketball cards. He divides them into 4 equal groups. How many cards are in each group?

____

13. The Wilsons drove 324 miles in 6 hours. If they drove the same number of miles each hour, how many miles did they drive in 1 hour?

____

14. Phil has 189 stamps to put into his stamp album. He puts the same number of stamps on each of 9 pages. How many stamps does Phil put on each page?

____

Name ____________________

COMMON CORE STANDARD CC.4.NBT.6

Lesson Objective: Use repeated subtraction and multiples to find quotients.

Divide Using Repeated Subtraction

You can use repeated subtraction to divide. Use repeated subtraction to solve the problem.

Nestor has 27 shells to make bracelets. He needs 4 shells for each bracelet. How many bracelets can he make?

Divide. 27 ÷ 4

Write $4\overline{)27}$.

Step 1

Subtract the divisor until the remainder is less than the divisor. Record a 1 each time you subtract.

$$
\begin{array}{rl}
4\overline{)27} & \\
-4 & \mathbf{1} \\
\hline
23 & \\
-4 & 1 \\
\hline
19 & \\
-4 & 1 \\
\hline
15 & \\
-4 & 1 \\
\hline
11 & \\
-4 & 1 \\
\hline
7 & \\
-4 & 1 \\
\hline
3 &
\end{array}
$$

Step 2

Count the number of times you subtracted the divisor, 4.

4 is subtracted six times with 3 left.

27 ÷ 4

6 r3

So, Nestor can make 6 bracelets.
He will have 3 shells left.

Use repeated subtraction to divide.

1. 30 ÷ 4 ________

2. 24 ÷ 5 ________

3. 47 ÷ 7 ________

Name ______________________________

Lesson 42

CC.4.NBT.6

Divide Using Repeated Subtraction

Use repeated subtraction to divide.

1. $42 \div 3 =$ **14**

$$\begin{array}{r|r} 3\overline{)42} & \\ -30 \leftarrow 10 \times 3 & 10 \\ 12 & \\ -12 \leftarrow 4 \times 3 & +4 \\ \hline 0 & 14 \end{array}$$

2. $72 \div 4 =$ ________

3. $93 \div 3 =$ ________

4. $35 \div 4$ ________

5. $93 \div 10$ ________

6. $86 \div 9$ ________

Draw a number line to divide.

7. $70 \div 5 =$ ________

Problem Solving REAL WORLD

8. Gretchen has 48 small shells. She uses 2 shells to make one pair of earrings. How many pairs of earrings can she make?

____

9. James wants to purchase a telescope for \$54. If he saves \$3 per week, in how many weeks will he have saved enough to purchase the telescope?

____

Name ___________________________

Lesson 43

COMMON CORE STANDARD CC.4.NBT.6

Lesson Objective: Use partial quotients to divide.

Divide Using Partial Quotients

You can use partial quotients to divide.

Divide. 492 ÷ 4

Step 1 Subtract greater multiples of the divisor. Repeat if needed.

Step 2 Subtract lesser multiples of the divisor. Repeat until the remaining number is less than the divisor.

Step 3 Add the partial quotients.

4)492		Partial quotients
− 400	100 × 4	100
92		
− 80	20 × 4	20
12		
− 12	3 × 4	+ 3
0		123

Use rectangular models to record partial quotients.

	100			
4	400	80	12	492 − 400 = 92

	100	20		
4	400	80	12	92 − 80 = 12

	100	20	3	
4	400	80	12	12 − 12 = 0

100 + 20 + 3 = 123

Divide. Use partial quotients.

1. 3)657

______	100 × ___	100
______	100 × ___	______
______	___ × ___	___
______	___ × ___	+ ______

Divide. Use rectangular models to record the partial quotients.

2. 852 ÷ 6 = ____

Name ___

Divide Using Partial Quotients

Divide. Use partial quotients.

1. $8\overline{)184}$

−80	10 × 8	10
104		
−80	10 × 8	10
24		
−24	3 × 8	+3
0		23

2. $6\overline{)258}$

3. $5\overline{)630}$

Divide. Use rectangular models to record the partial quotients.

4. $246 \div 3 =$ ___

5. $126 \div 2 =$ ___

6. $605 \div 5 =$ ___

Divide. Use either way to record the partial quotients.

7. $492 \div 3 =$ ___

8. $224 \div 7 =$ ___

9. $692 \div 4 =$ ___

Problem Solving REAL WORLD

10. Allison took 112 photos on vacation. She wants to put them in a photo album that holds 4 photos on each page. How many pages can she fill?

___

11. Hector saved $726 in 6 months. He saved the same amount each month. How much did Hector save each month?

___

Name ______________________________

Lesson 44

COMMON CORE STANDARD CC.4.NBT.6

Lesson Objective: Use base-ten blocks to model division with regrouping.

Model Division with Regrouping

You can use base-ten blocks to model division with regrouping.

Use base-ten blocks to find the quotient 65 ÷ 4.

Step 1 Show 65 with base-ten blocks.

Step 2 Draw 4 circles to represent dividing 65 into 4 equal groups. Share the tens equally among the 4 groups.

Step 3 Regroup leftover tens as ones.

Step 4 Share the ones equally among the 4 groups.

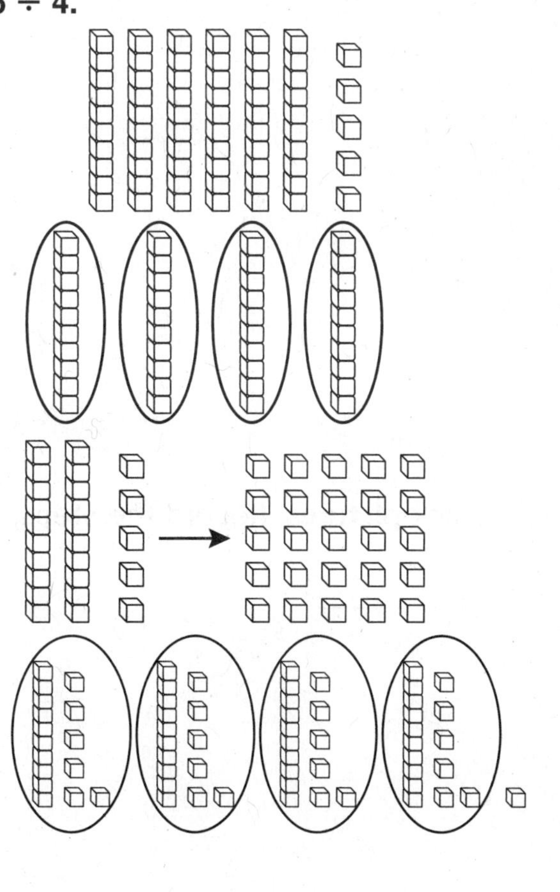

There are 1 ten(s) and 6 one(s) in each group with 1 left over.

So, the quotient is 16 r1.

Divide. Use base-ten blocks.

1. 37 ÷ 2 ________

2. 74 ÷ 3 ________

3. 66 ÷ 5 ________

Name ______________________

Lesson 44
CC.4.NBT.6

Model Division with Regrouping

Divide. Use base-ten blocks.

1. $63 \div 4$ 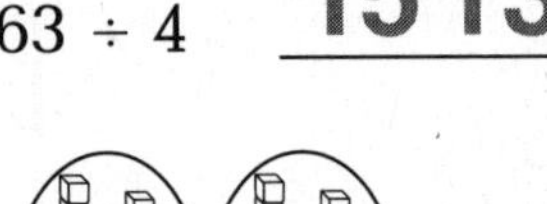

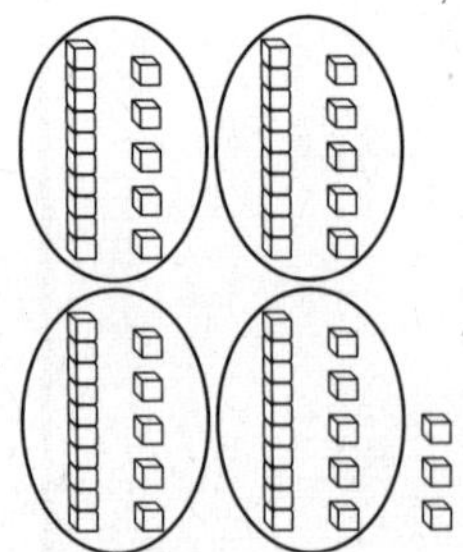

2. $83 \div 3$ __________

Divide. Draw quick pictures. Record the steps.

3. $85 \div 5$ __________

4. $97 \div 4$ __________

Problem Solving REAL WORLD

5. Tamara sold 92 cold drinks during her 2-hour shift at a festival food stand. If she sold the same number of drinks each hour, how many cold drinks did she sell each hour?

____

6. In 3 days Donald earned $42 running errands. He earned the same amount each day. How much did Donald earn from running errands each day?

____

Name ______________________________

Place the First Digit

Lesson 45

COMMON CORE STANDARD CC.4.NBT.6

Lesson Objective: Use place value to determine where to place the first digit of a quotient.

Divide. $763 \div 3 = \blacksquare$

Step 1 Estimate. Then divide the hundreds.

Think: 3 × 1 hundred = 3 hundreds
3 × 2 hundreds = 6 hundreds
3 × 3 hundreds = 9 hundreds

3 × **3 hundreds** is too large.
Use **2 hundreds** as an estimate.

$$\begin{array}{r} 2 \\ 3\overline{)763} \\ -6 \\ \hline 1 \end{array}$$

2 ← Divide 7 hundreds by 3.
−6 ← Multiply. 3 × 2 hundreds
1 ← Subtract.

Step 2 Bring down the tens digit. Then divide the tens.

$$\begin{array}{r} 2 \\ 3\overline{)763} \\ -6\downarrow \\ \hline 16 \end{array}$$

16 ← Bring down the 6.

$$\begin{array}{r} 25 \\ 3\overline{)763} \\ -6 \\ \hline 16 \\ -15 \\ \hline 1 \end{array}$$

25 ← Divide 16 tens by 3.
−15 ← Multiply. 3 × 5 tens
1 ← Subtract.

Step 3 Bring down the ones digit. Then divide the ones.

$$\begin{array}{r} 25 \\ 3\overline{)763} \\ -6 \\ \hline 16 \\ -15\downarrow \\ \hline 13 \end{array}$$

13 ← Bring down the 3.

$$\begin{array}{r} 254 \\ 3\overline{)763} \\ -6 \\ \hline 16 \\ -15 \\ \hline 13 \\ -12 \\ \hline 1 \end{array}$$

254 ← Divide 13 ones by 3.
−12 ← Multiply. 3 × 4 ones
1 ← Subtract.

Step 4 Check to make sure that the remainder is less than the divisor. Write the answer.

$$\begin{array}{r} 254 \text{ r1} \\ 3\overline{)763}\phantom{\text{ r1}} \end{array}$$

$1 < 3$

Divide.

1. $2\overline{)531}$

2. $4\overline{)628}$

3. $9\overline{)349}$

4. $7\overline{)794}$

Name ______________________________

Place the First Digit

Divide.

1. $3\overline{)186}$ = 62

   -18
   06
   -6
   0

2. $4\overline{)298}$

3. $3\overline{)461}$

4. $9\overline{)315}$

5. $2\overline{)766}$

6. $4\overline{)604}$

7. $6\overline{)796}$

8. $5\overline{)449}$

9. $6\overline{)756}$

10. $7\overline{)521}$

11. $5\overline{)675}$

12. $8\overline{)933}$

Problem Solving REAL WORLD

13. There are 132 projects in the science fair. If 8 projects can fit in a row, how many full rows of projects can be made? How many projects are in the row that is not full?

    ____

14. There are 798 calories in six 10-ounce bottles of apple juice. How many calories are there in one 10-ounce bottle of apple juice?

    ____

Name ______________________________

COMMON CORE STANDARD CC.4.NBT.6

Lesson Objective: Divide multidigit numbers by 1-digit divisors.

Divide by 1-Digit Numbers

Divide. 766 ÷ 6 = ■

Step 1 Use place value to place the first digit.
Think: 7 hundreds can be shared among 6 groups without regrouping.

$$6\overline{)766}\quad \text{quotient: } 1$$

Step 2 Bring down the tens digit. Then divide the tens.

$$\begin{array}{r} 1 \\ 6\overline{)766} \\ -6\downarrow \\ \hline 16 \end{array}$$

← Bring down the 6.

$$\begin{array}{r} 12 \\ 6\overline{)766} \\ -6 \\ \hline 16 \\ -12 \\ \hline 4 \end{array}$$

- 12 ← Divide 16 tens by 6.
- −12 ← Multiply. 6 × 2 tens
- 4 ← Subtract.

Step 3 Bring down the ones digit. Then divide the ones.

$$\begin{array}{r} 12 \\ 6\overline{)766} \\ -6 \\ \hline 16 \\ -12\downarrow \\ \hline 46 \end{array}$$

46 ← Bring down the 6.

$$\begin{array}{r} 127 \\ 6\overline{)766} \\ -6 \\ \hline 16 \\ -12 \\ \hline 46 \\ -42 \\ \hline 4 \end{array}$$

- 127 ← Divide 46 ones by 6.
- −42 ← Multiply. 6 × 7 ones
- 4 ← Subtract.

Step 4 Check to make sure that the remainder is less than the divisor. Write the answer.

$$\begin{array}{r} 127 \text{ r4} \\ 6\overline{)766} \end{array} \qquad 4 < 6$$

Step 5 Use multiplication and addition to check your answer.

$$\begin{array}{r} 127 \\ \times\ 6 \\ \hline 762 \\ +\ 4 \\ \hline 766 \end{array}$$

Divide and check.

1. $4\overline{)868}$

2. $2\overline{)657}$

3. $7\overline{)8{,}473}$

Name ____________________

Divide by 1-Digit Numbers

Lesson 46
CC.4.NBT.6

Divide and check.

1. $2\overline{)636}$ = 318

$$\begin{array}{r} 318 \\ 2\overline{)636} \\ -6\downarrow \\ \hline 03 \\ -2\downarrow \\ \hline 16 \\ -16 \\ \hline 0 \end{array} \qquad \begin{array}{r} 318 \\ \times\ \ 2 \\ \hline 636 \end{array}$$

2. $4\overline{)631}$

3. $8\overline{)906}$

4. $6\overline{)6{,}739}$

5. $4\overline{)2{,}328}$

6. $5\overline{)7{,}549}$

Problem Solving REAL WORLD

Use the table for 7 and 8.

7. The Briggs rented a car for 5 weeks. What was the cost of their rental car per week?

____

8. The Lees rented a car for 4 weeks. The Santos rented a car for 2 weeks. Whose weekly rental cost was lower? **Explain.**

____

____

Rental Car Costs	
Family	**Total Cost**
Lee	$632
Brigg	$985
Santo	$328

Name ______________________________

Lesson 47

COMMON CORE STANDARD CC.4.NF.1

Lesson Objective: Use models to show equivalent fractions.

Equivalent Fractions

Write two fractions that are equivalent to $\frac{2}{6}$.

Step 1 Make a model to represent $\frac{2}{6}$.

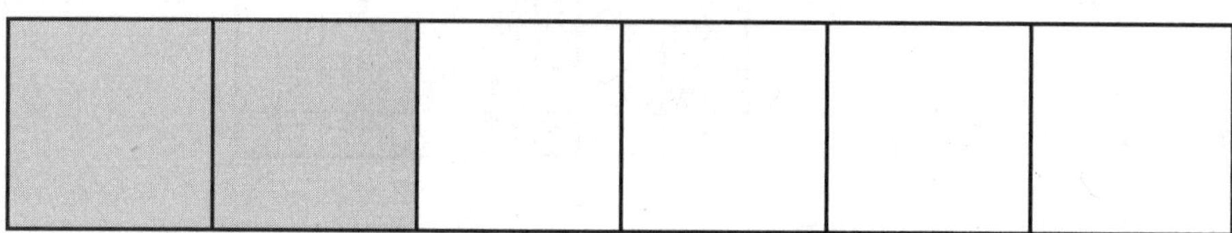

The rectangle is divided into 6 equal parts, with 2 parts shaded.

Step 2 Divide the rectangle from Step 1 in half.

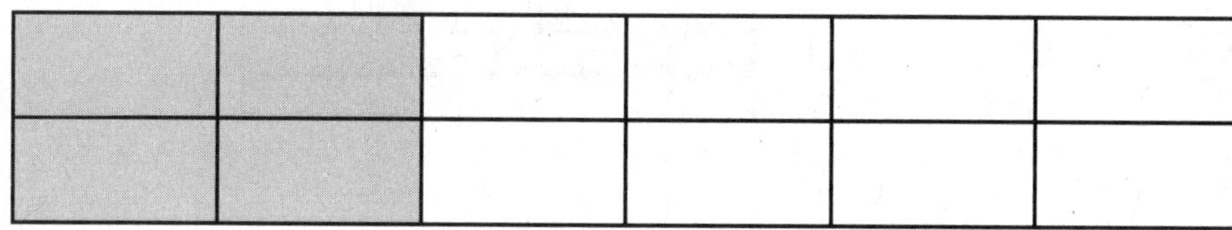

The rectangle is now divided into 12 equal parts, with 4 parts shaded.

The model shows the fraction $\frac{4}{12}$. So, $\frac{2}{6}$ and $\frac{4}{12}$ are equivalent.

Step 3 Draw the same rectangle as in Step 1, but with only 3 equal parts. Keep the same amount of the rectangle shaded.

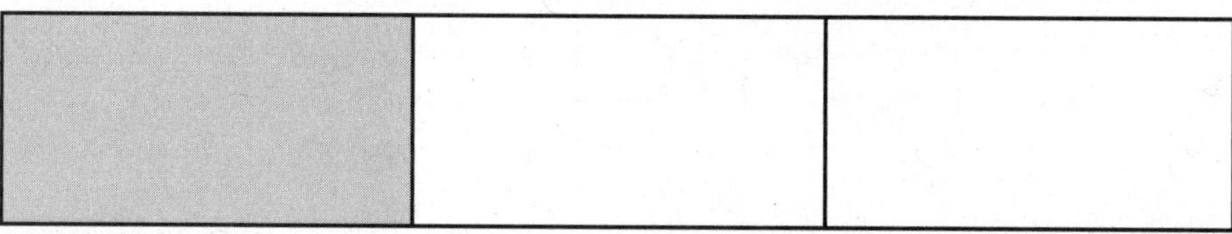

The rectangle is now divided into 3 equal parts, with 1 part shaded.

The model shows the fraction $\frac{1}{3}$. So, $\frac{2}{6}$ and $\frac{1}{3}$ are equivalent.

Use models to write two equivalent fractions.

1. $\frac{2}{4}$

____

2. $\frac{4}{6}$

____

Name ____________________

Equivalent Fractions

Use the model to write an equivalent fraction.

1. 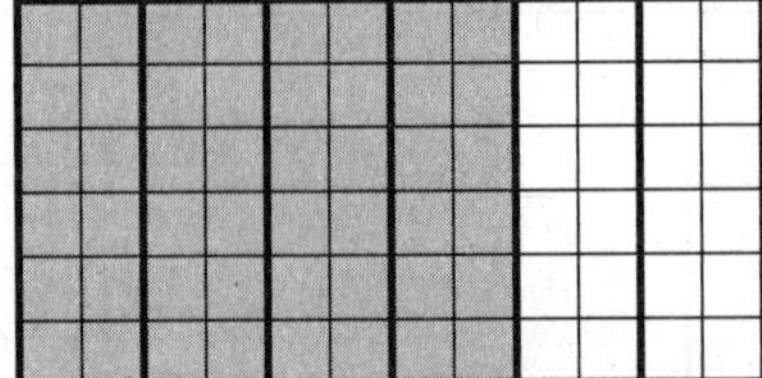 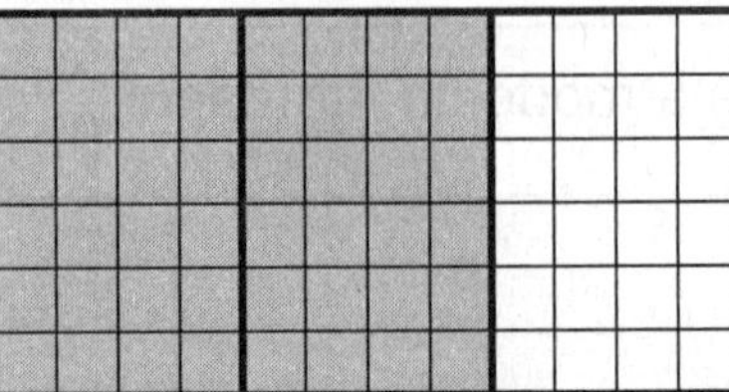

$\frac{4}{6}$ = $\frac{2}{3}$

2. 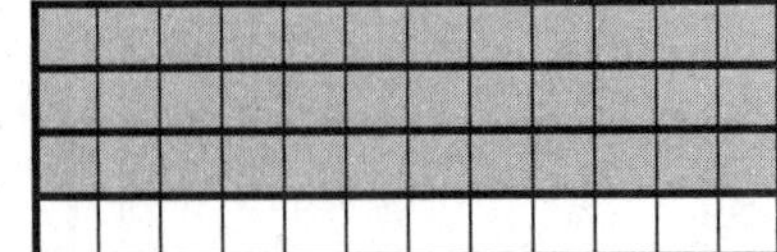 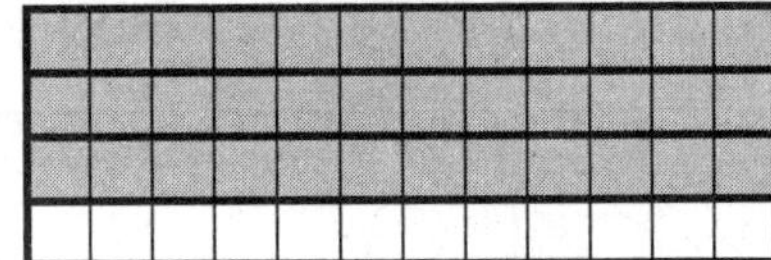

$\frac{3}{4}$ = ______

Tell whether the fractions are equivalent. Write = or ≠.

3. $\frac{8}{10} \bigcirc \frac{4}{5}$

4. $\frac{1}{2} \bigcirc \frac{7}{12}$

5. $\frac{3}{4} \bigcirc \frac{8}{12}$

6. $\frac{2}{3} \bigcirc \frac{4}{6}$

7. $\frac{5}{8} \bigcirc \frac{4}{10}$

8. $\frac{2}{6} \bigcirc \frac{4}{12}$

9. $\frac{20}{100} \bigcirc \frac{1}{5}$

10. $\frac{5}{8} \bigcirc \frac{9}{10}$

Problem Solving

11. Jamal finished $\frac{5}{6}$ of his homework. Margaret finished $\frac{3}{4}$ of her homework, and Steve finished $\frac{10}{12}$ of his homework. Which two students finished the same amount of homework?

____

12. Sophia's vegetable garden is divided into 12 equal sections. She plants carrots in 8 of the sections. Write two fractions that are equivalent to the part of Sophia's garden that is planted with carrots.

____

Name ___________________________

Lesson 48

COMMON CORE STANDARD CC.4.NF.1

Lesson Objective: Use multiplication to generate equivalent fractions.

Generate Equivalent Fractions

Write an equivalent fraction for $\frac{4}{5}$.

Step 1 Choose a whole number, like 2.
Step 2 Create a fraction using 2 as the numerator and denominator: $\frac{2}{2}$. This fraction is equal to 1. You can multiply a number by 1 without changing the value of the number.
Step 3 Multiply $\frac{4}{5}$ by $\frac{2}{2}$: $\frac{4 \times 2}{5 \times 2} = \frac{8}{10}$.
So, $\frac{4}{5}$ and $\frac{8}{10}$ are equivalent.

Write another equivalent fraction for $\frac{4}{5}$.

Step 1 Choose a different whole number, like 20.
Step 2 Create a fraction using 20 as the numerator and denominator: $\frac{20}{20}$.
Step 3 Multiply $\frac{4}{5}$ by $\frac{20}{20}$: $\frac{4 \times 20}{5 \times 20} = \frac{80}{100}$.
So, $\frac{4}{5}$ and $\frac{80}{100}$ are equivalent.

Write two equivalent fractions.

1. $\frac{2}{6}$ ___________________________

2. $\frac{4}{10}$ ___________________________

3. $\frac{3}{8}$ ___________________________

4. $\frac{3}{5}$ ___________________________

Name ______________________

Generate Equivalent Fractions

Write two equivalent fractions for each.

1. $\frac{1}{3}$

$\frac{1 \times 2}{3 \times 2} = \frac{2}{6}$

$\frac{1 \times 4}{3 \times 4} = \frac{4}{12}$

2. $\frac{2}{3}$ ______

3. $\frac{1}{2}$ ______

4. $\frac{4}{5}$ ______

Tell whether the fractions are equivalent. Write = or ≠.

5. $\frac{1}{4} \bigcirc \frac{3}{12}$

6. $\frac{4}{5} \bigcirc \frac{5}{10}$

7. $\frac{3}{8} \bigcirc \frac{2}{6}$

8. $\frac{3}{4} \bigcirc \frac{6}{8}$

9. $\frac{5}{6} \bigcirc \frac{10}{12}$

10. $\frac{6}{12} \bigcirc \frac{5}{8}$

11. $\frac{2}{5} \bigcirc \frac{4}{10}$

12. $\frac{2}{4} \bigcirc \frac{3}{12}$

Problem Solving

13. Jan has a 12-ounce milkshake. Four ounces in the milkshake are vanilla, and the rest is chocolate. What are two equivalent fractions that represent the fraction of the milkshake that is vanilla?

____

14. Kareem lives $\frac{4}{10}$ of a mile from the mall. Write two equivalent fractions that show what fraction of a mile Kareem lives from the mall.

____

Name ______________________________

Lesson 49

COMMON CORE STANDARD CC.4.NF.1

Lesson Objective: Write and identify equivalent fractions in simplest form.

Simplest Form

A fraction is in **simplest form** when 1 is the only factor that the numerator and denominator have in common.

Tell whether the fraction $\frac{7}{8}$ is in simplest form.

Look for common factors in the numerator and the denominator.

Step 1 The numerator of $\frac{7}{8}$ is 7. List all the factors of 7.	$1 \times 7 = 7$ The factors of 7 are 1 and 7.
Step 2 The denominator of $\frac{7}{8}$ is 8. List all the factors of 8.	$1 \times 8 = 8$ $2 \times 4 = 8$ The factors of 8 are 1, 2, 4, and 8.
Step 3 Check if the numerator and denominator of $\frac{7}{8}$ have any common factors greater than 1.	The only common factor of 7 and 8 is 1.
So, $\frac{7}{8}$ is in simplest form.	

Tell whether the fraction is in simplest form. Write *yes* or *no*.

1. $\frac{4}{10}$ ______________

2. $\frac{2}{8}$ ______________

3. $\frac{3}{5}$ ______________

Write the fraction in simplest form.

4. $\frac{4}{12}$ ______________

5. $\frac{6}{10}$ ______________

6. $\frac{3}{6}$ ______________

Name ______________________________

Lesson 49
CC.4.NF.1

Simplest Form

Write the fraction in simplest form.

1. $\frac{6}{10}$

$\frac{6}{10} = \frac{6 \div 2}{10 \div 2} = \frac{3}{5}$

2. $\frac{6}{8}$ ________

3. $\frac{5}{5}$ ________

4. $\frac{8}{12}$ ________

5. $\frac{100}{100}$ ________

6. $\frac{2}{6}$ ________

7. $\frac{2}{8}$ ________

8. $\frac{4}{10}$ ________

Tell whether the fractions are equivalent.
Write = or ≠.

9. $\frac{6}{12}$ ◯ $\frac{1}{12}$

10. $\frac{3}{4}$ ◯ $\frac{5}{6}$

11. $\frac{6}{10}$ ◯ $\frac{3}{5}$

12. $\frac{3}{12}$ ◯ $\frac{1}{3}$

13. $\frac{6}{10}$ ◯ $\frac{60}{100}$

14. $\frac{11}{12}$ ◯ $\frac{9}{10}$

15. $\frac{2}{5}$ ◯ $\frac{8}{20}$

16. $\frac{4}{8}$ ◯ $\frac{1}{2}$

Problem Solving REAL WORLD

17. At Memorial Hospital, 9 of the 12 babies born on Tuesday were boys. In simplest form, what fraction of the babies born on Tuesday were boys?

____

18. Cristina uses a ruler to measure the length of her math textbook. She says that the book is $\frac{4}{10}$ meter long. Is her measurement in simplest form? If not, what is the length of the book in simplest form?

____

Name ____________________

Common Denominators

Lesson 50

COMMON CORE STANDARD CC.4.NF.1

Lesson Objective: Use equivalent fractions to represent a pair of fractions with a common denominator.

A **common denominator** is a common multiple of the denominators of two or more fractions.

Write $\frac{2}{3}$ and $\frac{3}{4}$ as a pair of fractions with common denominators.

Step 1 Identify the denominators of $\frac{2}{3}$ and $\frac{3}{4}$.	$\frac{2}{3}$ and $\frac{3}{4}$ The denominators are 3 and 4.
Step 2 List multiples of 3 and 4. Circle common multiples.	**3:** 3, 6, 9, (12), 15, 18 **4:** 4, 8, (12), 16, 20 12 is a common multiple of 3 and 4.
Step 3 Rewrite $\frac{2}{3}$ as a fraction with a denominator of 12.	$\frac{2}{3} = \frac{2 \times 4}{3 \times 4} = \frac{8}{12}$
Step 4 Rewrite $\frac{3}{4}$ as a fraction with a denominator of 12.	$\frac{3}{4} = \frac{3 \times 3}{4 \times 3} = \frac{9}{12}$
So, you can rewrite $\frac{2}{3}$ and $\frac{3}{4}$ as $\frac{8}{12}$ and $\frac{9}{12}$.	

Write the pair of fractions as a pair of fractions with a common denominator.

1. $\frac{1}{2}$ and $\frac{1}{3}$ ____________________

2. $\frac{2}{4}$ and $\frac{5}{8}$ ____________________

3. $\frac{1}{2}$ and $\frac{3}{5}$ ____________________

4. $\frac{1}{4}$ and $\frac{5}{6}$ ____________________

5. $\frac{2}{5}$ and $\frac{2}{3}$ ____________________

6. $\frac{4}{5}$ and $\frac{7}{10}$ ____________________

Name ______________________

Common Denominators

Write the pair of fractions as a pair of fractions with a common denominator.

1. $\frac{2}{3}$ and $\frac{3}{4}$

Think: Find a common multiple.
3: 3, 6, 9, (12), 15
4: 4, 8, (12), 16, 20

$\frac{8}{12}$, $\frac{9}{12}$

2. $\frac{1}{4}$ and $\frac{2}{3}$ ______

3. $\frac{3}{10}$ and $\frac{1}{2}$ ______

4. $\frac{3}{5}$ and $\frac{3}{4}$ ______

5. $\frac{2}{4}$ and $\frac{7}{8}$ ______

6. $\frac{2}{3}$ and $\frac{5}{12}$ ______

7. $\frac{1}{4}$ and $\frac{1}{6}$ ______

Tell whether the fractions are equivalent. Write = or ≠.

8. $\frac{1}{2}$ ◯ $\frac{2}{5}$

9. $\frac{1}{2}$ ◯ $\frac{3}{6}$

10. $\frac{3}{4}$ ◯ $\frac{5}{6}$

11. $\frac{6}{10}$ ◯ $\frac{3}{5}$

12. $\frac{6}{8}$ ◯ $\frac{3}{4}$

13. $\frac{3}{4}$ ◯ $\frac{2}{3}$

14. $\frac{2}{10}$ ◯ $\frac{4}{5}$

15. $\frac{1}{4}$ ◯ $\frac{3}{12}$

Problem Solving REAL WORLD

16. Adam drew two same size rectangles and divided them into the same number of equal parts. He shaded $\frac{1}{3}$ of one rectangle and $\frac{1}{4}$ of other rectangle. What is the least number of parts into which both rectangles could be divided?

____

17. Mera painted equal sections of her bedroom wall to make a pattern. She painted $\frac{2}{5}$ of the wall white and $\frac{1}{2}$ of the wall lavender. Write an equivalent fraction for each using a common denominator.

____

Name ________________________________

Lesson 51

COMMON CORE STANDARD CC.4.NF.1

Lesson Objective: Use the strategy *make a table* to solve problems using equivalent fractions.

Problem Solving • Find Equivalent Fractions

Kyle's mom bought bunches of balloons for a family party. Each bunch has 4 balloons, and $\frac{1}{4}$ of the balloons are blue. If Kyle's mom bought 5 bunches of balloons, how many balloons did she buy? How many of the balloons are blue?

Read the Problem		
What do I need to find?	**What information do I need to use?**	**How will I use the information?**
I need to find how many balloons Kyle's mom bought and how many of the balloons are blue.	Each bunch has 1 out of 4 balloons that are blue, and there are 5 bunches.	I will make a table to find the total number balloons Kyle's mom bought and the fraction of balloons that are blue.

Solve the Problem

I can make a table.

Number of Bunches	1	2	3	4	5
$\frac{\text{Total Number of Blue Balloons}}{\text{Total Number of Balloons}}$	$\frac{1}{4}$	$\frac{2}{8}$	$\frac{3}{12}$	$\frac{4}{16}$	$\frac{5}{20}$

Kyle's mom bought 20 balloons. 5 of the balloons are blue.

Make a table to solve.

1. Jackie is making a beaded bracelet. The bracelet will have no more than 12 beads. $\frac{1}{3}$ of the beads on the bracelet will be green. What other fractions could represent the part of the beads on the bracelet that will be green?

____

2. Ben works in his dad's bakery packing bagels. Each package can have no more than 16 bagels. $\frac{3}{4}$ of the bagels in each package are plain. What other fractions could represent the part of the bagels in each package that will be plain?

____

Name ______________________________

Problem Solving • Find Equivalent Fractions

Solve each problem.

1. Miranda is braiding her hair. Then she will attach beads to the braid. She wants $\frac{1}{3}$ of the beads to be red. If the greatest number of beads that will fit on the braid is 12, what other fractions could represent the part of the beads that are red?

$\frac{2}{6}, \frac{3}{9}, \frac{4}{12}$

2. Ms. Groves has trays of paints for students in her art class. Each tray has 5 colors. One of the colors is purple. What fraction of the colors in 20 trays is purple?

____

3. Miguel is making an obstacle course for field day. At the end of every sixth of the course, there is a tire. At the end of every third of the course, there is a cone. At the end of every half of the course, there is a hurdle. At which locations of the course will people need to go through more than one obstacle?

____

4. Preston works in a bakery where he puts muffins in boxes. He makes the following table to remind himself how many blueberry muffins should go in each box.

Number of Blueberry Muffins	2	4	8	■
Total Number of Muffins	6	12	24	36

How many blueberry muffins should Preston put in a box with 36 muffins?

____

Name ______________________________

Lesson 52

COMMON CORE STANDARD CC.4.NF.2

Lesson Objective: Compare fractions using benchmarks.

Compare Fractions Using Benchmarks

A **benchmark** is a known size or amount that helps you understand a different size or amount. You can use $\frac{1}{2}$ as a benchmark.

Sara reads for $\frac{3}{6}$ hour every day after school. Connor reads for $\frac{2}{3}$ hour. Who reads for a longer amount of time?

Compare the fractions. $\frac{3}{6}$ ● $\frac{2}{3}$

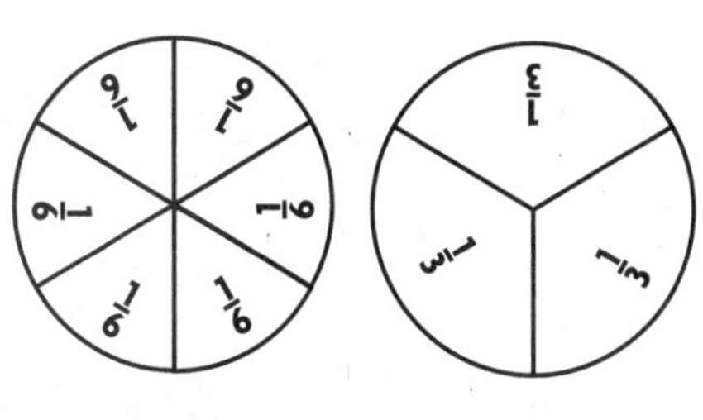

Step 1 Divide one circle into 6 equal parts. Divide another circle into 3 equal parts.

Step 2 Shade $\frac{3}{6}$ of the first circle. How many parts will you shade? **3 parts**

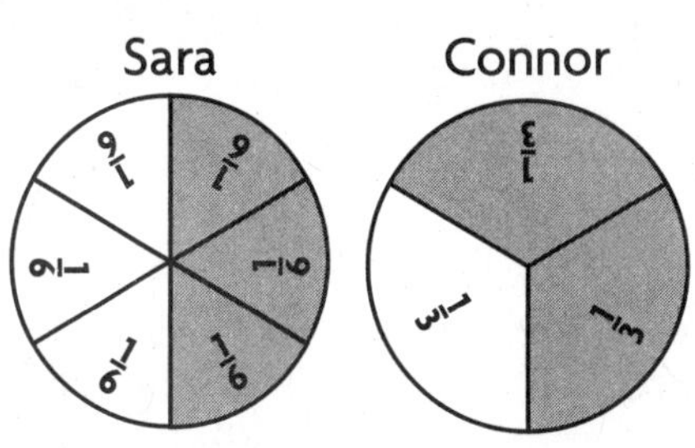

Step 3 Shade $\frac{2}{3}$ of the second circle. How many parts will you shade? **2 parts**

Step 4 Compare the shaded parts of each circle. Half of Sara's circle is shaded. More than half of Connor's circle is shaded.

$\frac{3}{6}$ is less than $\frac{2}{3}$. $\frac{3}{6} < \frac{2}{3}$

So, **Connor** reads for a longer amount of time.

1. Compare $\frac{2}{8}$ and $\frac{3}{4}$. Write $<$ or $>$.

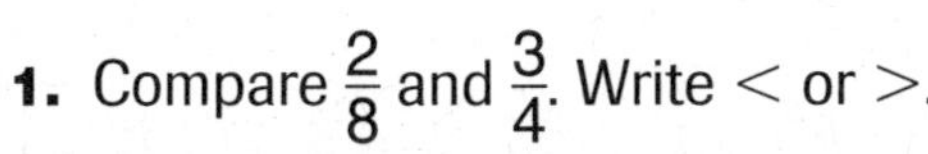

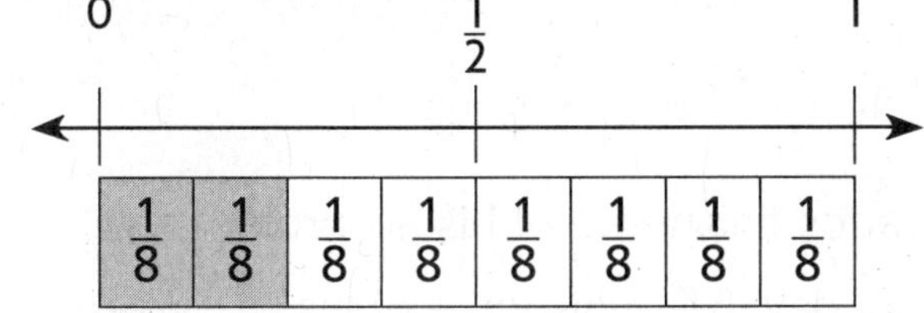

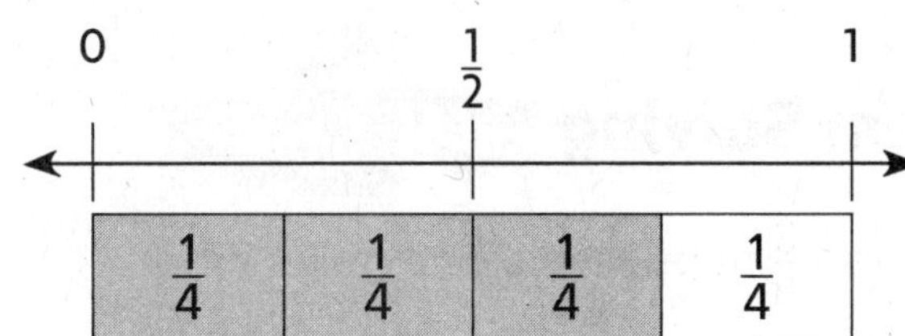

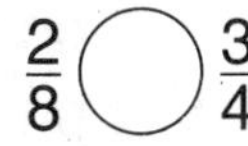

$\frac{2}{8}$ ◯ $\frac{3}{4}$

Compare. Write $<$ or $>$.

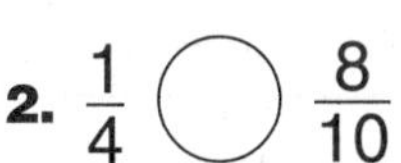

2. $\frac{1}{4}$ ◯ $\frac{8}{10}$

3. $\frac{7}{8}$ ◯ $\frac{1}{3}$

4. $\frac{5}{12}$ ◯ $\frac{1}{2}$

5. $\frac{2}{8}$ ◯ $\frac{8}{12}$

6. $\frac{4}{6}$ ◯ $\frac{4}{8}$

7. $\frac{7}{12}$ ◯ $\frac{2}{4}$

Name ______________________

Compare Fractions Using Benchmarks

Compare. Write < or >.

1. $\frac{1}{8}$ (<) $\frac{6}{10}$

Think: $\frac{1}{8}$ is less than $\frac{1}{2}$.
$\frac{6}{10}$ is more than $\frac{1}{2}$.

2. $\frac{4}{12}$ ◯ $\frac{4}{6}$

3. $\frac{2}{8}$ ◯ $\frac{1}{2}$

4. $\frac{3}{5}$ ◯ $\frac{3}{3}$

5. $\frac{7}{8}$ ◯ $\frac{5}{10}$

6. $\frac{9}{12}$ ◯ $\frac{1}{3}$

7. $\frac{4}{6}$ ◯ $\frac{7}{8}$

8. $\frac{2}{4}$ ◯ $\frac{2}{3}$

9. $\frac{3}{5}$ ◯ $\frac{1}{4}$

10. $\frac{6}{10}$ ◯ $\frac{2}{5}$

11. $\frac{1}{8}$ ◯ $\frac{2}{10}$

12. $\frac{2}{3}$ ◯ $\frac{5}{12}$

13. $\frac{4}{5}$ ◯ $\frac{5}{6}$

14. $\frac{3}{5}$ ◯ $\frac{5}{8}$

15. $\frac{8}{8}$ ◯ $\frac{3}{4}$

Problem Solving REAL WORLD

16. Erika ran $\frac{3}{8}$ mile. Maria ran $\frac{3}{4}$ mile. Who ran farther?

____

17. Carlos finished $\frac{1}{3}$ of his art project on Monday. Tyler finished $\frac{1}{2}$ of his art project on Monday. Who finished more of his art project on Monday?

____

Name ______________________

Lesson 53

COMMON CORE STANDARD CC.4.NF.2

Lesson Objective: Compare fractions by first writing them as fractions with a common numerator or a common denominator.

Compare Fractions

Theo filled a beaker $\frac{2}{4}$ full with water. Angelica filled a beaker $\frac{3}{8}$ full with water. Whose beaker has more water?

Compare $\frac{2}{4}$ and $\frac{3}{8}$.

Step 1 Divide one beaker into 4 equal parts. Divide another beaker into 8 equal parts.

Step 2 Shade $\frac{2}{4}$ of the first beaker.

Step 3 Shade $\frac{3}{8}$ of the second beaker.

Step 4 Compare the shaded parts of each beaker. Half of Theo's beaker is shaded. Less than half of Angelica's beaker is shaded.

$\frac{2}{4}$ is greater than $\frac{3}{8}$.

$\frac{2}{4} > \frac{3}{8}$

So, Theo's beaker has more water.

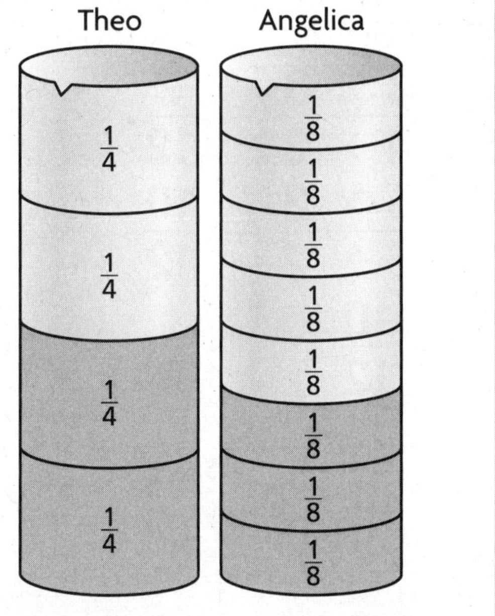

1. Compare $\frac{1}{2}$ and $\frac{1}{4}$.

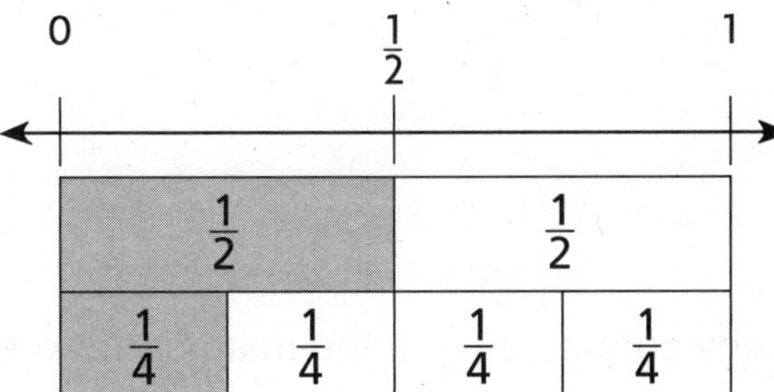

Which is greater? ______________

2. Compare $\frac{2}{3}$ and $\frac{3}{6}$.

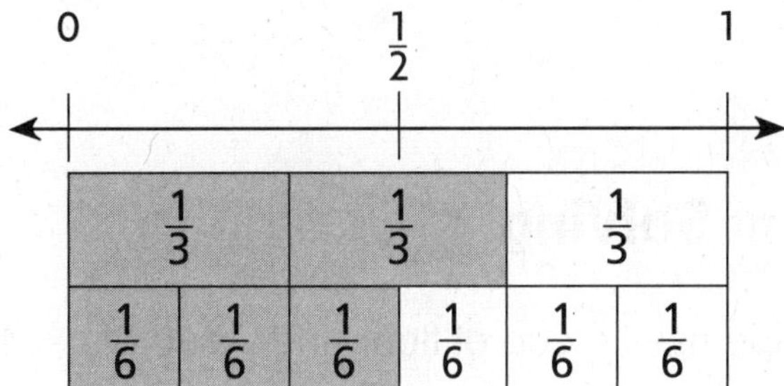

Which is less? ______________

Compare. Write <, >, or =.

3. $\frac{1}{2}$ ◯ $\frac{3}{4}$

4. $\frac{6}{12}$ ◯ $\frac{5}{8}$

5. $\frac{2}{3}$ ◯ $\frac{4}{6}$

6. $\frac{3}{8}$ ◯ $\frac{1}{4}$

Name ______________________________

Compare Fractions

Compare. Write <, >, or =.

1. $\frac{3}{4}$ (<) $\frac{5}{6}$

Think: 12 is a common denominator.

$$\frac{3}{4} = \frac{3 \times 3}{4 \times 3} = \frac{9}{12}$$
$$\frac{5}{6} = \frac{5 \times 2}{6 \times 2} = \frac{10}{12}$$
$$\frac{9}{12} < \frac{10}{12}$$

2. $\frac{1}{5}$ ◯ $\frac{2}{10}$

3. $\frac{2}{4}$ ◯ $\frac{2}{5}$

4. $\frac{3}{5}$ ◯ $\frac{7}{10}$

5. $\frac{4}{12}$ ◯ $\frac{1}{6}$

6. $\frac{2}{6}$ ◯ $\frac{1}{3}$

7. $\frac{1}{3}$ ◯ $\frac{2}{4}$

8. $\frac{2}{5}$ ◯ $\frac{1}{2}$

9. $\frac{4}{8}$ ◯ $\frac{2}{4}$

10. $\frac{7}{12}$ ◯ $\frac{2}{4}$

11. $\frac{1}{8}$ ◯ $\frac{3}{4}$

Problem Solving REAL WORLD

12. A recipe uses $\frac{2}{3}$ cup of flour and $\frac{5}{8}$ cup of blueberries. Is there more flour or more blueberries in the recipe?

____

13. Peggy completed $\frac{5}{6}$ of the math homework and Al completed $\frac{4}{5}$ of the math homework. Did Peggy or Al complete more of the math homework?

____

Name ______________________________

Lesson 54

COMMON CORE STANDARD CC.4.NF.2

Lesson Objective: Compare and order fractions.

Compare and Order Fractions

Write $\frac{3}{8}$, $\frac{1}{4}$, and $\frac{1}{2}$ in order from least to greatest.

Step 1 Identify a common denominator.	Multiples of 8: (8), 16, 24 Multiples of 4: 4, (8), 16, Multiples of 2: 2, 4, 6, (8) Use 8 as a common denominator.
Step 2 Use the common denominator to write equivalent fractions.	$\frac{3}{8}$ $\frac{1}{4} = \frac{1 \times 2}{4 \times 2} = \frac{2}{8}$ $\frac{1}{2} = \frac{1 \times 4}{2 \times 4} = \frac{4}{8}$
Step 3 Compare the numerators.	$2 < 3 < 4$
Step 4 Order the fractions from least to greatest, using $<$ or $>$ symbols. So, $\frac{1}{4} < \frac{3}{8} < \frac{1}{2}$.	$\frac{2}{8} < \frac{3}{8} < \frac{4}{8}$

Write the fraction with the greatest value.

1. $\frac{2}{3}, \frac{1}{4}, \frac{1}{6}$ ______________

2. $\frac{3}{10}, \frac{1}{2}, \frac{2}{5}$ ______________

3. $\frac{1}{8}, \frac{5}{12}, \frac{9}{10}$ ______________

Write the fractions in order from least to greatest.

4. $\frac{9}{10}, \frac{1}{2}, \frac{4}{5}$ ______________

5. $\frac{3}{4}, \frac{7}{8}, \frac{1}{2}$ ______________

6. $\frac{2}{3}, \frac{3}{4}, \frac{5}{6}$ ______________

Name ______________________________

Lesson 54

CC.4.NF.2

Compare and Order Fractions

Write the fractions in order from least to greatest.

1. $\frac{5}{8}, \frac{2}{12}, \frac{8}{10}$

Use benchmarks and a number line.

Think: $\frac{5}{8}$ is close to $\frac{1}{2}$. $\frac{2}{12}$ is close to 0.
$\frac{8}{10}$ is close to 1.

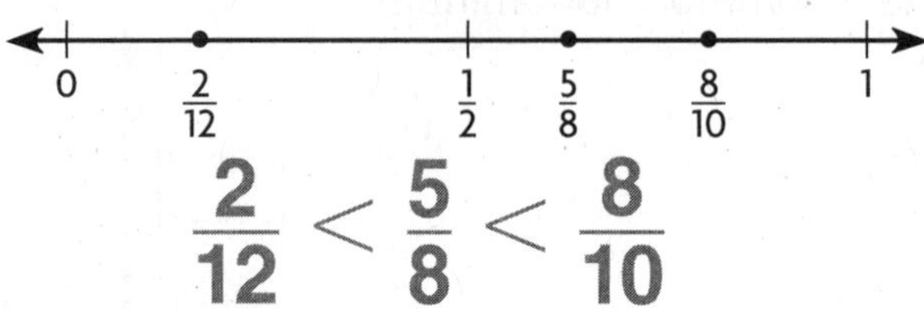

$\frac{2}{12} < \frac{5}{8} < \frac{8}{10}$

2. $\frac{1}{5}, \frac{2}{3}, \frac{5}{8}$

____

3. $\frac{1}{2}, \frac{2}{5}, \frac{6}{10}$

____

4. $\frac{4}{6}, \frac{7}{12}, \frac{5}{10}$

____

5. $\frac{1}{4}, \frac{3}{6}, \frac{1}{8}$

____

6. $\frac{1}{8}, \frac{3}{6}, \frac{7}{12}$

____

7. $\frac{8}{100}, \frac{3}{5}, \frac{7}{10}$

____

8. $\frac{3}{4}, \frac{7}{8}, \frac{1}{5}$

____

Problem Solving REAL WORLD

9. Amy's math notebook weighs $\frac{1}{2}$ pound, her science notebook weighs $\frac{7}{8}$ pound, and her history notebook weighs $\frac{3}{4}$ pound. What are the weights in order from lightest to heaviest?

____

____

10. Carl has three picture frames. The thicknesses of the frames are $\frac{4}{5}$ inch, $\frac{3}{12}$ inch, and $\frac{5}{6}$ inch. What are the thicknesses in order from least to greatest?

____

____

Name ________________________________

Lesson 55

COMMON CORE STANDARD CC.4.NF.3a

Lesson Objective: Understand that to add or subtract fractions, they must refer to parts of the same wholes.

Add and Subtract Parts of a Whole

Justin has $\frac{3}{8}$ pound of cheddar cheese and $\frac{2}{8}$ pound of brick cheese. How much cheese does he have in all?

Step 1 Use fraction strips to model the problem. Use three $\frac{1}{8}$-strips to represent $\frac{3}{8}$ pound of cheddar cheese.

Step 2 Join two more $\frac{1}{8}$-strips to represent the amount of brick cheese.

Step 3 Count the number of $\frac{1}{8}$-strips. There are __five__ $\frac{1}{8}$-strips. Write the amount as a fraction. Justin has __$\frac{5}{8}$__ pound of cheese.

Step 4 Use the model to write an equation. __$\frac{3}{8} + \frac{2}{8} = \frac{5}{8}$__

Suppose Justin eats $\frac{1}{8}$ pound of cheese. How much cheese is left?

Step 1 Use five $\frac{1}{8}$-strips to represent the $\frac{5}{8}$ pound of cheese.

Step 2 Remove one $\frac{1}{8}$-strip to show the amount eaten.

Step 3 Count the number of $\frac{1}{8}$-strips left. There are __four__ $\frac{1}{8}$ fraction strips. There is __$\frac{4}{8}$__ pound left.

Step 4 Write an equation for the model. __$\frac{5}{8} - \frac{1}{8} = \frac{4}{8}$__

Use the model to write an equation.

1. [1 | $\frac{1}{5}$] + [1 | $\frac{1}{5}$ $\frac{1}{5}$ $\frac{1}{5}$] = [1 | $\frac{1}{5}$ $\frac{1}{5}$ $\frac{1}{5}$ $\frac{1}{5}$]

____

2. 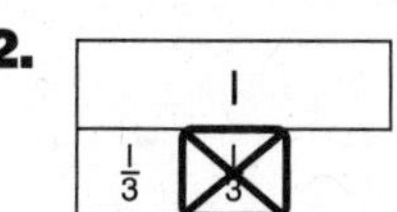

____

3. [1 | $\frac{1}{4}$ $\frac{1}{4}$ $\frac{1}{4}$] + [1 | $\frac{1}{4}$] = [1 | $\frac{1}{4}$ $\frac{1}{4}$ $\frac{1}{4}$ $\frac{1}{4}$]

____

4. 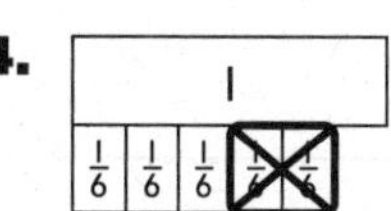

____

Name ______________________

Add and Subtract Parts of a Whole

Use the model to write an equation.

1. 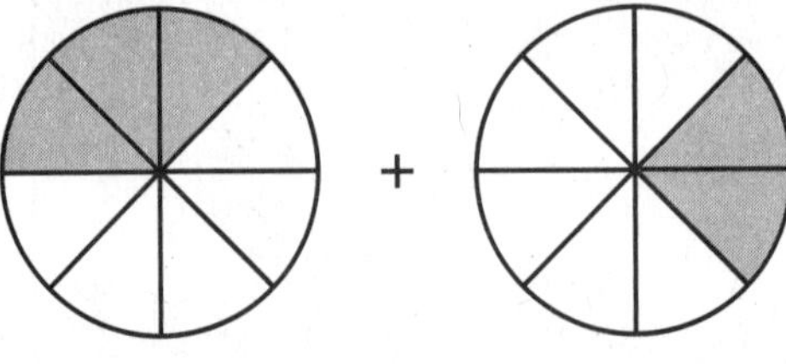

Think: $\frac{3}{8}$ + $\frac{2}{8}$ = $\frac{5}{8}$

$\frac{3}{8} + \frac{2}{8} = \frac{5}{8}$

2. 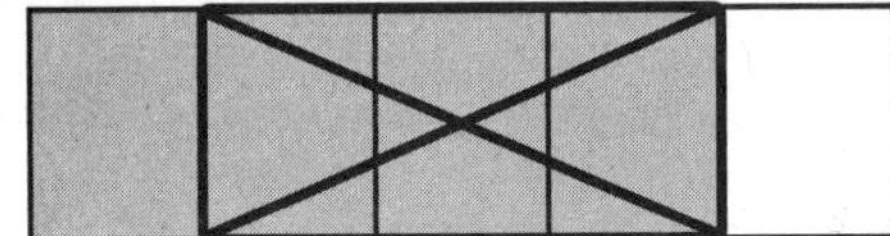

____

3. 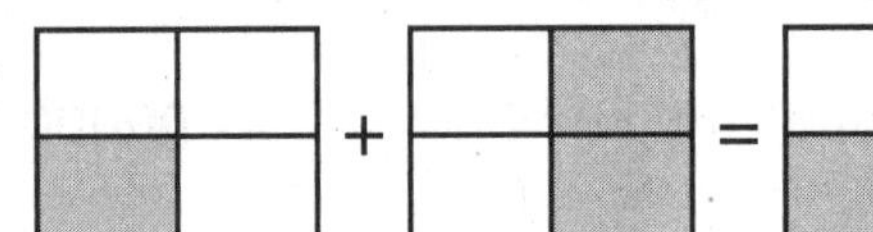

____

Use the model to solve the equation.

4. 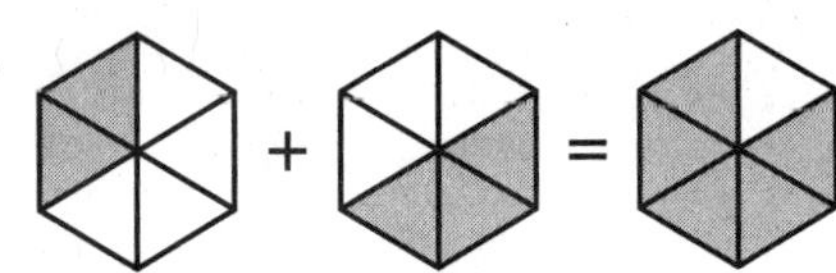

$\frac{2}{6} + \frac{3}{6} =$ __________

5. 

$\frac{3}{5} - \frac{2}{5} =$ __________

6. Jake ate $\frac{4}{8}$ of a pizza. Millie ate $\frac{3}{8}$ of the same pizza. How much of the pizza was eaten by Jake and Millie?

____

7. Kate ate $\frac{1}{4}$ of her orange. Ben ate $\frac{2}{4}$ of his banana. Did Kate and Ben eat $\frac{1}{4} + \frac{2}{4} = \frac{3}{4}$ of their fruit? **Explain.**

____

____

____

Name ______________________________

Lesson 56

COMMON CORE STANDARD CC.4.NF.3b

Lesson Objective: Decompose a fraction by writing it as a sum of fractions with the same denominators.

Write Fractions as Sums

A **unit fraction** tells the part of the whole that 1 piece represents.
A unit fraction always has a numerator of 1.

Bryan has $\frac{4}{10}$ pound of clay for making clay figures. He wants to use $\frac{1}{10}$ pound of clay for each figure. How many clay figures can he make?

Use fraction strips to write $\frac{4}{10}$ as a sum of unit fractions.

Step 1 Represent $\frac{4}{10}$ with fraction strips.

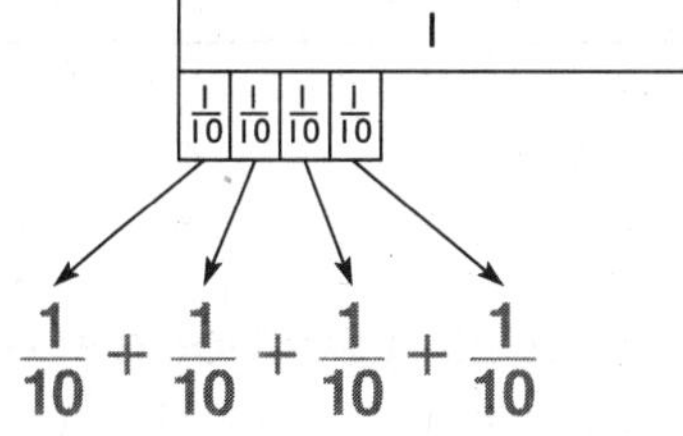

Step 2 Each $\frac{1}{10}$ is a unit fraction. Write a $\frac{1}{10}$ addend for each $\frac{1}{10}$-strip you used to show $\frac{4}{10}$.

Step 3 Count the number of addends. The number of addends represents the number of clay figures Bryan can make.

So, Bryan can make __4__ clay figures.

Write the fraction as the sum of unit fractions.

1. 1 | 1/6 1/6 1/6

$\frac{3}{6}$ = ____ + ____ + ____

2.

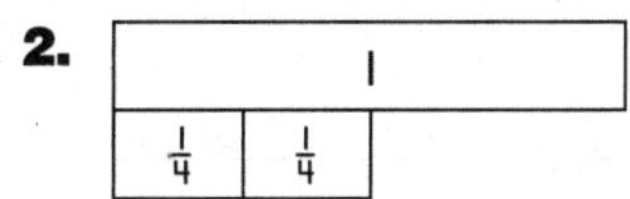

$\frac{2}{4}$ = ____ + ____

3. 1 | 1/8 1/8 1/8 1/8

$\frac{4}{8}$ = ____ + ____ + ____ + ____

4. 1 | 1/5 1/5 1/5 1/5 1/5

$\frac{5}{5}$ = ____ + ____ + ____ + ____ + ____

Name ______________________

Lesson 56

CC.4.NF.3b

Write Fractions as Sums

Write the fraction as a sum of unit fractions.

1. $\frac{4}{5}$ = $\frac{1}{5} + \frac{1}{5} + \frac{1}{5} + \frac{1}{5}$

   Think: Add $\frac{1}{5}$ four times.

2. $\frac{3}{8}$ = ______________________

3. $\frac{6}{12}$ = ______________________

   ____

4. $\frac{4}{4}$ = ______________________

Write the fraction as a sum of fractions three different ways.

5. $\frac{7}{10}$

   ____

   ____

   ____

6. $\frac{6}{6}$

   ____

   ____

   ____

Problem Solving REAL WORLD

7. Miguel's teacher asks him to color $\frac{4}{8}$ of his grid. He must use 3 colors: red, blue, and green. There must be more green sections than red sections. How can Miguel color the sections of his grid to follow all the rules?

   ____

   ____

   ____

8. Petra is asked to color $\frac{6}{6}$ of her grid. She must use 3 colors: blue, red, and pink. There must be more blue sections than red sections or pink sections. What are the different ways Petra can color the sections of her grid and follow all the rules?

   ____

   ____

   ____

   ____

Name ________________________________

Lesson 57

COMMON CORE STANDARD CC.4.NF.3b

Lesson Objective: Write fractions greater than 1 as mixed numbers and write mixed numbers as fractions greater than 1.

Rename Fractions and Mixed Numbers

A **mixed number** is made up of a whole number and a fraction. You can use multiplication and addition to rename a mixed number as a fraction greater than 1.

Rename $2\frac{5}{6}$ as a fraction.

First, multiply the denominator, or the number of parts in the whole, by the whole number.

$6 \times 2 = 12$

Then, add the numerator to your product.

$12 + 5 = 17$

$2\frac{5}{6} = \frac{\boxed{17}}{6}$ — total number of parts (numerator); number of parts in the whole (denominator)

So, $2\frac{5}{6} = \frac{17}{6}$.

You can use division to write a fraction greater than 1 as a mixed number.

Rename $\frac{16}{3}$ as a mixed number.

To rename $\frac{16}{3}$ as a mixed number, divide the numerator by the denominator.

Use the quotient and remainder to write a mixed number.

$$\begin{array}{r} 5 \\ 3\overline{)16} \\ -15 \\ \hline 1 \end{array}$$

So, $\frac{16}{3} = 5\frac{1}{3}$.

Write the mixed number as a fraction.

1. $3\frac{2}{3} =$ _____

2. $4\frac{3}{5} =$ _____

3. $4\frac{3}{8} =$ _____

4. $2\frac{1}{6} =$ _____

Write the fraction as a mixed number.

5. $\frac{32}{5} =$ _____

6. $\frac{19}{3} =$ _____

7. $\frac{15}{4} =$ _____

8. $\frac{51}{10} =$ _____

Name ____________________

Rename Fractions and Mixed Numbers

Write the mixed number as a fraction.

1. $2\frac{3}{5}$
Think: Find $\frac{5}{5} + \frac{5}{5} + \frac{3}{5}$.
$\frac{13}{5}$

2. $4\frac{1}{3}$

3. $1\frac{2}{5}$

4. $3\frac{2}{3}$

5. $4\frac{1}{8}$

6. $1\frac{7}{10}$

7. $5\frac{1}{2}$

8. $2\frac{3}{8}$

Write the fraction as a mixed number.

9. $\frac{31}{6}$

10. $\frac{20}{10}$

11. $\frac{15}{8}$

12. $\frac{13}{6}$

13. $\frac{23}{10}$

14. $\frac{19}{5}$

15. $\frac{11}{3}$

16. $\frac{9}{2}$

Problem Solving REAL WORLD

17. A recipe calls for $2\frac{2}{4}$ cups of raisins, but Julie only has a $\frac{1}{4}$-cup measuring cup. How many $\frac{1}{4}$ cups does Julie need to measure out $2\frac{2}{4}$ cups of raisins?

18. If Julie needs $3\frac{1}{4}$ cups of oatmeal, how many $\frac{1}{4}$ cups of oatmeal will she use?

Name ______________________________

Lesson 58

COMMON CORE STANDARD CC.4.NF.3c

Lesson Objective: Add and subtract mixed numbers.

Add and Subtract Mixed Numbers

Find the sum. $3\frac{1}{4} + 2\frac{1}{4}$

Add the whole number and fraction parts.

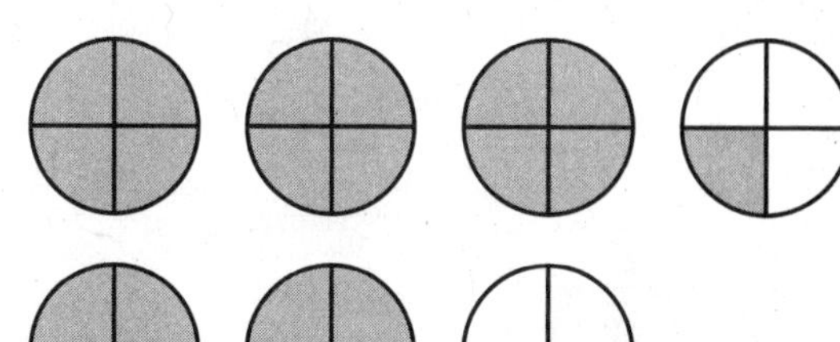

- Add the whole numbers: $3 + 2 = 5$
- Add the fractions: $\frac{1}{4} + \frac{1}{4} = \frac{2}{4}$

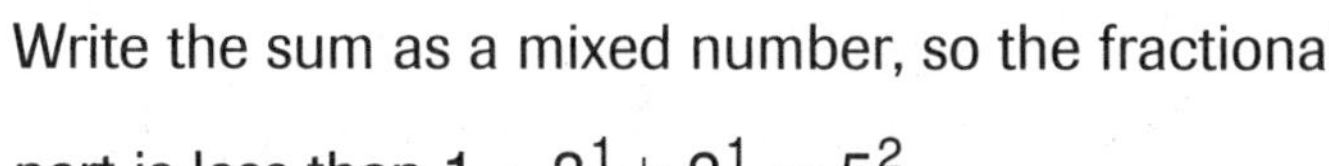

Write the sum as a mixed number, so the fractional part is less than 1. $3\frac{1}{4} + 2\frac{1}{4} = 5\frac{2}{4}$

Find the difference. $4\frac{5}{8} - 3\frac{1}{8}$

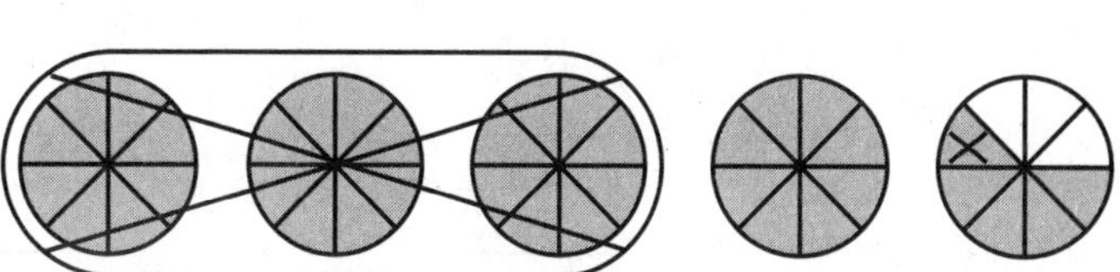

Subtract the fraction and the whole number parts.

- Subtract the fractions: $\frac{5}{8} - \frac{1}{8} = \frac{4}{8}$
- Subtract the whole numbers: $4 - 3 = 1$

$4\frac{5}{8} - 3\frac{1}{8} = 1\frac{4}{8}$

Find the sum or difference.

1. $3\frac{4}{5} + 4\frac{3}{5}$ = ______
2. $7\frac{2}{3} - 3\frac{1}{3}$ = ______
3. $4\frac{7}{12} + 6\frac{5}{12}$ = ______
4. $12\frac{3}{4} - 6\frac{1}{4}$ = ______
5. $2\frac{3}{8} + 8\frac{1}{8}$ = ______
6. $11\frac{9}{10} - 3\frac{7}{10}$ = ______
7. $7\frac{3}{5} + 4\frac{3}{5}$ = ______
8. $8\frac{3}{6} - 3\frac{1}{6}$ = ______

Name ______________________

Lesson 58
CC.4.NF.3c

Add and Subtract Mixed Numbers

Find the sum. Write the sum as a mixed number, so the fractional part is less than 1.

1. $6\frac{4}{5} + 3\frac{3}{5}$ = $9\frac{7}{5} = 10\frac{2}{5}$

2. $4\frac{1}{2} + 2\frac{1}{2}$

3. $2\frac{2}{3} + 3\frac{2}{3}$

4. $6\frac{4}{5} + 7\frac{4}{5}$

5. $9\frac{3}{6} + 2\frac{2}{6}$

6. $8\frac{4}{12} + 3\frac{6}{12}$

7. $4\frac{3}{8} + 1\frac{5}{8}$

8. $9\frac{5}{10} + 6\frac{3}{10}$

Find the difference.

9. $6\frac{7}{8} - 4\frac{3}{8}$

10. $4\frac{2}{3} - 3\frac{1}{3}$

11. $6\frac{4}{5} - 3\frac{3}{5}$

12. $7\frac{3}{4} - 2\frac{1}{4}$

Problem Solving REAL WORLD

13. James wants to send two gifts by mail. One package weighs $2\frac{3}{4}$ pounds. The other package weighs $1\frac{3}{4}$ pounds. What is the total weight of the packages?

____

14. Tierra bought $4\frac{3}{8}$ yards blue ribbon and $2\frac{1}{8}$ yards yellow ribbon for a craft project. How much more blue ribbon than yellow ribbon did Tierra buy?

____

Lesson 59

COMMON CORE STANDARD CC.4.NF.3c

Lesson Objective: Rename mixed numbers to subtract.

Subtraction with Renaming

Fraction strips can help you subtract mixed numbers or subtract a mixed number from a whole number.

Find the difference. $3\frac{1}{3} - 2\frac{2}{3}$

Step 1 Model the number you are subtracting from, $3\frac{1}{3}$.

Step 2 Because you cannot subtract $\frac{2}{3}$ from $\frac{1}{3}$ without renaming, change one of the 1 strips to three $\frac{1}{3}$ strips. Then subtract by crossing out two wholes and two $\frac{1}{3}$ strips.

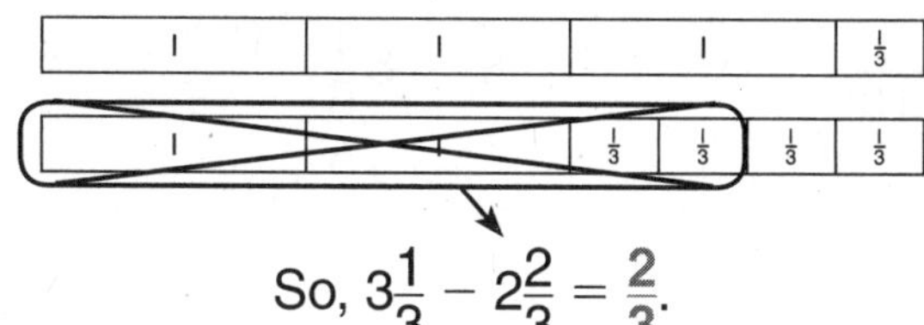

So, $3\frac{1}{3} - 2\frac{2}{3} = \frac{2}{3}$.

Find the difference. $2 - 1\frac{1}{4}$

Step 1 Model the number you are subtracting from, 2.

Step 2 Because you cannot subtract $\frac{1}{4}$ from 1 without renaming, change one of the 1 strips to four $\frac{1}{4}$ strips. Then subtract by crossing out one whole and one $\frac{1}{4}$ strip.

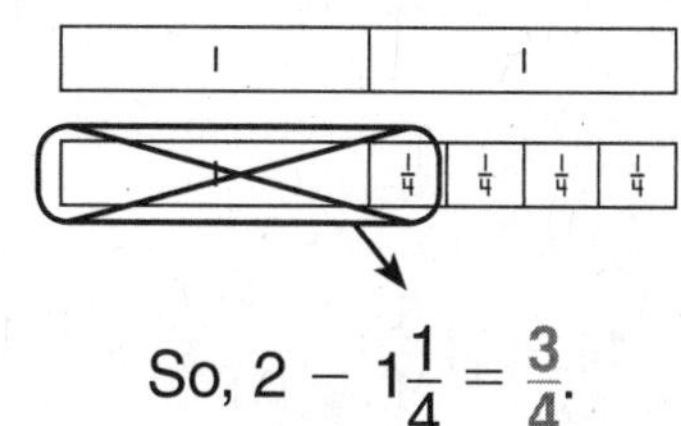

So, $2 - 1\frac{1}{4} = \frac{3}{4}$.

Find the difference.

1. $3 - 2\frac{2}{5} =$ ______

1	1	1
1	1	$\frac{1}{5}$ $\frac{1}{5}$ $\frac{1}{5}$ $\frac{1}{5}$ $\frac{1}{5}$

2. $2\frac{1}{4} - 1\frac{3}{4} =$ ______

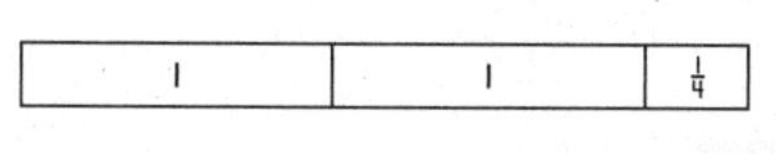

3. $3\frac{3}{5} - 2\frac{4}{5}$ = ______

4. $3\frac{1}{12} - 2\frac{11}{12}$ = ______

5. $4\frac{5}{8} - 2\frac{7}{8}$ = ______

Name ____________________

Lesson 59

CC.4.NF.3c

Subtraction with Renaming

Find the difference.

1. $\begin{array}{r} 5\frac{1}{3} \\ -3\frac{2}{3} \\ \hline \end{array}$ → $\begin{array}{r} 4\frac{4}{3} \\ 3\frac{2}{3} \\ \hline 1\frac{2}{3} \end{array}$

2. $\begin{array}{r} 6 \\ -3\frac{2}{5} \\ \hline \end{array}$

3. $\begin{array}{r} 5\frac{1}{4} \\ -2\frac{3}{4} \\ \hline \end{array}$

4. $\begin{array}{r} 9\frac{3}{8} \\ -8\frac{7}{8} \\ \hline \end{array}$

5. $\begin{array}{r} 12\frac{3}{10} \\ -7\frac{7}{10} \\ \hline \end{array}$

6. $\begin{array}{r} 8\frac{1}{6} \\ -3\frac{5}{6} \\ \hline \end{array}$

7. $\begin{array}{r} 7\frac{3}{5} \\ -4\frac{4}{5} \\ \hline \end{array}$

8. $\begin{array}{r} 10\frac{1}{2} \\ -8\frac{1}{2} \\ \hline \end{array}$

9. $\begin{array}{r} 7\frac{1}{6} \\ -2\frac{5}{6} \\ \hline \end{array}$

10. $\begin{array}{r} 9\frac{3}{12} \\ -4\frac{7}{12} \\ \hline \end{array}$

11. $\begin{array}{r} 9\frac{1}{10} \\ -8\frac{7}{10} \\ \hline \end{array}$

12. $\begin{array}{r} 9\frac{1}{3} \\ -\frac{2}{3} \\ \hline \end{array}$

13. $\begin{array}{r} 3\frac{1}{4} \\ -1\frac{3}{4} \\ \hline \end{array}$

14. $\begin{array}{r} 4\frac{5}{8} \\ -1\frac{7}{8} \\ \hline \end{array}$

15. $\begin{array}{r} 5\frac{1}{12} \\ -3\frac{8}{12} \\ \hline \end{array}$

16. $\begin{array}{r} 7 \\ -1\frac{3}{5} \\ \hline \end{array}$

Problem Solving REAL WORLD

17. Alicia buys a 5-pound bag of rocks for a fish tank. She uses $1\frac{1}{8}$ pounds for a small fish bowl. How much is left?

____

18. Xavier made 25 pounds of roasted almonds for a fair. He has $3\frac{1}{2}$ pounds left at the end of the fair. How many pounds of roasted almonds did he sell at the fair?

____

Name ____________________

COMMON CORE STANDARD CC.4.NF.3c

Lesson Objective: Use the properties of addition to add fractions.

Algebra • Fractions and Properties of Addition

Properties of addition can help you group and order addends so you can use mental math to find sums.

The **Commutative Property of Addition** states that when the order of two addends is changed, the sum is the same. $6 + 3 = 3 + 6$

The **Associative Property of Addition** states that when the grouping of addends is changed, the sum is the same. $(3 + 6) + 4 = 3 + (6 + 4)$

Use the properties and mental math to add $10\frac{3}{8} + 4\frac{7}{8} + 6\frac{5}{8}$.

Step 1 Look for fractions that combine to make 1. $10\frac{3}{8} + 4\frac{7}{8} + 6\frac{5}{8}$

Step 2 Use the Commutative Property to order the addends so that the fractions with a sum of 1 are together. $10\frac{3}{8} + 4\frac{7}{8} + 6\frac{5}{8} = 10\frac{3}{8} + 6\frac{5}{8} + 4\frac{7}{8}$

Step 3 Use the Associative Property to group the addends that you can add mentally. $= \left(10\frac{3}{8} + 6\frac{5}{8}\right) + 4\frac{7}{8}$

Step 4 Add the grouped numbers and then add the other mixed number. $= (17) + 4\frac{7}{8}$

Step 5 Write the sum. $= 21\frac{7}{8}$

Use the properties and mental math to find the sum.

1. $\left(3\frac{1}{5} + 1\frac{2}{5}\right) + 4\frac{4}{5}$ ________

2. $\left(5\frac{7}{10} + 1\frac{4}{10}\right) + 6\frac{3}{10}$ ________

3. $7\frac{3}{4} + \left(5 + 3\frac{1}{4}\right)$ ________

4. $\left(2\frac{5}{12} + 3\frac{11}{12}\right) + 1\frac{7}{12}$ ________

5. $4\frac{7}{8} + \left(6\frac{3}{8} + \frac{1}{8}\right)$ ________

6. $9\frac{2}{6} + \left(4\frac{1}{6} + 7\frac{4}{6}\right)$ ________

Name ______________________

Fractions and Properties of Addition

Lesson 60
CC.4.NF.3c

Use the properties and mental math to find the sum.

1. $5\frac{1}{3} + \left(2\frac{2}{3} + 1\frac{1}{3}\right)$

   $5\frac{1}{3} + (4)$

   $9\frac{1}{3}$

2. $10\frac{1}{8} + \left(3\frac{5}{8} + 2\frac{7}{8}\right)$ ______

3. $8\frac{1}{5} + \left(3\frac{2}{5} + 5\frac{4}{5}\right)$ ______

4. $6\frac{3}{4} + \left(4\frac{2}{4} + 5\frac{1}{4}\right)$ ______

5. $\left(6\frac{3}{6} + 10\frac{4}{6}\right) + 9\frac{2}{6}$ ______

6. $\left(6\frac{2}{5} + 1\frac{4}{5}\right) + 3\frac{1}{5}$ ______

7. $7\frac{7}{8} + \left(3\frac{1}{8} + 1\frac{1}{8}\right)$ ______

8. $14\frac{1}{10} + \left(20\frac{2}{10} + 15\frac{7}{10}\right)$ ______

9. $\left(13\frac{2}{12} + 8\frac{7}{12}\right) + 9\frac{5}{12}$ ______

Problem Solving REAL WORLD

10. Nate's classroom has three tables of different lengths. One has a length of $4\frac{1}{2}$ feet, another has a length of 4 feet, and a third has a length of $2\frac{1}{2}$ feet. What is the length of all three tables when pushed end to end?

    ____

11. Mr. Warren uses $2\frac{1}{4}$ bags of mulch for his garden and another $4\frac{1}{4}$ bags for his front yard. He also uses $\frac{3}{4}$ bag around a fountain. How many total bags of mulch does Mr. Warren use?

    ____

Name ____________________

Lesson 61

COMMON CORE STANDARD CC.4.NF.3d

Lesson Objective: Use models to represent and find sums involving fractions.

Add Fractions Using Models

Fractions with like denominators have the same denominator. You can add fractions with like denominators using a number line.

Model $\frac{4}{6} + \frac{1}{6}$.

Step 1 Draw a number line labeled with sixths. Model the fraction $\frac{4}{6}$ by starting at 0 and shading 4 sixths.

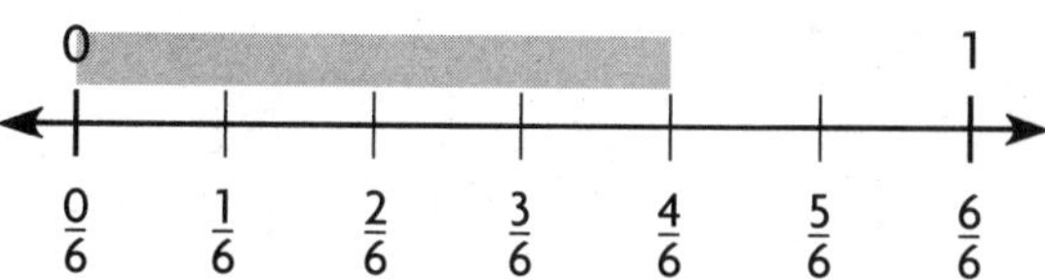

Step 2 Add the fraction $\frac{1}{6}$ by shading 1 more sixth.

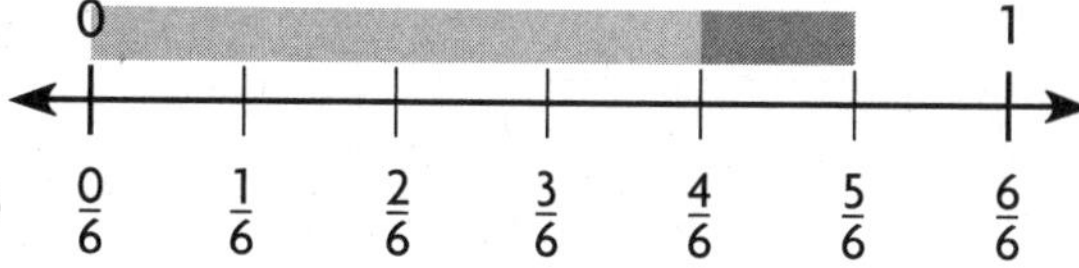

Step 3 How many sixths are there in all? 5 sixths

Write the number of sixths as a fraction.

5 sixths $= \frac{5}{6}$ $\qquad \frac{4}{6} + \frac{1}{6} = \frac{5}{6}$

1. Model $\frac{1}{5} + \frac{4}{5}$.

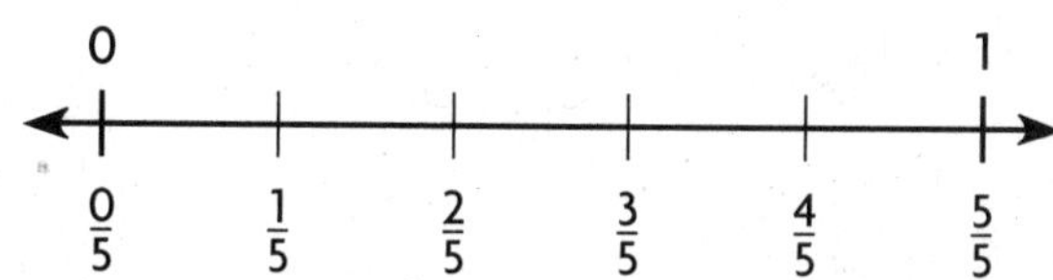

$\frac{1}{5} + \frac{4}{5} =$ ____________________

Find the sum. Use a model to help.

2. $\frac{2}{10} + \frac{4}{10}$

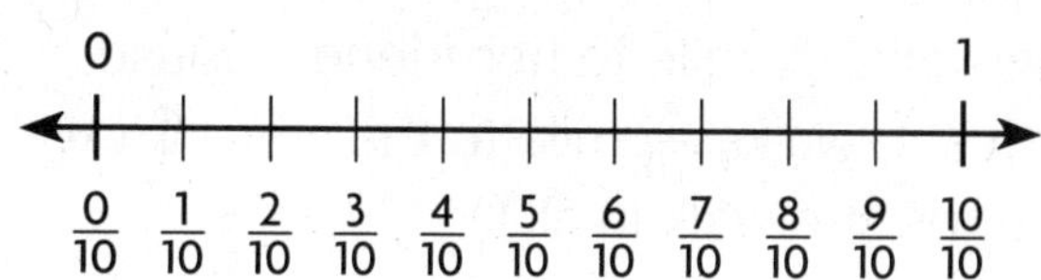

____

3. $\frac{1}{4} + \frac{1}{4}$

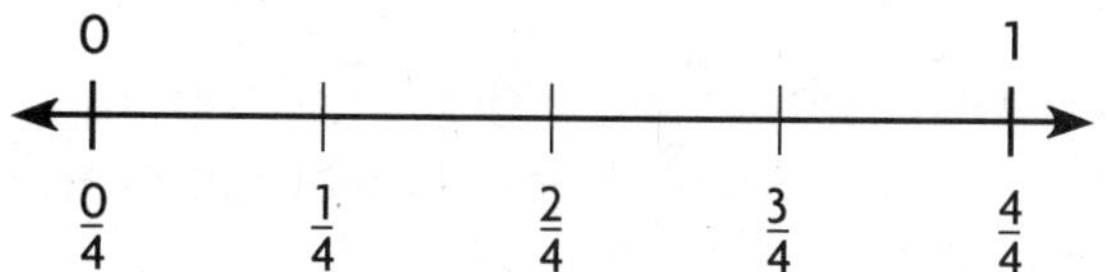

____

Name ____________________

Add Fractions Using Models

Lesson 61
CC.4.NF.3d

Find the sum. Use fraction strips to help.

1. $\frac{2}{6} + \frac{1}{6} =$ $\frac{3}{6}$

1

$\frac{1}{6}$	$\frac{1}{6}$	$\frac{1}{6}$

$\frac{2}{6}$ $\frac{1}{6}$

2. $\frac{4}{10} + \frac{5}{10} =$ ________

3. $\frac{1}{3} + \frac{2}{3} =$ ________

4. $\frac{2}{4} + \frac{1}{4} =$ ________

5. $\frac{2}{12} + \frac{4}{12} =$ ________

6. $\frac{1}{6} + \frac{2}{6} =$ ________

7. $\frac{3}{12} + \frac{9}{12} =$ ________

8. $\frac{3}{8} + \frac{4}{8} =$ ________

9. $\frac{3}{4} + \frac{1}{4} =$ ________

10. $\frac{1}{5} + \frac{2}{5} =$ ________

Problem Solving REAL WORLD

11. Lola walks $\frac{4}{10}$ mile to her friend's house. Then she walks $\frac{5}{10}$ mile to the store. How far does she walk in all?

____

12. Evan eats $\frac{1}{8}$ of a pan of lasagna and his brother eats $\frac{2}{8}$ of it. What fraction of the pan of lasagna do they eat in all?

____

13. Jacqueline buys $\frac{2}{4}$ yard of green ribbon and $\frac{1}{4}$ yard of pink ribbon. How many yards of ribbon does she buy in all?

____

14. Shu mixes $\frac{2}{3}$ pound of peanuts with $\frac{1}{3}$ pound of almonds. How many pounds of nuts does Shu mix in all?

____

Name ____________________

Lesson 62

COMMON CORE STANDARD CC.4.NF.3d

Lesson Objective: Use models to represent and find differences involving fractions.

Subtract Fractions Using Models

You can subtract fractions with like denominators using fraction strips.

Model $\frac{5}{8} - \frac{2}{8}$.

Step 1 Shade the eighths you start with.
Shade 5 eighths.

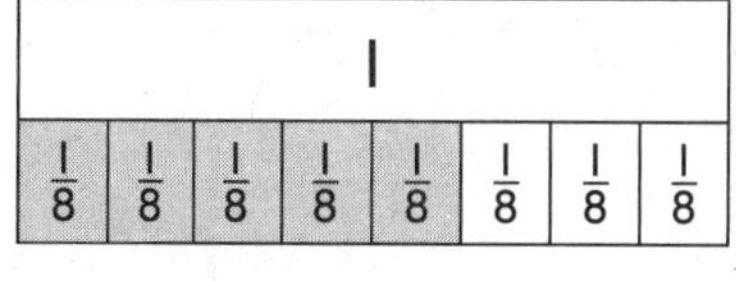

Step 2 Subtract $\frac{2}{8}$.

Think: How many eighths are taken away?
Cross out 2 of the shaded eighths.

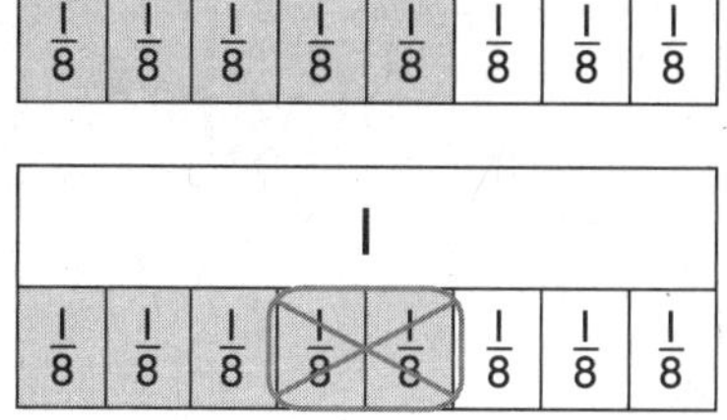

Step 3 Count the shaded eighths that remain.
There are 3 eighths remaining.

Step 4 Write the number of eighths that remain as a fraction.

3 eighths $= \frac{3}{8}$ $\qquad \frac{5}{8} - \frac{2}{8} = \frac{3}{8}$

1. Model $\frac{3}{3} - \frac{2}{3}$.

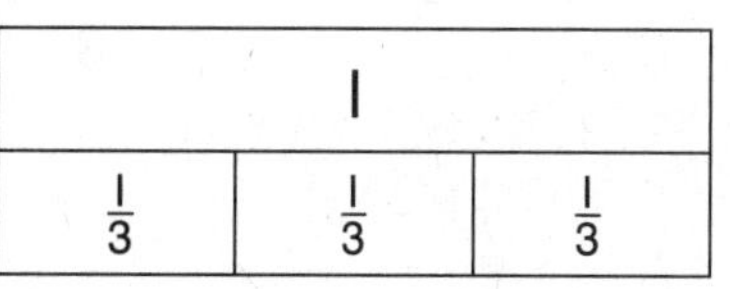

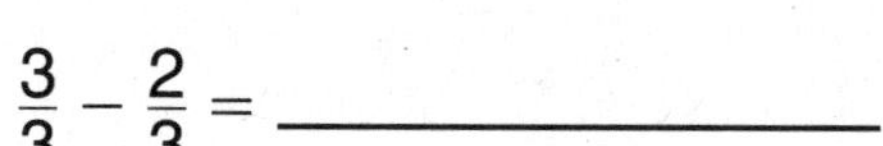

$\frac{3}{3} - \frac{2}{3} =$ ____________

Subtract. Use fraction strips to help.

2. $\frac{5}{6} - \frac{1}{6}$

1					
1/6	1/6	1/6	1/6	1/6	1/6

$\frac{5}{6} - \frac{1}{6} =$ ____________

3. $\frac{6}{10} - \frac{3}{10}$

1									
1/10	1/10	1/10	1/10	1/10	1/10	1/10	1/10	1/10	1/10

$\frac{6}{10} - \frac{3}{10} =$ ____________

Lesson 62

CC.4.NF.3d

Name ______________________________

Subtract Fractions Using Models

Subtract. Use fraction strips to help.

1. $\frac{4}{5} - \frac{1}{5} =$ $\frac{3}{5}$

1			
$\frac{1}{5}$	$\frac{1}{5}$	$\frac{1}{5}$	$\frac{1}{5}$

2. $\frac{3}{4} - \frac{1}{4} =$ ______

1		
$\frac{1}{4}$	$\frac{1}{4}$	$\frac{1}{4}$
$\frac{1}{4}$		

$\frac{2}{4}$

3. $\frac{5}{6} - \frac{1}{6} =$ ______

4. $\frac{7}{8} - \frac{1}{8} =$ ______

5. $1 - \frac{2}{3} =$ ______

6. $\frac{8}{10} - \frac{2}{10} =$ ______

7. $\frac{3}{4} - \frac{1}{4} =$ ______

8. $\frac{7}{6} - \frac{5}{6} =$ ______

Problem Solving REAL WORLD

Use the table for 9 and 10.

9. Ena is making trail mix. She buys the items shown in the table. How many more pounds of pretzels than raisins does she buy?

____

10. How many more pounds of granola than banana chips does she buy?

____

Item	Weight (in pounds)
Pretzels	$\frac{7}{8}$
Peanuts	$\frac{4}{8}$
Raisins	$\frac{2}{8}$
Banana Chips	$\frac{3}{8}$
Granola	$\frac{5}{8}$

Name ______________________

Add and Subtract Fractions

Lesson 63

COMMON CORE STANDARD CC.4.NF.3d

Lesson Objective: Solve word problems involving addition and subtraction with fractions.

<table>
<tr><td colspan="3">You can find and record the sums and the differences of fractions.

Add. $\frac{2}{6} + \frac{4}{6}$</td></tr>
<tr><td>Step 1 Model it.
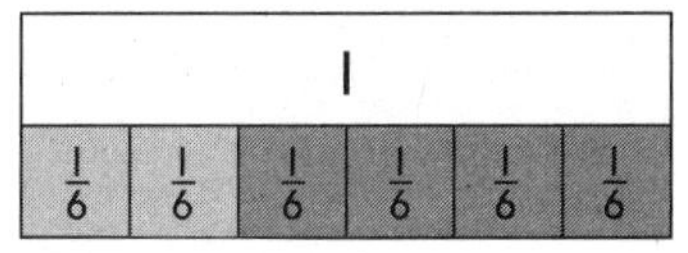
</td><td>Step 2 Think: How many sixths are there in all?

There are 6 sixths.

6 sixths = $\frac{6}{6}$</td><td>Step 3 Record it.

Write the sum as an addition equation.

$\frac{2}{6} + \frac{4}{6} = \frac{6}{6}$</td></tr>
<tr><td colspan="3">Subtract. $\frac{6}{10} - \frac{2}{10}$</td></tr>
<tr><td>Step 1 Model it.
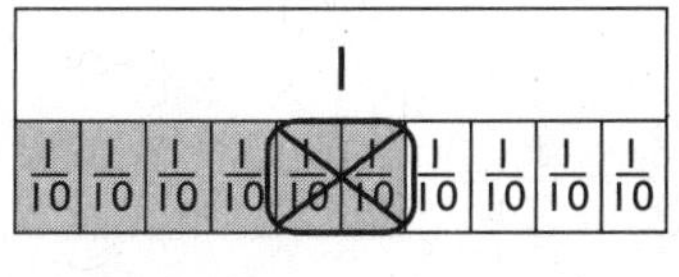
</td><td>Step 2 Think: There are 6 tenths. I take away 2 tenths. How many tenths are left?

There are 4 tenths left.

4 tenths = $\frac{4}{10}$</td><td>Step 3 Record it.

Write the difference as a subtraction equation.

$\frac{6}{10} - \frac{2}{10} = \frac{4}{10}$</td></tr>
</table>

Find the sum or difference.

1. 7 eighth-size parts − 4 eighth-size parts = ______________________

$\frac{7}{8} - \frac{4}{8} =$ ____________

2. $\frac{11}{12} - \frac{4}{12} =$ ____________

3. $\frac{2}{10} + \frac{2}{10} =$ ____________

4. $\frac{6}{8} - \frac{4}{8} =$ ____________

5. $\frac{2}{4} + \frac{2}{4} =$ ____________

6. $\frac{4}{5} - \frac{3}{5} =$ ____________

7. $\frac{1}{3} + \frac{2}{3} =$ ____________

Name ______________________________

Lesson 63

CC.4.NF.3d

Add and Subtract Fractions

Find the sum or difference.

1. $\frac{4}{12} + \frac{8}{12} =$ $\frac{12}{12}$

1

$\frac{1}{12}$ $\frac{1}{12}$ $\frac{1}{12}$ $\frac{1}{12}$ $\frac{1}{12}$ $\frac{1}{12}$ $\frac{1}{12}$ $\frac{1}{12}$ $\frac{1}{12}$ $\frac{1}{12}$ $\frac{1}{12}$ $\frac{1}{12}$

$\frac{4}{12}$ $\frac{8}{12}$

2. $\frac{3}{6} - \frac{1}{6} =$ ____________

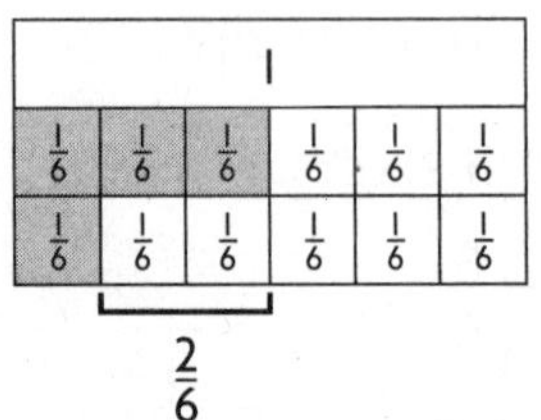

3. $\frac{4}{5} - \frac{3}{5} =$ ____________

4. $\frac{6}{10} + \frac{3}{10} =$ ____________

5. $1 - \frac{3}{8} =$ ____________

6. $\frac{1}{4} + \frac{2}{4} =$ ____________

7. $\frac{9}{12} - \frac{5}{12} =$ ____________

8. $\frac{5}{6} - \frac{2}{6} =$ ____________

9. $\frac{2}{3} + \frac{1}{3} =$ ____________

Problem Solving REAL WORLD

Use the table for 10 and 11.

10. Guy finds how far his house is from several locations and makes the table shown. How much farther away from Guy's house is the library than the cafe?

____

11. If Guy walks from his house to school and back, how far does he walk?

____

Distance from Guy's House	
Location	Distance (in miles)
Library	$\frac{9}{10}$
School	$\frac{5}{10}$
Store	$\frac{7}{10}$
Cafe	$\frac{4}{10}$
Yogurt Shop	$\frac{6}{10}$

Name ___________________________

COMMON CORE STANDARD CC.4.NF.3d

Lesson Objective: Use the strategy *act it out* to solve multistep fraction problems.

Problem Solving • Multistep Fraction Problems

Jeff runs $\frac{3}{5}$ mile each day. He wants to know how many days he has to run before he has run a whole number of miles.

Read the Problem	Solve the Problem
What do I need to find? I need to find how many days Jeff needs to run $\frac{3}{5}$ mile until he has run a whole number of miles.	**Describe how to act it out.** **Use a number line.** 0 $\frac{1}{5}$ $\frac{2}{5}$ $\frac{3}{5}$ $\frac{4}{5}$ 1 $\frac{6}{5}$ $\frac{7}{5}$ $\frac{8}{5}$ $\frac{9}{5}$ 2 $\frac{11}{5}$ $\frac{12}{5}$ $\frac{13}{5}$ $\frac{14}{5}$ 3 $\frac{16}{5}$
What information do I need to use? Jeff runs $\frac{3}{5}$ mile a day. He wants the distance run to be a whole number.	Day 1: $\frac{3}{5}$ mile Day 2: $\frac{6}{5}$ mile $\frac{3}{5} + \frac{3}{5} = \frac{6}{5}$ 1 whole mile and $\frac{1}{5}$ mile more Day 3: $\frac{9}{5}$ mile $\frac{3}{5} + \frac{3}{5} + \frac{3}{5} = \frac{9}{5}$ 1 whole mile and $\frac{4}{5}$ mile more
How will I use the information? I can use a number line and patterns to act out the problem.	Day 4: $\frac{12}{5}$ mile $\frac{3}{5} + \frac{3}{5} + \frac{3}{5} + \frac{3}{5} = \frac{12}{5}$ 2 whole miles and $\frac{2}{5}$ mile more Day 5: $\frac{15}{5}$ mile $\frac{3}{5} + \frac{3}{5} + \frac{3}{5} + \frac{3}{5} + \frac{3}{5} = \frac{15}{5}$ 3 whole miles So, Jeff will run a total of 3 miles in 5 days.

1. Lena runs $\frac{2}{3}$ mile each day. She wants to know how many days she has to run before she has run a whole number of miles.

   ____

2. Mack is repackaging $\frac{6}{8}$-pound bags of birdseed into 1-pound bags of birdseed. What is the least number of $\frac{6}{8}$-pound bags of birdseed he needs in order to fill 1-pound bags without leftovers?

   ____

Name ______________________

Lesson 64
CC.4.NF.3d

Problem Solving • Multistep Fraction Problems

Read each problem and solve.

1. Each child in the Smith family was given an orange cut into 8 equal sections. Each child ate $\frac{5}{8}$ of the orange. After combining the leftover sections, Mrs. Smith noted that there were exactly 3 full oranges left. How many children are in the Smith family?

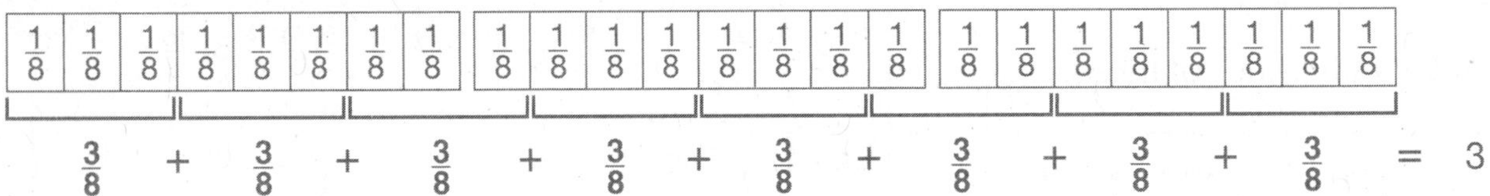

$\frac{3}{8} + \frac{3}{8} + \frac{3}{8} + \frac{3}{8} + \frac{3}{8} + \frac{3}{8} + \frac{3}{8} + \frac{3}{8} = 3$

There are 8 addends, so there are 8 children in the Smith family.

8 children

2. Val walks $2\frac{3}{5}$ miles each day. Bill runs 10 miles once every 4 days. In 4 days, who covers the greater distance?

____

3. Chad buys peanuts in 2-pound bags. He repackages them into bags that hold $\frac{5}{6}$ pound of peanuts. How many 2-pound bags of peanuts should Chad buy so that he can fill the $\frac{5}{6}$-pound bags without having any peanuts left over?

____

4. A carpenter has several boards of equal length. He cuts $\frac{3}{5}$ of each board. After cutting the boards, the carpenter notices that he has enough pieces left over to make up the same length as 4 of the original boards. How many boards did the carpenter start with?

____

Name ______________________

Lesson 65

COMMON CORE STANDARD CC.4.NF.4a

Lesson Objective: Write a fraction as a product of a whole number and a unit fraction.

Multiples of Unit Fractions

A unit fraction is a fraction with a numerator of 1. You can write a fraction as the product of a whole number and a unit fraction.

Write $\frac{7}{10}$ as the product of a whole number and a unit fraction.

Write $\frac{7}{10}$ as the sum of unit fractions.

$\frac{7}{10} = \underline{\frac{1}{10}} + \underline{\frac{1}{10}} + \underline{\frac{1}{10}} + \underline{\frac{1}{10}} + \underline{\frac{1}{10}} + \underline{\frac{1}{10}} + \underline{\frac{1}{10}}$

Use multiplication to show repeated addition.

$\frac{7}{10} = \underline{7} \times \frac{1}{10}$

So, $\frac{7}{10} = \underline{7} \times \underline{\frac{1}{10}}$.

The product of a number and a counting number is a multiple of the number. You can find multiples of unit fractions.

List the next 4 multiples of $\frac{1}{8}$.

Make a table and use repeated addition.

$1 \times \frac{1}{8}$	$2 \times \frac{1}{8}$	$3 \times \frac{1}{8}$	$4 \times \frac{1}{8}$	$5 \times \frac{1}{8}$
$\frac{1}{8}$	$\frac{1}{8} + \frac{1}{8}$	$\frac{1}{8} + \frac{1}{8} + \frac{1}{8}$	$\frac{1}{8} + \frac{1}{8} + \frac{1}{8} + \frac{1}{8}$	$\frac{1}{8} + \frac{1}{8} + \frac{1}{8} + \frac{1}{8} + \frac{1}{8}$
$\frac{1}{8}$	$\frac{2}{8}$	$\frac{3}{8}$	$\frac{4}{8}$	$\frac{5}{8}$

The next 4 multiples of $\frac{1}{8}$ are $\underline{\frac{2}{8}}$, $\underline{\frac{3}{8}}$, $\underline{\frac{4}{8}}$, and $\underline{\frac{5}{8}}$.

Write the fraction as the product of a whole number and a unit fraction.

1. $\frac{2}{5} =$ ______

2. $\frac{5}{12} =$ ______

3. $\frac{7}{2} =$ ______

List the next four multiples of the unit fraction.

4. $\frac{1}{4}$, ____, ____, ____, ____

5. $\frac{1}{6}$, ____, ____, ____, ____

Name ______________________

Multiples of Unit Fractions

Lesson 65
CC.4.NF.4a

Write the fraction as a product of a whole number and a unit fraction.

1. $\frac{5}{6}$ = $5 \times \frac{1}{6}$

2. $\frac{7}{8}$ = ______

3. $\frac{5}{3}$ = ______

4. $\frac{9}{10}$ = ______

5. $\frac{3}{4}$ = ______

6. $\frac{11}{12}$ = ______

7. $\frac{4}{6}$ = ______

8. $\frac{8}{20}$ = ______

9. $\frac{13}{100}$ = ______

List the next four multiples of the unit fraction.

10. $\frac{1}{5}$, ____, ____, ____, ____

11. $\frac{1}{8}$, ____, ____, ____, ____

Problem Solving REAL WORLD

12. So far, Monica has read $\frac{5}{6}$ of a book. She has read the same number of pages each day for 5 days. What fraction of the book does Monica read each day?

____

13. Nicholas buys $\frac{3}{8}$ pound of cheese. He puts the same amount of cheese on 3 sandwiches. How much cheese does Nicholas put on each sandwich?

____

Name ____________________

Multiples of Fractions

Lesson 66

COMMON CORE STANDARD CC.4.NF.4b

Lesson Objective: Write a product of a whole number and a fraction as a product of a whole number and a unit fraction.

You have learned to write multiples of unit fractions. You can also write multiples of other fractions.

Write the next 4 multiples of $\frac{2}{5}$.

Make a table.

$1 \times \frac{2}{5}$	$2 \times \frac{2}{5}$	$3 \times \frac{2}{5}$	$4 \times \frac{2}{5}$	$5 \times \frac{2}{5}$
$\frac{2}{5}$	$\frac{2}{5} + \frac{2}{5}$	$\frac{2}{5} + \frac{2}{5} + \frac{2}{5}$	$\frac{2}{5} + \frac{2}{5} + \frac{2}{5} + \frac{2}{5}$	$\frac{2}{5} + \frac{2}{5} + \frac{2}{5} + \frac{2}{5} + \frac{2}{5}$
$\frac{2}{5}$	$\frac{4}{5}$	$\frac{6}{5}$	$\frac{8}{5}$	$\frac{10}{5}$

So, the next 4 multiples of $\frac{2}{5}$ are $\frac{4}{5}$, $\frac{6}{5}$, $\frac{8}{5}$, and $\frac{10}{5}$.

Write $3 \times \frac{2}{5}$ as the product of a whole number and a unit fraction.

Use a number line. Make three jumps of $\frac{2}{5}$.

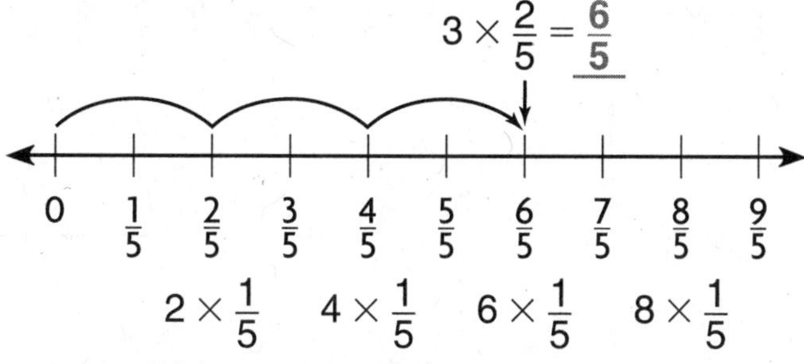

So, $3 \times \frac{2}{5} = \frac{6}{5}$, or $6 \times \frac{1}{5}$.

List the next four multiples of the fraction.

1. $\frac{3}{4}$, ____, ____, ____, ____

2. $\frac{5}{6}$, ____, ____, ____, ____

Write as the product of a whole number and a unit fraction.

3. 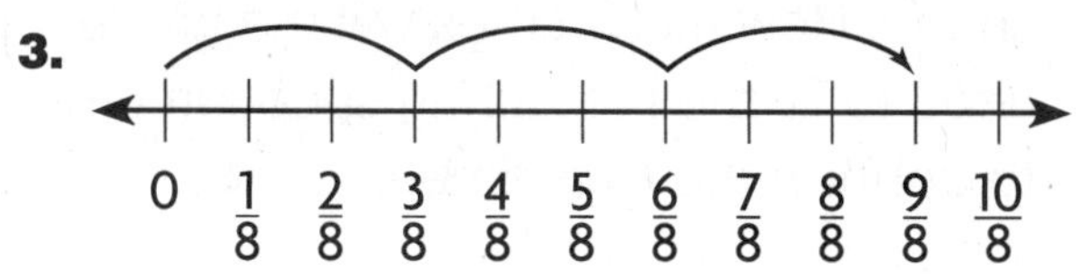

$3 \times \frac{3}{8} =$ ____________

4. 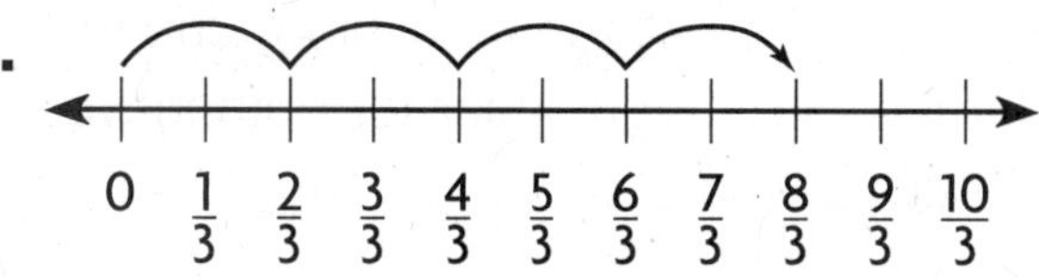

$4 \times \frac{2}{3} =$ ____________

Name ______________________________

Lesson 66
CC.4.NF.4b

Multiples of Fractions

List the next four multiples of the fraction.

1. $\frac{3}{5}$, ____, ____, ____, ____

2. $\frac{2}{6}$, ____, ____, ____, ____

3. $\frac{4}{8}$, ____, ____, ____, ____

4. $\frac{5}{10}$, ____, ____, ____, ____

Write the product as the product of a whole number and a unit fraction.

5. 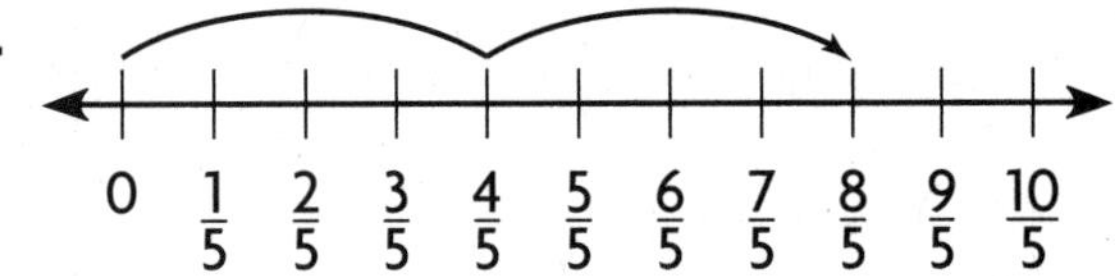

$2 \times \frac{4}{5} =$ ______________

6. 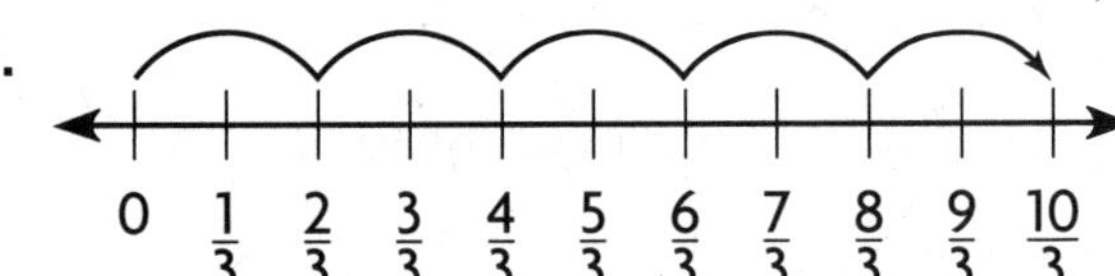

$5 \times \frac{2}{3} =$ ______________

Problem Solving REAL WORLD

7. Jessica is making 2 loaves of banana bread. She needs $\frac{3}{4}$ cup of sugar for each loaf. Her measuring cup can only hold $\frac{1}{4}$ cup of sugar. How many times will Jessica need to fill the measuring cup in order to get enough sugar for both loaves of bread?

____

8. A group of four students is performing an experiment with salt. Each student must add $\frac{3}{8}$ teaspoon of salt to a solution. The group only has a $\frac{1}{8}$-teaspoon measuring spoon. How many times will the group need to fill the measuring spoon in order to perform the experiment?

____

Name ______________________________

Lesson 67

COMMON CORE STANDARD CC.4.NF.4b

Lesson Objective: Use a model to multiply a fraction by a whole number.

Multiply a Fraction by a Whole Number Using Models

You can use a model to multiply a fraction by a whole number.

Find the product of $4 \times \frac{3}{5}$.

Use fraction strips. Show 4 groups of $\frac{3}{5}$ each.

$\frac{1}{5}$	$\frac{1}{5}$	$\frac{1}{5}$	$\frac{1}{5}$	$\frac{1}{5}$

1 group of $\frac{3}{5} = \frac{3}{5}$

$\frac{1}{5}$	$\frac{1}{5}$	$\frac{1}{5}$	$\frac{1}{5}$	$\frac{1}{5}$

2 groups of $\frac{3}{5} = \frac{6}{5}$

$\frac{1}{5}$	$\frac{1}{5}$	$\frac{1}{5}$	$\frac{1}{5}$	$\frac{1}{5}$

3 groups of $\frac{3}{5} = \frac{9}{5}$

$\frac{1}{5}$	$\frac{1}{5}$	$\frac{1}{5}$	$\frac{1}{5}$	$\frac{1}{5}$

4 groups of $\frac{3}{5} = \frac{12}{5}$

So, $4 \times \frac{3}{5} = \frac{12}{5}$.

Multiply.

1.

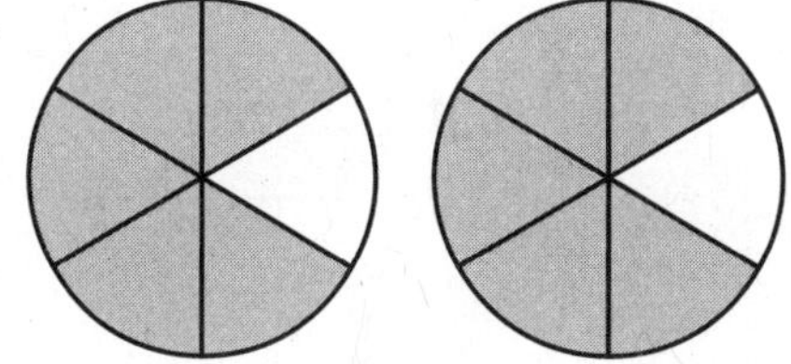

$2 \times \frac{5}{6} =$ ______

2.

$\frac{1}{8}$	$\frac{1}{8}$	$\frac{1}{8}$	$\frac{1}{8}$	$\frac{1}{8}$	$\frac{1}{8}$	$\frac{1}{8}$	$\frac{1}{8}$
$\frac{1}{8}$	$\frac{1}{8}$	$\frac{1}{8}$	$\frac{1}{8}$	$\frac{1}{8}$	$\frac{1}{8}$	$\frac{1}{8}$	$\frac{1}{8}$
$\frac{1}{8}$	$\frac{1}{8}$	$\frac{1}{8}$	$\frac{1}{8}$	$\frac{1}{8}$	$\frac{1}{8}$	$\frac{1}{8}$	$\frac{1}{8}$

$3 \times \frac{7}{8} =$ ______

3. $6 \times \frac{2}{3} =$ ______

4. $2 \times \frac{9}{10} =$ ______

5. $5 \times \frac{3}{4} =$ ______

6. $4 \times \frac{5}{8} =$ ______

7. $7 \times \frac{2}{5} =$ ______

8. $8 \times \frac{4}{6} =$ ______

Name ______________________

Multiply a Fraction by a Whole Number Using Models

Multiply.

1. $2 \times \frac{5}{6} =$ $\frac{10}{6}$

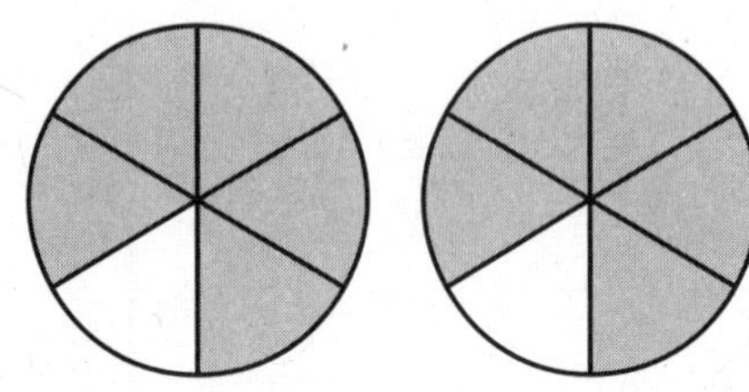

2. $3 \times \frac{2}{5} =$ __________

3. $7 \times \frac{3}{10} =$ __________

4. $3 \times \frac{5}{12} =$ __________

5. $6 \times \frac{3}{4} =$ __________

6. $4 \times \frac{2}{8} =$ __________

7. $5 \times \frac{2}{3} =$ __________

8. $2 \times \frac{7}{8} =$ __________

9. $6 \times \frac{4}{5} =$ __________

Problem Solving REAL WORLD

10. Matthew walks $\frac{5}{8}$ mile to the bus stop each morning. How far will he walk in 5 days?

____

11. Emily uses $\frac{2}{3}$ cup of milk to make one batch of muffins. How many cups of milk will Emily use if she makes 3 batches of muffins?

____

Name ______________________________

Lesson 68

COMMON CORE STANDARD CC.4.NF.4c

Lesson Objective: Multiply a fraction by a whole number to solve a problem.

Multiply a Fraction or Mixed Number by a Whole Number

To multiply a fraction by a whole number, multiply the numerators. Then multiply the denominators.

A recipe for one loaf of bread calls for $2\frac{1}{4}$ cups of flour. How many cups of flour will you need for 2 loaves of bread?

Step 1 Write and solve an equation.

$2 \times 2\frac{1}{4} = \frac{2}{1} \times \frac{9}{4}$ Write 2 as $\frac{2}{1}$. Write $2\frac{1}{4}$ as a fraction.

$= \frac{2 \times 9}{1 \times 4}$ Multiply the numerators. Then multiply the denominators.

$= \frac{18}{4}$ Simplify.

Step 2 Write the product as a mixed number.

$$\frac{18}{4} = \underbrace{\frac{1}{4}+\frac{1}{4}+\frac{1}{4}+\frac{1}{4}}_{1} + \underbrace{\frac{1}{4}+\frac{1}{4}+\frac{1}{4}+\frac{1}{4}}_{1} + \underbrace{\frac{1}{4}+\frac{1}{4}+\frac{1}{4}+\frac{1}{4}}_{1} + \underbrace{\frac{1}{4}+\frac{1}{4}+\frac{1}{4}+\frac{1}{4}}_{1} + \frac{1}{4}+\frac{1}{4}$$

$= \underline{4} + \underline{\frac{1}{4}} + \underline{\frac{1}{4}}$ Combine the wholes. Then combine the remaining parts.

$= \underline{4\frac{2}{4}}$, or $\underline{4\frac{1}{2}}$ Add. Write the sum as a mixed number.

So, you will need $\underline{4\frac{1}{2}}$ cups of flour.

Multiply. Write the product as a mixed number.

1. $3 \times \frac{2}{5} =$ _____

2. $4 \times \frac{3}{8} =$ _____

3. $5 \times \frac{1}{3} =$ _____

4. $2 \times 1\frac{3}{10} =$ _____

5. $4 \times 1\frac{2}{3} =$ _____

6. $7 \times 1\frac{1}{6} =$ _____

Name ___________________________

Multiply a Fraction or Mixed Number by a Whole Number

Multiply. Write the product as a mixed number.

1. $5 \times \frac{3}{10} =$ $1\frac{5}{10}$

2. $3 \times \frac{3}{5} =$ ________

3. $5 \times \frac{3}{4} =$ ________

4. $4 \times 1\frac{1}{5} =$ ________

5. $2 \times 2\frac{1}{3} =$ ________

6. $5 \times 1\frac{1}{6} =$ ________

7. $2 \times 2\frac{7}{8} =$ ________

8. $7 \times 1\frac{3}{4} =$ ________

9. $8 \times 1\frac{3}{5} =$ ________

Problem Solving REAL WORLD

10. Brielle exercises for $\frac{3}{4}$ hour each day for 6 days in a row. Altogether, how many hours does she exercise during the 6 days?

____

11. A recipe for quinoa calls for $2\frac{2}{3}$ cups of milk. Conner wants to make 4 batches of quinoa. How much milk does he need?

____

Name ______________________________

Lesson 69

COMMON CORE STANDARD CC.4.NF.4c

Lesson Objective: Use the strategy *draw a diagram* to solve comparison problems with fractions.

Problem Solving • Comparison Problems with Fractions

The Great Salt Lake in Utah is about $\frac{4}{5}$ mile above sea level. Lake Titicaca in South America is about 3 times as high above sea level as the Great Salt Lake. About how high above sea level is Lake Titicaca?

Read the Problem	Solve the Problem
What do I need to find? I need to find <u>about how high above sea level Lake Titicaca is.</u>	Draw a comparison model. Compare the heights above sea level of the Great Salt Lake and Lake Titicaca, in miles. <u>Great Salt Lake</u> $\boxed{\frac{4}{5}}$ <u>Lake Titicaca</u> $\boxed{\frac{4}{5}}\boxed{\frac{4}{5}}\boxed{\frac{4}{5}}$ → t
What information do I need to use? The Great Salt Lake is about <u>$\frac{4}{5}$</u> mile above sea level. Lake Titicaca is about <u>3</u> times as high above sea level.	Write an equation and solve. t is the height above sea level of <u>Lake Titicaca</u>, in miles.
How will I use the information? I can <u>draw a diagram</u> to compare the heights.	$t = \underline{3} \times \underline{\frac{4}{5}}$ Write an equation. $t = \underline{\frac{12}{5}}$ Multiply. $t = \underline{2\frac{2}{5}}$ Write the fraction as a mixed number.
So, Lake Titicaca is about <u>$2\frac{2}{5}$</u> miles above sea level.	

1. Amelia is training for a triathlon. She swims $\frac{3}{5}$ mile. Then she runs about 6 times farther than she swims. About how far does Amelia run?

   ____

2. Last week, Meg bought $1\frac{3}{4}$ pounds of fruit at the market. This week, she buys 4 times as many pounds of fruit as last week. In pounds, how much fruit does Meg buy this week?

   ____

Name ______________________________

Problem Solving • Comparison Problems with Fractions

Read each problem and solve.

1. A shrub is $1\frac{2}{3}$ feet tall. A small tree is 3 times as tall as the shrub. How tall is the tree?

t is the height of the tree, in feet.

$t = 3 \times 1\frac{2}{3}$

$t = 3 \times \frac{5}{3}$

$t = \frac{15}{3}$

$t = 5$

So, the tree is 5 feet tall.

shrub	$1\frac{2}{3}$		
tree	$1\frac{2}{3}$	$1\frac{2}{3}$	$1\frac{2}{3}$

5 feet

2. You run $1\frac{3}{4}$ miles each day. Your friend runs 4 times as far as you do. How far does your friend run each day?

____

3. At the grocery store, Ayla buys $1\frac{1}{3}$ pounds of ground turkey. Tasha buys 2 times as much ground turkey as Ayla. How much ground turkey does Tasha buy?

____

4. When Nathan's mother drives him to school, it takes $\frac{1}{5}$ hour. When Nathan walks to school, it takes him 4 times as long to get to school. How long does it take Nathan to walk to school?

____

Name ______________________

Lesson 70

COMMON CORE STANDARD CC.4.NF.5

Lesson Objective: Record tenths and hundredths as fractions and decimals.

Equivalent Fractions and Decimals

Lori ran $\frac{20}{100}$ mile. How many tenths of a mile did she run?

Write $\frac{20}{100}$ as an equivalent fraction with a denominator of 10.

Step 1 **Think:** 10 is a common factor of the numerator and the denominator.

Step 2 Divide the numerator and denominator by 10.

$$\frac{20}{100} = \frac{20 \div 10}{100 \div 10} = \frac{2}{10}$$

So, Lori ran $\frac{2}{10}$ mile.

Use a place-value chart.

Step 1 Write $\frac{20}{100}$ as an equivalent decimal.

Ones	.	Tenths	Hundredths
0	.	2	0

Step 2 **Think:** 20 hundredths is __2__ tenths __0__ hundredths

Ones	.	Tenths
0	.	2

So, Lori ran **0.2** mile.

Write the number as hundredths in fraction form and decimal form.

1. $\frac{9}{10}$ ______________

2. 0.6 ______________

3. $\frac{4}{10}$ ______________

Write the number as tenths in fraction form and decimal form.

4. $\frac{70}{100}$ ______________

5. $\frac{80}{100}$ ______________

6. 0.50 ______________

Name ______________________

Equivalent Fractions and Decimals

Write the number as hundredths in fraction form and decimal form.

1. $\frac{5}{10}$

$\frac{5}{10} = \frac{5 \times 10}{10 \times 10} = \frac{50}{100}$

Think: 5 tenths is the same as 5 tenths and 0 hundredths. Write 0.50.

$\frac{50}{100}$; 0.50

2. $\frac{9}{10}$ ______

3. 0.2 ______

4. 0.8 ______

Write the number as tenths in fraction form and decimal form.

5. $\frac{40}{100}$ ______

6. $\frac{10}{100}$ ______

7. 0.60 ______

Problem Solving REAL WORLD

8. Billy walks $\frac{6}{10}$ mile to school each day. Write $\frac{6}{10}$ as hundredths in fraction form and in decimal form.

______

9. Four states have names that begin with the letter A. This represents 0.08 of all the states. Write 0.08 as a fraction.

______

Name ______________________________

Lesson 71

COMMON CORE STANDARD CC.4.NF.5

Lesson Objective: Add fractions when the denominators are 10 or 100.

Add Fractional Parts of 10 and 100

Sam uses 100 glass beads for a project. Of the beads, $\frac{35}{100}$ are gold and $\frac{4}{10}$ are silver. What fraction of the glass beads are gold or silver?

Add $\frac{35}{100}$ and $\frac{4}{10}$.

Step 1 Decide on a common denominator. Use 100.

Step 2 Write $\frac{4}{10}$ as an equivalent fraction with a denominator of 100.

$$\frac{4}{10} = \frac{4 \times 10}{10 \times 10} = \frac{40}{100}$$

Step 3 Add $\frac{35}{100}$ and $\frac{40}{100}$.

$$\frac{35}{100} + \frac{40}{100} = \frac{75}{100}$$

← Add the numerators.
← Use 100 as the denominator.

So, $\frac{75}{100}$ of the glass beads are gold or silver.

Add $0.26 and $0.59.

Step 1 Write each amount as a fraction of a dollar.

$0.26 = $\frac{26}{100}$ of a dollar $0.59 = $\frac{59}{100}$ of a dollar

Step 2 Add $\frac{26}{100}$ and $\frac{59}{100}$.

$$\frac{26}{100} + \frac{59}{100} = \frac{85}{100}$$

← Add the numerators.
← 100 is the common denominator.

Step 3 Write the sum as a decimal.

$$\frac{85}{100} = 0.85$$

So, $0.26 + $0.59 = $0.85.

Find the sum.

1. $\frac{75}{100} + \frac{2}{10} =$ ________

2. $0.73 + $0.25 = $ ________

$$\frac{73}{100} + \frac{25}{100} = \frac{}{}$$

Name ______________________

Add Fractional Parts of 10 and 100

Find the sum.

1. $\frac{2}{10} + \frac{43}{100}$

$\frac{20}{100} + \frac{43}{100} = \frac{63}{100}$

$\frac{63}{100}$

Think: Write $\frac{2}{10}$ as a fraction with a denominator of 100:

$\frac{2 \times 10}{10 \times 10} = \frac{20}{100}$

2. $\frac{17}{100} + \frac{6}{10}$ ______

3. $\frac{9}{100} + \frac{4}{10}$ ______

4. $\frac{7}{10} + \frac{23}{100}$ ______

5. \$0.48 + \$0.30 ______

6. \$0.25 + \$0.34 ______

7. \$0.66 + \$0.06 ______

Problem Solving REAL WORLD

8. Ned's frog jumped $\frac{38}{100}$ meter. Then his frog jumped $\frac{4}{10}$ meter. How far did Ned's frog jump in all?

______

9. Keiko walks $\frac{5}{10}$ kilometer from school to the park. Then she walks $\frac{19}{100}$ kilometer from the park to her home. How far does Keiko walk in all?

______

Name ______________________

Lesson 72

COMMON CORE STANDARD CC.4.NF.6

Lesson Objective: Record tenths as fractions and as decimals.

Relate Tenths and Decimals

Write the fraction and the decimal that are shown by the point on the number line.

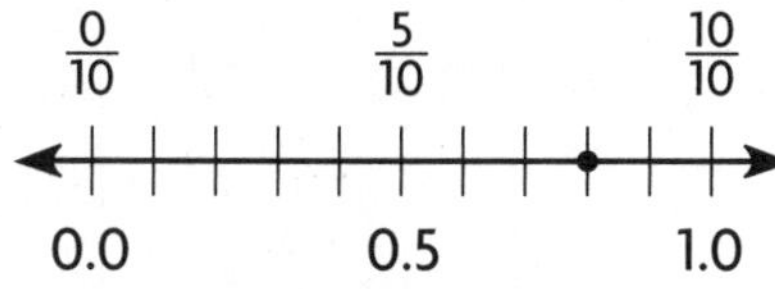

Step 1 Count the number of equal parts of the whole shown on the number line. There are ten equal parts.

This tells you that the number line shows tenths.

Step 2 Label the number line with the missing fractions. What fraction is shown by the point on the number line?

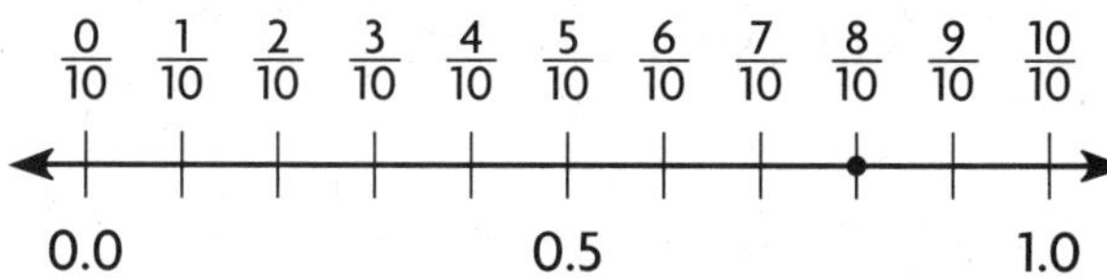

The fraction shown by the point on the number line is $\frac{8}{10}$.

Step 3 Label the number line with the missing decimals. What decimal is shown by the point on the number line?

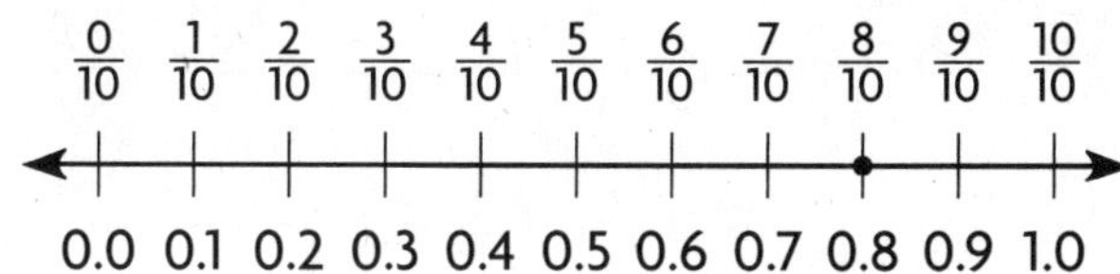

The decimal shown by the point on the number line is 0.8.

So, the fraction and decimal shown by the point on the number line are $\frac{8}{10}$ and 0.8.

Write the fraction or mixed number and the decimal shown by the model.

1.

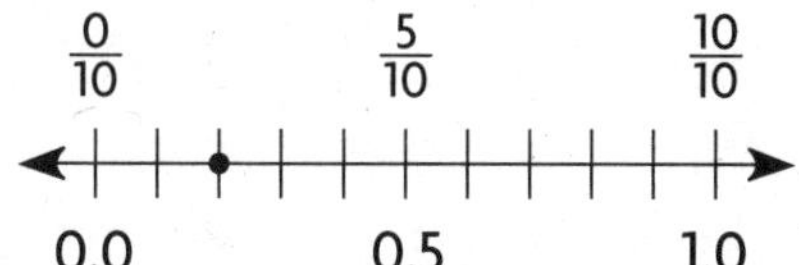

____

2.

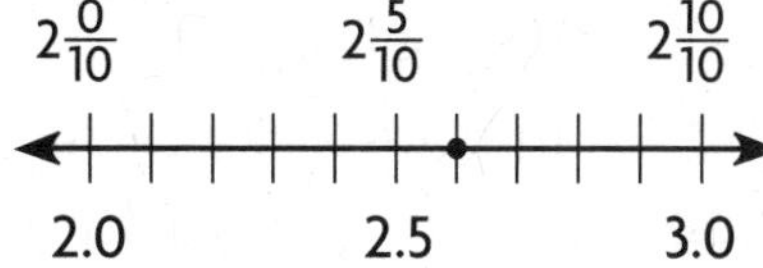

____

Name ____________________

Relate Tenths and Decimals

Lesson 72
CC.4.NF.6

Write the fraction or mixed number and the decimal shown by the model.

1. 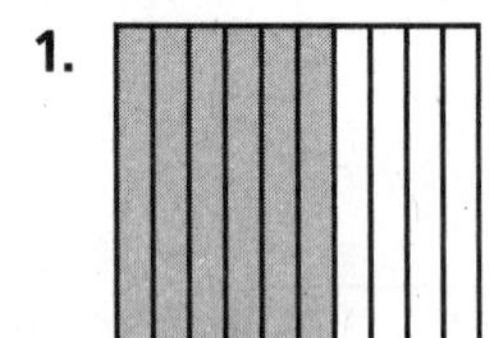

Think: The model is divided into 10 equal parts. Each part represents one tenth.

$\frac{6}{10}$; 0.6

2. 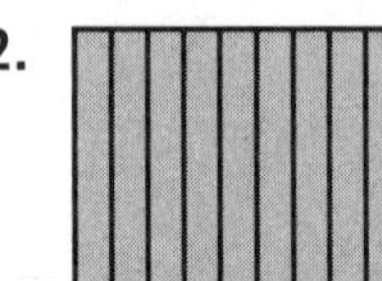 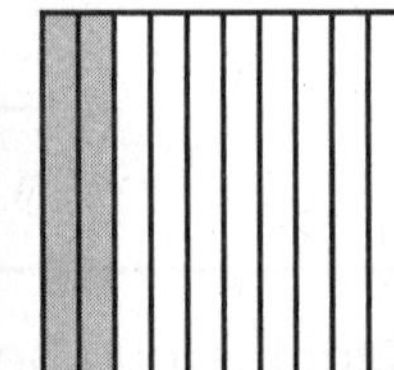

____

3. 

____

4. 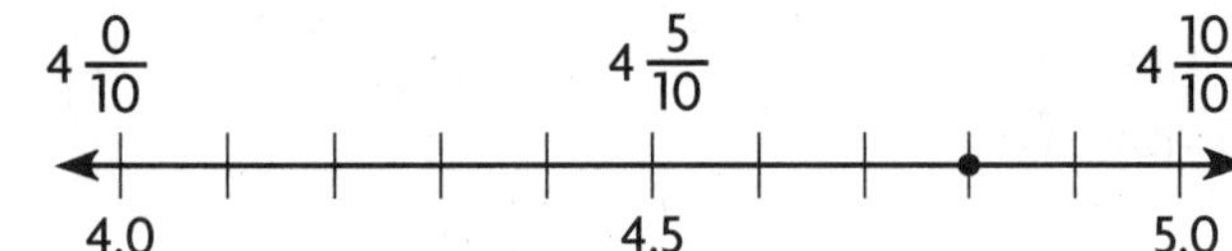

____

Write the fraction or mixed number as a decimal.

5. $\frac{4}{10}$ ______
6. $3\frac{1}{10}$ ______
7. $\frac{7}{10}$ ______
8. $6\frac{5}{10}$ ______
9. $\frac{9}{10}$ ______

Problem Solving REAL WORLD

10. There are 10 sports balls in the equipment closet. Three are kickballs. Write the portion of the balls that are kickballs as a fraction, as a decimal, and in word form.

____

11. Peyton has 2 pizzas. Each pizza is cut into 10 equal slices. She and her friends eat 14 slices. What part of the pizzas did they eat? Write your answer as a decimal.

____

Name ___________________________

Lesson 73

COMMON CORE STANDARD CC.4.NF.6

Lesson Objective: Record hundredths as fractions and as decimals.

Relate Hundredths and Decimals

Write the fraction or mixed number and the decimal shown by the model.

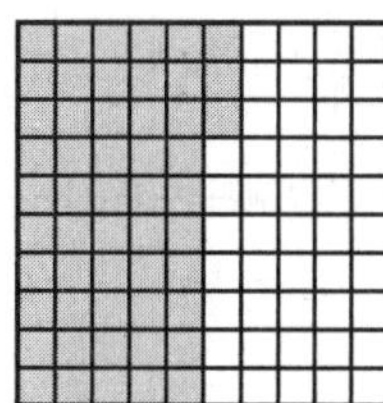

Step 1 Count the number of shaded squares in the model and the total number of squares in the whole model.	Number of shaded squares: 53 Total number of squares: 100
Step 2 Write a fraction to represent the part of the model that is shaded.	$\frac{\text{Number of Shaded Squares}}{\text{Total Number of Squares}} = \frac{53}{100}$ The fraction shown by the model is $\frac{53}{100}$.
Step 3 Write the fraction in decimal form.	**Think:** The fraction shown by the model is $\frac{53}{100}$. 0.53 names the same amount as $\frac{53}{100}$. The decimal shown by the model is 0.53.
The fraction and decimal shown by the model are $\frac{53}{100}$ and 0.53.	

Write the fraction or mixed number and the decimal shown by the model.

1.

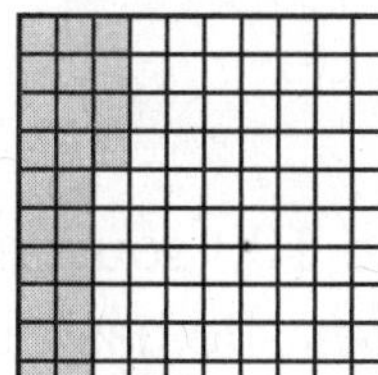

____

2.

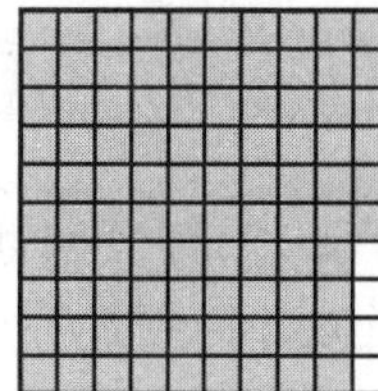

____

Name ______________________

Relate Hundredths and Decimals

Write the fraction or mixed number and the decimal shown by the model.

1. 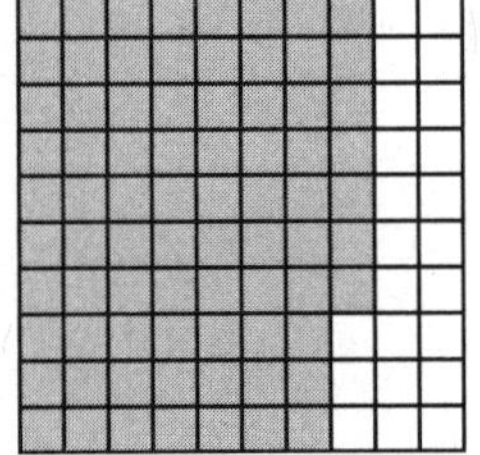

Think: The whole is divided into one hundred equal parts, so each part is one hundredth.

$\frac{77}{100}$; 0.77

2.

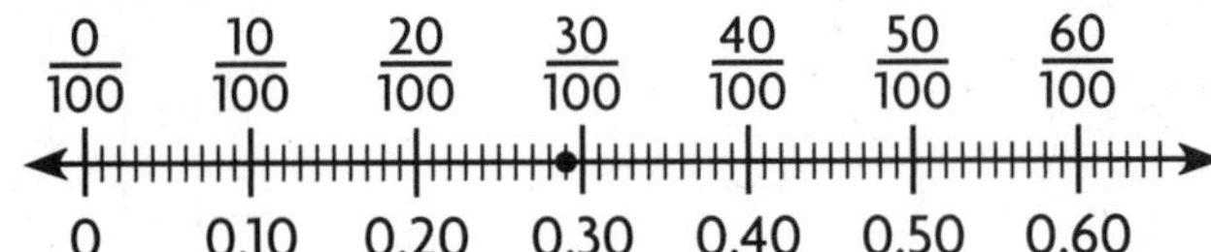

____

3. 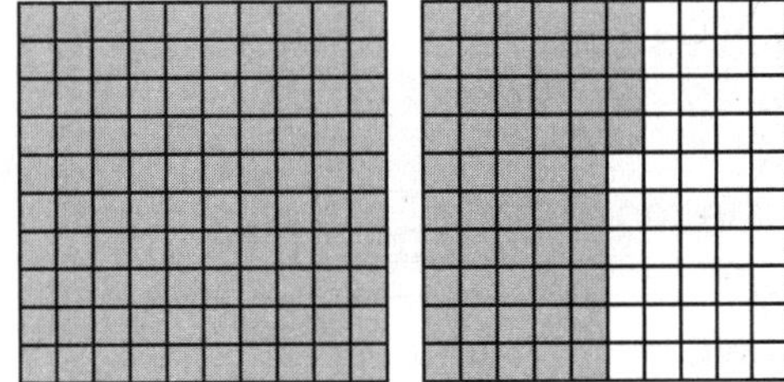

____

4.

$4\frac{20}{100}$ $4\frac{30}{100}$ $4\frac{40}{100}$ $4\frac{50}{100}$ $4\frac{60}{100}$ $4\frac{70}{100}$ $4\frac{80}{100}$

4.20 4.30 4.40 4.50 4.60 4.70 4.80

____

Write the fraction or mixed number as a decimal.

5. $\frac{37}{100}$ ______________

6. $8\frac{11}{100}$ ______________

7. $\frac{98}{100}$ ______________

8. $25\frac{50}{100}$ ______________

9. $\frac{6}{100}$ ______________

Problem Solving REAL WORLD

10. There are 100 pennies in a dollar. What fraction of a dollar is 61 pennies? Write it as a fraction, as a decimal, and in word form.

____

____

11. Kylee has collected 100 souvenir thimbles from different places she has visited with her family. Twenty of the thimbles are carved from wood. Write the fraction of thimbles that are wooden as a decimal.

____

Name ___________________________

Lesson 74

COMMON CORE STANDARD CC.4.NF.6

Lesson Objective: Translate among representations of fractions, decimals, and money.

Relate Fractions, Decimals, and Money

Write the total money amount. Then write the amount as a fraction and as a decimal in terms of a dollar.

Step 1 Count the value of coins from greatest to least. Write the total money amount.

\$0.25 ⟶ \$0.35 ⟶ \$0.40 ⟶ \$0.45 ⟶ \$0.50

Step 2 Write the total money amount as a fraction of a dollar.

The total money amount is \$0.50, which is the same as 50 cents.

Think: There are 100 cents in a dollar.

So, the total amount written as a fraction of a dollar is:

$\frac{50 \text{ cents}}{100 \text{ cents}} = \frac{50}{100}$

Step 3 Write the total money amount as a decimal.

Think: I can write \$0.50 as 0.50.

The total money amount is $\frac{50}{100}$ written as a fraction of a dollar, and 0.50 written as a decimal.

Write the total money amount. Then write the amount as a fraction or a mixed number and as a decimal in terms of a dollar.

1.

____

2.

____

Name ______________________________

Lesson 74

CC.4.NF.6

Relate Fractions, Decimals, and Money

Write the total money amount. Then write the amount as a fraction or a mixed number and as a decimal in terms of dollars.

1.

$0.18; $\frac{18}{100}$; 0.18

2.

____

Write as a money amount and as a decimal in terms of dollars.

3. $\frac{25}{100}$ ________

4. $\frac{79}{100}$ ________

5. $\frac{31}{100}$ ________

6. $\frac{8}{100}$ ________

7. $\frac{42}{100}$ ________

Write the money amount as a fraction in terms of dollars.

8. $0.87 ________

9. $0.03 ________

10. $0.66 ________

11. $0.95 ________

12. $1.00 ________

Write the total money amount. Then write the amount as a fraction and as a decimal in terms of dollars.

13. 2 quarters 2 dimes ________

14. 3 dimes 4 pennies ________

15. 8 nickels 12 pennies ________

Problem Solving REAL WORLD

16. Kate has 1 dime, 4 nickels, and 8 pennies. Write Kate's total amount as a fraction in terms of a dollar.

____

17. Nolan says he has $\frac{75}{100}$ of a dollar. If he only has 3 coins, what are the coins?

____

Name ______________________

Lesson 75

COMMON CORE STANDARD CC.4.NF.7

Lesson Objective: Compare decimals to hundredths by reasoning about their size.

Compare Decimals

Alfie found 0.2 of a dollar and Gemma found 0.23 of a dollar. Which friend found more money?

To compare decimals, you can use a number line.

Step 1 Locate each decimal on a number line.

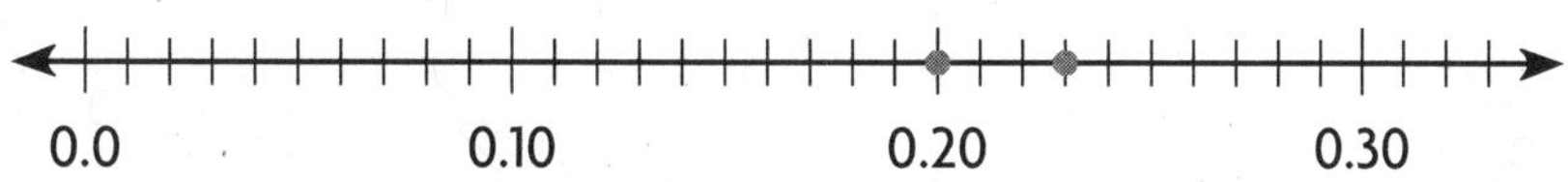

Step 2 The number farther to the right is greater.

0.23 > 0.2, so __Gemma__ found more money.

To compare decimals, you can compare equal-size parts.

Step 1 Write 0.2 as a decimal in hundredths.

0.2 is 2 tenths, which is equivalent to __20__ hundredths.

0.2 = __0.20__

Step 2 Compare.

23 hundredths __is greater than__ 20 hundredths,
so **0.23 > 0.2**.

So, __Gemma__ found more money.

Compare. Write <, >, or =.

1. 0.17 ◯ 0.13 **2.** 0.8 ◯ 0.08 **3.** 0.36 ◯ 0.63 **4.** 0.4 ◯ 0.40

5. 0.75 ◯ 0.69 **6.** 0.3 ◯ 0.7 **7.** 0.45 ◯ 0.37 **8.** 0.96 ◯ 0.78

Name ______________________________

Lesson 75

CC.4.NF.7

Compare Decimals

Compare. Write $<$, $>$, or $=$.

1. $0.35 \;(<)\; 0.53$

   Think: 3 tenths is less than 5 tenths.
   So, $0.35 < 0.53$

2. $0.6 \;\bigcirc\; 0.60$

3. $0.24 \;\bigcirc\; 0.31$

4. $0.94 \;\bigcirc\; 0.9$

5. $0.3 \;\bigcirc\; 0.32$

6. $0.45 \;\bigcirc\; 0.28$

7. $0.39 \;\bigcirc\; 0.93$

Use the number line to compare. Write *true* or *false*.

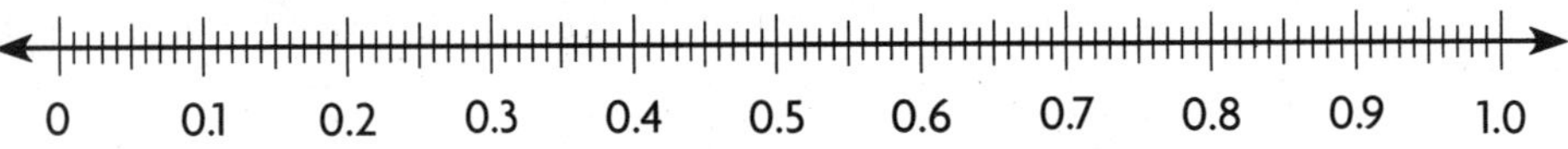

8. $0.8 > 0.78$ ______________

9. $0.4 > 0.84$ ______________

10. $0.7 < 0.70$ ______________

11. $0.4 > 0.04$ ______________

Compare. Write *true* or *false*.

12. $0.09 > 0.1$ ______________

13. $0.24 = 0.42$ ______________

14. $0.17 < 0.32$ ______________

15. $0.85 > 0.82$ ______________

Problem Solving REAL WORLD

16. Kelly walks 0.7 mile to school. Mary walks 0.49 mile to school. Write an inequality using $<$, $>$, or $=$ to compare the distances they walk to school.

    ____

17. Tyrone shades two decimal grids. He shades 0.03 of the squares on one grid blue. He shades 0.3 of another grid red. Which grid has the greater part shaded?

    ____

Name ______________________________

Lesson 76

COMMON CORE STANDARD CC.4.MD.1

Lesson Objective: Use benchmarks to understand the relative sizes of measurement units.

Measurement Benchmarks

You can use benchmarks to estimate measurements.

The chart shows benchmarks for customary units of measurement.

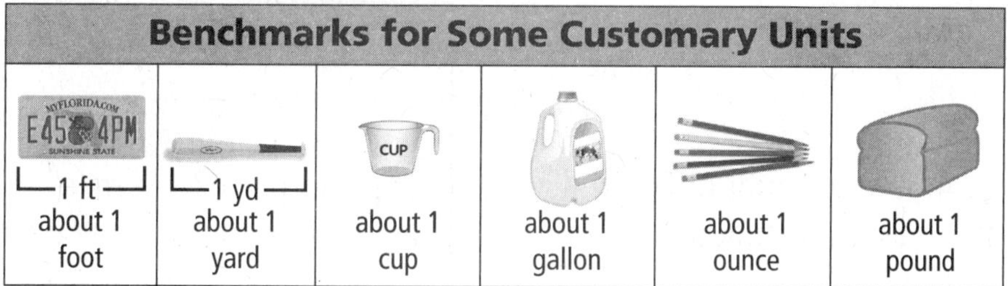

Benchmarks for Some Customary Units					
1 ft about 1 foot	1 yd about 1 yard	about 1 cup	about 1 gallon	about 1 ounce	about 1 pound

Here are some more examples of estimating with customary units.

- The width of a professional football is about 1 foot.
- A large fish bowl holds about 1 gallon of water.
- A box of cereal weighs about 1 pound.

The chart shows benchmarks for metric units of measurement.

Benchmarks for Some Metric Units					
about 1 centimeter	about 1 meter	about 1 milliliter	about 1 liter	about 1 gram	about 1 kilogram

Here are some more examples of estimating with metric units.

- The width of a large paper clip is about 1 centimeter.
- A pitcher holds about 1 liter of juice.
- Three laps around a track is about 1 kilometer.

Use benchmarks to choose the customary unit you would use to measure each.

1. length of a school bus

____

2. weight of a computer

____

Use benchmarks to choose the metric unit you would use to measure each.

3. the amount of liquid a bottle of detergent holds

____

4. distance between two cities

____

Name ______________________________

Lesson 76

CC.4.MD.1

Measurement Benchmarks

Use benchmarks to choose the customary unit you would use to measure each.

1. height of a computer

foot

2. weight of a table

____

3. length of a semi-truck

____

4. the amount of liquid a bathtub holds

____

Customary Units	
ounce	yard
pound	mile
inch	gallon
foot	cup

Use benchmarks to choose the metric unit you would use to measure each.

5. mass of a grasshopper

____

6. the amount of liquid a water bottle holds

____

7. length of a soccer field

____

8. length of a pencil

____

Metric Units	
milliliter	centimeter
liter	meter
gram	kilometer
kilogram	

Circle the better estimate.

9. mass of a chicken egg

50 grams   50 kilograms

10. length of a car

12 miles   12 feet

11. amount of liquid a drinking glass holds

8 ounces   8 quarts

Complete the sentence. Write *more* or *less*.

12. A camera has a length of ________ than one centimeter.

13. A bowling ball weighs ________ than one pound.

Problem Solving REAL WORLD

14. What is the better estimate for the mass of a textbook, 1 gram or 1 kilogram?

____

15. What is the better estimate for the height of a desk, 1 meter or 1 kilometer?

____

Name ______________________________

Lesson 77

COMMON CORE STANDARD CC.4.MD.1

Lesson Objective: Use models to compare customary units of length.

Customary Units of Length

A ruler is used to measure length. A ruler that is 1 foot long shows 12 inches in 1 foot. A ruler that is 3 feet long is called a yardstick. There are 3 feet in 1 yard.

How does the size of a foot compare to the size of an inch?

Step 1 A small paper clip is about 1 inch long. Below is a drawing of a chain of paper clips that is about 1 foot long. Number each paper clip, starting with 1.

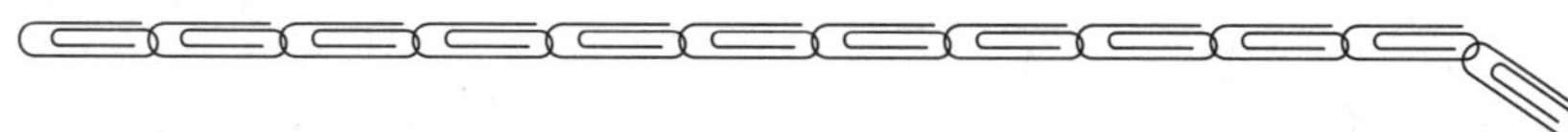

Step 2 Complete this sentence.

In the chain of paper clips shown, there are __12__ paper clips.

Step 3 Compare the size of 1 inch to the size of 1 foot.

There are __12__ inches in __1__ foot.

So, 1 foot is __12__ times as long as 1 inch.

Complete.

1. 5 feet = ________ inches

2. 3 yards = ________ feet

3. 5 yards = ________ feet

4. 4 feet = ________ inches

5. 6 feet = ________ inches

6. 8 yards = ________ feet

Name ______________________________

Lesson 77
CC.4.MD.1

Customary Units of Length

Complete.

1. 3 feet = __36__ inches Think: 1 foot = 12 inches, so 3 feet = 3×12 inches, or 36 inches

2. 2 yards = ______ feet
3. 8 feet = ______ inches
4. 7 yards = ______ feet

5. 4 feet = ______ inches
6. 15 yards = ______ feet
7. 10 feet = ______ inches

Compare using <, >, or =.

8. 3 yards ◯ 10 feet
9. 5 feet ◯ 60 inches
10. 8 yards ◯ 20 feet

11. 3 feet ◯ 10 inches
12. 3 yards ◯ 21 feet
13. 6 feet ◯ 72 inches

Problem Solving REAL WORLD

14. Carla has two lengths of ribbon. One ribbon is 2 feet long. The other ribbon is 30 inches long. Which length of ribbon is longer? **Explain.**

____

____

____

____

15. A football player gained 2 yards on one play. On the next play, he gained 5 feet. Was his gain greater on the first play or the second play? **Explain.**

____

____

____

____

Name ______________________________

Lesson 78

COMMON CORE STANDARD CC.4.MD.1

Lesson Objective: Use models to compare customary units of weight.

Customary Units of Weight

Ounces and **pounds** are customary units of weight. A **ton** is a unit of weight that is equal to 2,000 pounds.

A slice of bread weighs about 1 ounce. Some loaves of bread weigh about 1 pound.

How does the size of 1 ounce compare to the size of 1 pound?

Step 1 You know a slice of bread weighs about 1 ounce. Below is a drawing of a loaf of bread that weighs about 1 pound. Number each slice of bread, starting with 1.

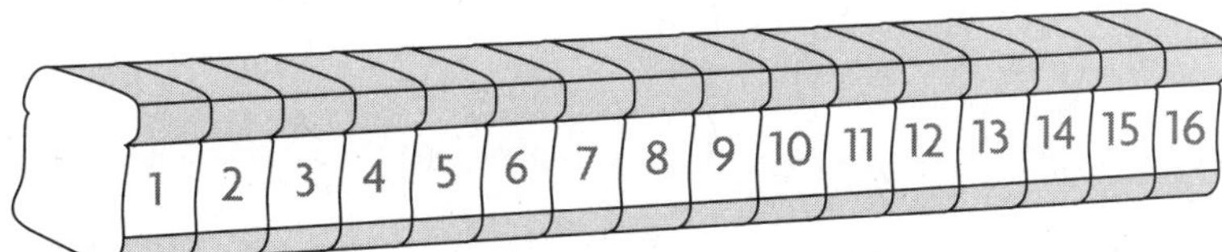

Step 2 Complete this sentence.

In the loaf of bread shown above, there are <u>16</u> slices of bread.

Step 3 Compare the size of 1 ounce to the size of 1 pound.

There are <u>16</u> ounces in <u>1</u> pound.

So, 1 pound is <u>16</u> times as heavy as 1 ounce.

Complete.

1. 2 pounds = ________ ounces

   Think: 2 × 16 = 32

2. 2 tons = ________ pounds

3. 7 pounds = ________ ounces

4. 4 pounds = ________ ounces

5. 3 tons = ________ pounds

6. 10 pounds = ________ ounces

Name ______________________

Lesson 78
CC.4.MD.1

Customary Units of Weight

Complete.

1. 5 pounds = ___80___ ounces

Think: 1 pound = 16 ounces, so
5 pounds = 5 × 16 ounces, or 80 ounces

2. 7 tons = __________ pounds

3. 2 pounds = __________ ounces

4. 3 tons = __________ pounds

5. 10 pounds = __________ ounces

6. 5 tons = __________ pounds

7. 7 pounds = __________ ounces

Compare using <, >, or =.

8. 8 pounds ◯ 80 ounces

9. 1 ton ◯ 100 pounds

10. 3 pounds ◯ 50 ounces

11. 5 tons ◯ 1,000 pounds

12. 16 pounds ◯ 256 ounces

13. 8 tons ◯ 16,000 pounds

Problem Solving REAL WORLD

14. A company that makes steel girders can produce 6 tons of girders in one day. How many pounds is this?

____

15. Larry's baby sister weighed 6 pounds at birth. How many ounces did the baby weigh?

____

Name ______________________________

Lesson 79

COMMON CORE STANDARD CC.4.MD.1

Lesson Objective: Use models to compare customary units of liquid volume.

Customary Units of Liquid Volume

Liquid volume is the measure of the space a liquid occupies. Some basic units for measuring liquid volume are **gallons, half gallons, quarts, pints, cups,** and **fluid ounces**. The table at the right shows the relationships among some units of liquid volume.

1 cup = 8 fluid ounces
1 pint = 2 cups
1 quart = 2 pints
1 half gallon = 2 quarts
1 gallon = 4 quarts

How does the size of a gallon compare to the size of a pint?

Step 1 Use the information in the table. Draw a bar to represent 1 gallon.

1 gallon

Step 2 The table shows that 1 gallon is equal to 4 quarts. Draw a bar to show 4 quarts.

1 quart	1 quart	1 quart	1 quart

Step 3 The table shows that 1 quart is equal to 2 pints. Draw a bar to show 2 pints for each of the 4 quarts.

1 pint	1 pint	1 pint	1 pint	1 pint	1 pint	1 pint	1 pint

Step 4 Compare the size of 1 gallon to the size of 1 pint.

There are __8__ pints in __1__ gallon.

So, 1 gallon is __8__ times as much as 1 pint.

Complete. Draw a model to help.

1. 2 quarts = ________ pints

2. 1 gallon = ________ cups

3. 1 pint = ________ fluid ounces

4. 3 pints = ________ cups

5. 3 quarts = ________ cups

6. 1 half gallon = ________ pints

Name ______________________________

Customary Units of Liquid Volume

Complete.

1. 6 gallons = __24__ quarts

Think: 1 gallon = 4 quarts,
so 6 gallons = 6 × 4 quarts, or 24 quarts

2. 12 quarts = ______ pints

3. 6 cups = ______ fluid ounces

4. 9 pints = ______ cups

5. 10 quarts = ______ cups

6. 5 gallons = ______ pints

7. 3 gallons = ______ cups

Compare using <, >, or =.

8. 6 pints ◯ 60 fluid ounces

9. 3 gallons ◯ 30 quarts

10. 5 quarts ◯ 20 cups

11. 6 cups ◯ 12 pints

12. 8 quarts ◯ 16 pints

13. 6 gallons ◯ 96 pints

Problem Solving REAL WORLD

14. A chef makes $1\frac{1}{2}$ gallons of soup in a large pot. How many 1-cup servings can the chef get from this large pot of soup?

____

15. Kendra's water bottle contains 2 quarts of water. She wants to add drink mix to it, but the directions for the drink mix give the amount of water in fluid ounces. How many fluid ounces are in her bottle?

____

Name ________________________________

Lesson 80

COMMON CORE STANDARD CC.4.MD.1

Lesson Objective: Use models to compare metric units of length.

Metric Units of Length

Meters (m), **decimeters** (dm), centimeters (cm), and **millimeters** (mm) are all metric units of length. You can use a ruler and a meterstick to find out how these units are related.

Materials: ruler, meterstick

Step 1 Look at a metric ruler. Most look like the one below.

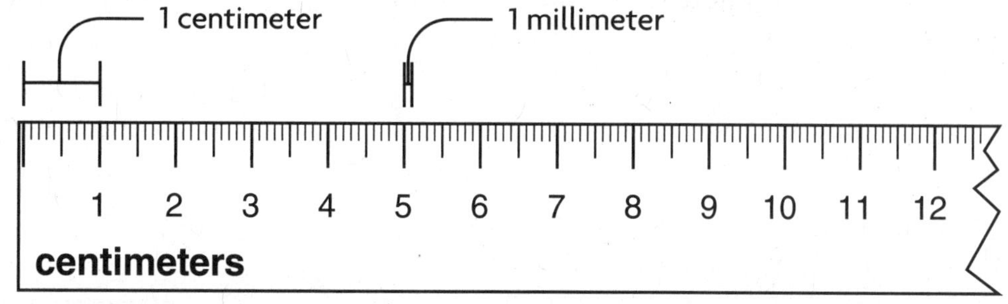

The short marks between each centimeter mark show millimeters. 1 centimeter has the same length as a group of 10 millimeters.

Step 2 Look at a meterstick. Most look like the one below.

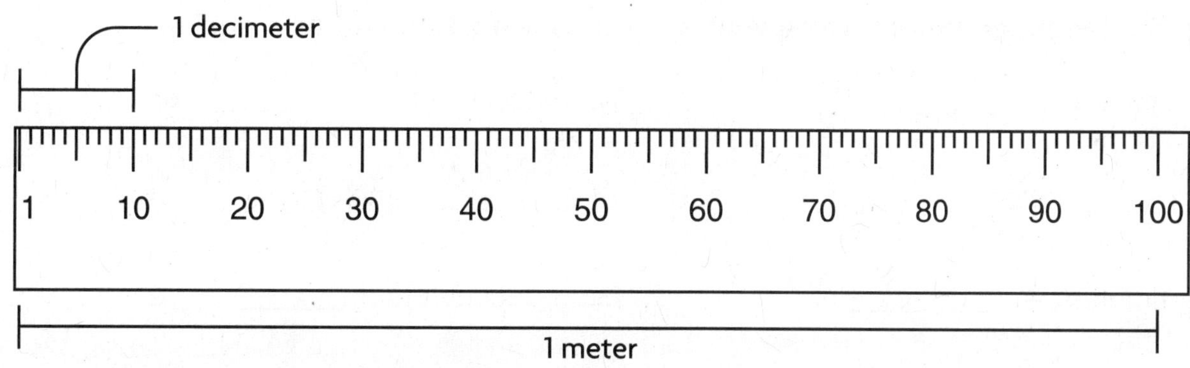

1 decimeter has the same length as a group of 10 centimeters.

Step 3 Use the ruler and the meterstick to compare metric units of length.

1 centimeter = 10 millimeters   1 decimeter = 10 centimeters

1 meter = 10 decimeters   1 meter = 100 centimeters

Complete.

1. 3 meters = ________ decimeters

2. 5 meters = ________ centimeters

3. 4 centimeters = ________ millimeters

4. 9 decimeters = ________ centimeters

Name ______________________

Metric Units of Length

Lesson 80
CC.4.MD.1

Complete.

1. 4 meters = **400** centimeters

   Think: 1 meter = 100 centimeters, so 4 meters = 4 × 100 centimeters, or 400 centimeters

2. 8 centimeters = __________ millimeters

3. 5 meters = __________ decimeters

4. 9 meters = __________ millimeters

5. 7 meters = __________ centimeters

Compare using <, >, or =.

6. 8 meters ◯ 80 centimeters

7. 3 decimeters ◯ 30 centimeters

8. 4 meters ◯ 450 centimeters

9. 90 centimeters ◯ 9 millimeters

Describe the length in meters. Write your answer as a fraction and as a decimal.

10. 43 centimeters = __________ or __________ meter

11. 6 decimeters = __________ **or** __________ meter

12. 8 centimeters = __________ or __________ meter

13. 3 decimeters = __________ or __________ meter

Problem Solving REAL WORLD

14. A flagpole is 4 meters tall. How many centimeters tall is the flagpole?

    ____

15. A new building is 25 meters tall. How many decimeters tall is the building?

    ____

Name ______________________

COMMON CORE STANDARD CC.4.MD.1

Lesson Objective: Use models to compare metric units of mass and liquid volume.

Metric Units of Mass and Liquid Volume

Mass is the amount of matter in an object. Metric units of mass include grams (g) and kilograms (kg). 1 kilogram represents the same mass as 1,000 grams.

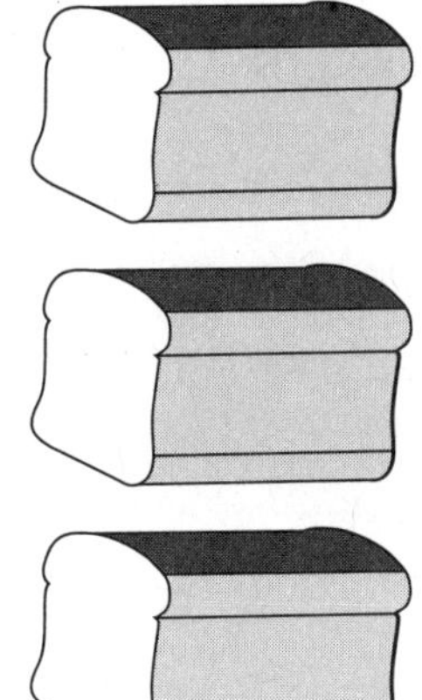

One large loaf of bread has a mass of about 1 kilogram. Jacob has 3 large loaves of bread. About how many grams is the mass of the loaves?

3 kilograms = 3 × **1,000** grams

= **3,000** grams

Liters (L) and **milliliters** (mL) are metric units of liquid volume. 1 liter represents the same liquid volume as 1,000 milliliters.

A large bowl holds about 2 liters of juice. Carmen needs to know the liquid volume in milliliters.

2 liters = 2 × **1,000** milliliters

= **2,000** milliliters

Complete.

1. 4 kilograms = ________ grams

2. 9 liters = ________ milliliters

3. 3 liters = ________ milliliters

4. 7 kilograms = ________ grams

5. 5 kilograms = ________ grams

6. 8 liters = ________ milliliters

Name ______________________________

Lesson 81
CC.4.MD.1

Metric Units of Mass and Liquid Volume

Complete.

1. 5 liters = **5,000** milliliters

Think: 1 liter = 1,000 milliliters, so 5 liters = 5 × 1,000 milliliters, or 5,000 milliliters

2. 3 kilograms = __________ grams
3. 8 liters = __________ milliliters
4. 7 kilograms = __________ grams
5. 9 liters = __________ milliliters
6. 2 liters = __________ milliliters
7. 6 kilograms = __________ grams

Compare using <, >, or =.

8. 8 kilograms ◯ 850 grams
9. 3 liters ◯ 3,500 milliliters
10. 1 kilogram ◯ 1,000 grams
11. 5 liters ◯ 520 milliliters

Problem Solving

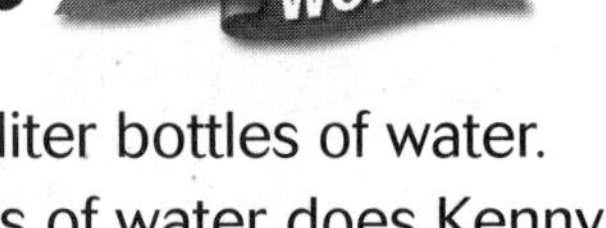

12. Kenny buys four 1-liter bottles of water. How many milliliters of water does Kenny buy?

____

13. Mrs. Jones bought three 2-kilogram packages of flour. How many grams of flour did she buy?

____

14. Colleen bought 8 kilograms of apples and 2.5 kilograms of pears. How many more grams of apples than pears did she buy?

____

15. Dave uses 500 milliliters of juice for a punch recipe. He mixes it with 2 liters of ginger ale. How many milliliters of punch does he make?

____

Name ______________________________

Lesson 82

COMMON CORE STANDARD CC.4.MD.1

Lesson Objective: Use models to compare units of time.

Units of Time

Some analog clocks have an hour hand, a minute hand, and a **second** hand.

There are 60 seconds in a minute. The second hand makes 1 full turn every minute. There are 60 minutes in an hour. The minute hand makes 1 full turn every hour. The hour hand makes 1 full turn every 12 hours.

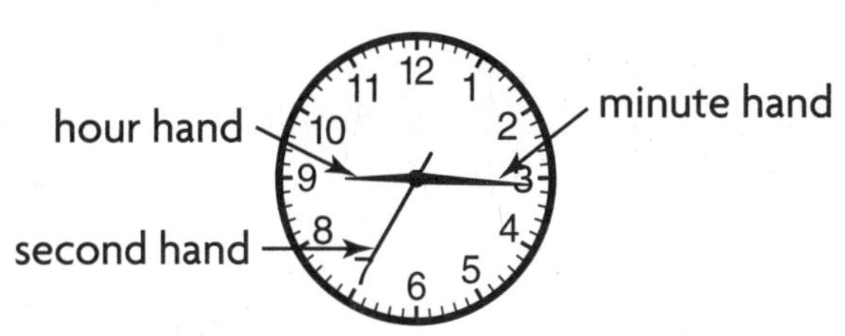

You can think of the clock as unrolling to become a number line.

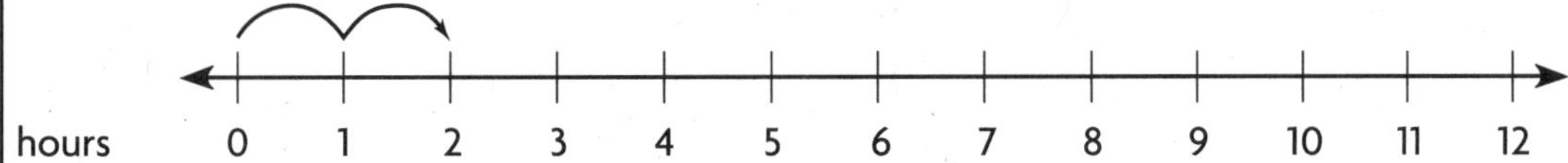

hours 0 1 2 3 4 5 6 7 8 9 10 11 12

The hour hand moves from one number to the next in 1 hour.

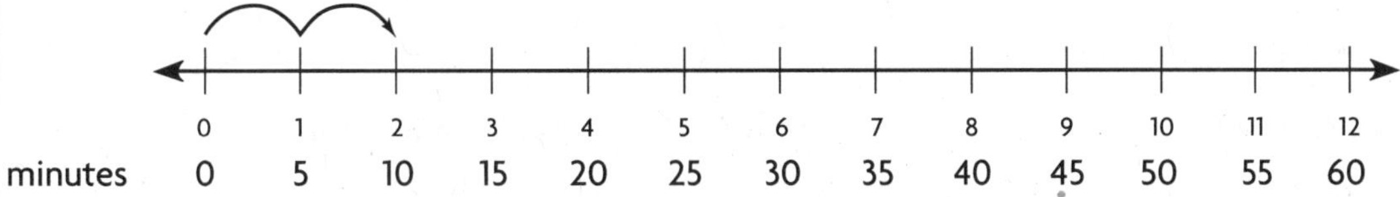

	0	1	2	3	4	5	6	7	8	9	10	11	12
minutes	0	5	10	15	20	25	30	35	40	45	50	55	60

The minute hand moves from one number to the next in 5 minutes.

Use the table at the right to change between units of time.

Units of Time
1 minute = 60 seconds
1 hour = 60 minutes
1 day = 24 hours
1 week = 7 days
1 year = 12 months
1 year = 52 weeks

1 hour = 60 minutes, or 60 × 60 seconds, or <u>3,600</u> seconds.

So, 1 hour is <u>3,600</u> times as long as 1 second.

1 day = 24 hours, so 3 days = 3 × 24 hours, or <u>72</u> hours.

1 year = 12 months, so 5 years = 5 × 12 months, or <u>60</u> months.

Complete.

1. 3 hours = ________ minutes

2. 2 years = ________ weeks

3. 6 days = ________ hours

4. 5 weeks = ________ days

5. 8 minutes = ________ seconds

6. 7 years = ________ months

Name ______________________________

Units of Time

Complete.

1. 6 minutes = 360 seconds

Think: 1 minute = 60 seconds, so 6 minutes = 6 × 60 seconds, or 360 seconds

2. 5 weeks = __________ days

3. 3 years = __________ weeks

4. 9 hours = __________ minutes

5. 9 minutes = __________ seconds

6. 5 years = __________ months

7. 7 days = __________ hours

Compare using <, >, or =.

8. 2 years ◯ 14 months

9. 3 hours ◯ 300 minutes

10. 2 days ◯ 48 hours

11. 6 years ◯ 300 weeks

12. 4 hours ◯ 400 minutes

13. 5 minutes ◯ 300 seconds

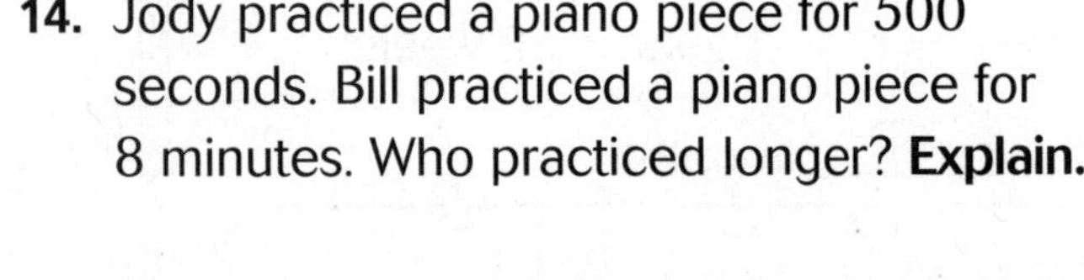

14. Jody practiced a piano piece for 500 seconds. Bill practiced a piano piece for 8 minutes. Who practiced longer? **Explain.**

____

____

____

____

15. Yvette's younger brother just turned 3 years old. Fred's brother is now 30 months old. Whose brother is older? **Explain.**

____

____

____

____

Name ________________________

Lesson 83

COMMON CORE STANDARD CC.4.MD.1

Lesson Objective: Use patterns to write number pairs for measurement units.

Algebra • Patterns in Measurement Units

Use the relationship between the number pairs to label the columns in the table.

?	?
1	8
2	16
3	24
4	32

Step 1 List the number pairs. 1 and 8; 2 and 16; 3 and 24; 4 and 32

Step 2 Describe the relationship between the numbers in each pair.

The second number is 8 times as great as the first number.

Step 3 Look for a relationship involving 1 and 8 in the table below.

Length	Weight	Liquid Volume	Time
1 foot = 12 inches 1 yard = 3 feet 1 yard = 36 inches	1 pound = 16 ounces 1 ton = 2,000 pounds	**1 cup = 8 fluid ounces** 1 pint = 2 cups 1 quart = 2 pints 1 gallon = 4 quarts	1 minute = 60 seconds 1 hour = 60 minutes 1 day = 24 hours 1 week = 7 days 1 year = 12 months 1 year = 52 weeks

So, the label for the first column is Cups.

The label for the second column is Fluid Ounces.

Each table shows a pattern for two customary units. Label the columns of the table.

1.

1	12
2	24
3	36
4	48

2.

1	2,000
2	4,000
3	6,000
4	8,000

Name ______________________

Patterns in Measurement Units

Lesson 83
CC.4.MD.1

Each table shows a pattern for two customary units of time or volume. Label the columns of the table.

1.

Gallons	Quarts
1	4
2	8
3	12
4	16
5	20

2.

1	12
2	24
3	36
4	48
5	60

3.

1	2
2	4
3	6
4	8
5	10

4.

1	7
2	14
3	21
4	28
5	35

Problem Solving REAL WORLD

Use the table for 5 and 6.

?	?
1	10
2	20
3	30
4	40
5	50

5. Marguerite made the table to compare two metric measures of length. Name a pair of units Marguerite could be comparing.

____

6. Name another pair of metric units of length that have the same relationship.

____

Name ______________________________

Lesson 84

COMMON CORE STANDARD CC.4.MD.2

Lesson Objective: Solve problems by using the strategy *act it out.*

Problem Solving • Money

Use the strategy *act it out* to solve the problem.

Jessica, Brian, and Grace earned $7.50. They want to share the money equally. How much will each person get?

Read the Problem	Solve the Problem
What do I need to find? I need to find the amount of money each person should get.	• Show the total amount, $7.50, using 7 one-dollar bills and 2 quarters.
What information do I need to use? I need to use the total amount, $7.50, and divide it by 3, the number of people sharing the money equally.	• Share the one-dollar bills equally. There is 1 one-dollar bill left.
How will I use the information? I will use dollar bills and coins to model the total amount and act out the problem.	• Change the dollar bill that is left for 4 quarters. Now there are 6 quarters. • Share the quarters equally. So, each person gets 2 one-dollar bills and 2 quarters, or $2.50.

1. Jacob, Dan, and Nathan were given $6.90 to share equally. How much money will each boy get?

____

2. Becky, Marlis, and Hallie each earned $2.15 raking leaves. How much did they earn together?

____

Name ______________________

Problem Solving • Money

Lesson 84
CC.4.MD.2

Use the *act it out* strategy to solve.

1. Carl wants to buy a bicycle bell that costs $4.50. Carl has saved $2.75 so far. How much more money does he need to buy the bell?

Use 4 $1 bills and 2 quarters to model $4.50. Remove bills and coins that have a value of $2.75. First, remove 2 $1 bills and 2 quarters.

Next, exchange one $1 bill for 4 quarters and remove 1 quarter.

Count the amount that is left.
So, Carl needs to save $1.75 more.

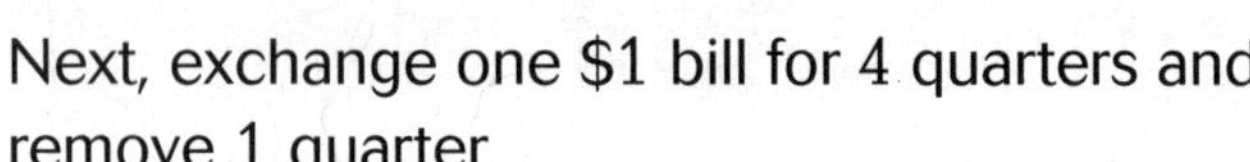

$1.75

2. Together, Xavier, Yolanda, and Zachary have $4.44. If each person has the same amount, how much money does each person have?

____

3. Marcus, Nan, and Olive each have $1.65 in their pockets. They decide to combine the money. How much money do they have altogether?

____

4. Jessie saves $6 each week. In how many weeks will she have saved at least $50?

____

5. Becca has $12 more than Cece. Dave has $3 less than Cece. Cece has $10. How much money do they have altogether?

____

Name ______________________________

Lesson 85

COMMON CORE STANDARD CC.4.MD.2

Lesson Objective: Use the strategy *draw a diagram* to solve elapsed time problems.

Problem Solving • Elapsed Time

Opal finished her art project at 2:25 P.M. She spent 50 minutes working on her project. What time did she start working on her project?

Read the Problem		
What do I need to find?	**What information do I need to use?**	**How will I use the information?**
I need to find Opal's start time.	End time: 2:25 P.M. Elapsed time: 50 minutes	I can draw a diagram of a clock. I can then count back 5 minutes at a time until I reach 50 minutes.

Solve the Problem

I start by showing 2:25 P.M. on the clock.
Then I count back 50 minutes by 5s.

Think: As I count back, I go past the 12.
The hour must be 1 hour less than the ending time.

The hour will be 1 o'clock.

So, Opal started on her project at 1:35 P.M.

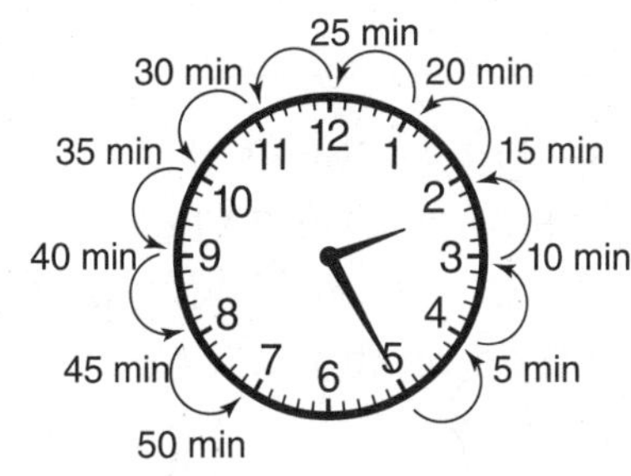

Draw hands on the clock to help you solve the problem.

1. Bill wants to be at school at 8:05 A.M. It takes him 20 minutes to walk to school. At what time should Bill leave his house?

Bill should leave his house at ______________.

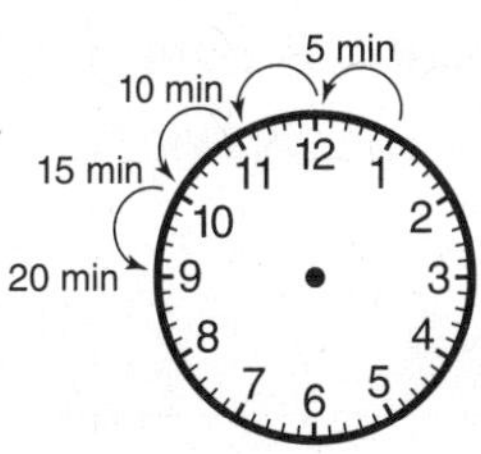

2. Mr. Gleason's math class lasts 40 minutes. Math class starts at 9:55 A.M. At what time does math class end?

Math class ends at ______________.

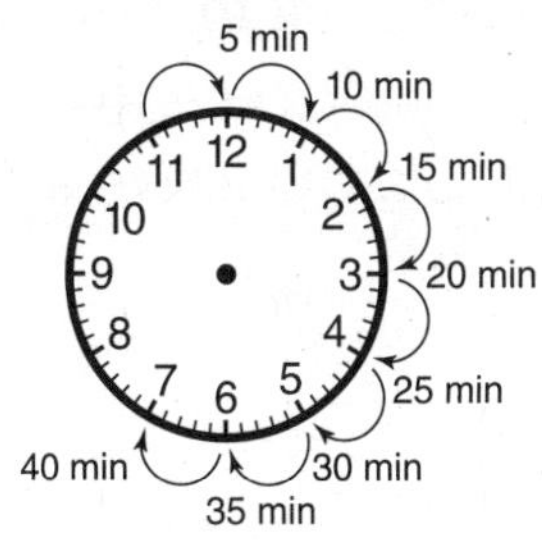

3. Hannah rode her bike for 1 hour and 15 minutes until she got a flat tire at 2:30 P.M. What time did Hannah start riding her bike?

Hannah started riding her bike at ______________.

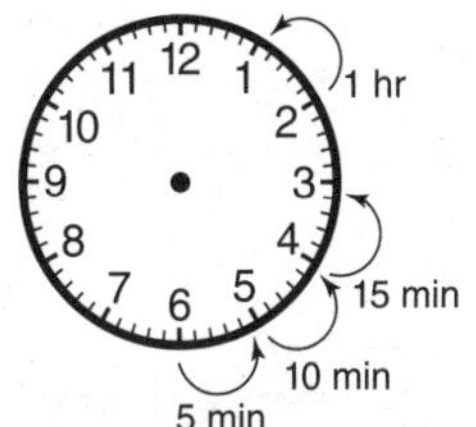

Name ______________________________

Lesson 85

CC.4.MD.2

Problem Solving • Elapsed Time

Read each problem and solve.

1. Molly started her piano lesson at 3:45 P.M. The lesson lasted 20 minutes. What time did the piano lesson end?

   Think: What do I need to find?
   How can I draw a diagram to help?

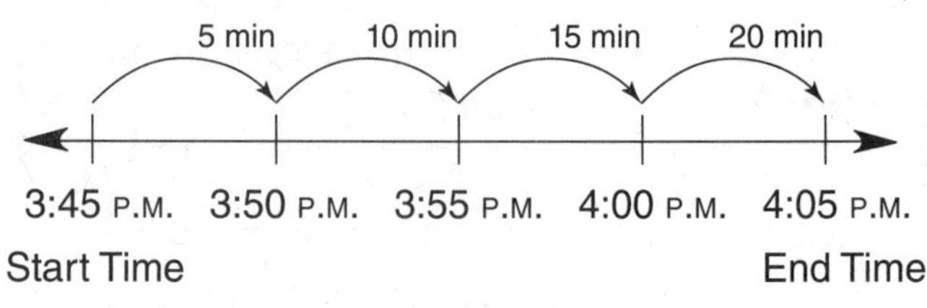

4:05 P.M.

2. Brendan spent 24 minutes playing a computer game. He stopped playing at 3:55 P.M and went outside to ride his bike. What time did he start playing the computer game?

____

3. Aimee's karate class lasts 1 hour and 15 minutes and is over at 5:00 P.M. What time does Aimee's karate class start?

____

4. Mr. Giarmo left for work at 7:15 A.M. Twenty-five minutes later, he arrived at his work. What time did Mr. Giarmo arrive at his work?

____

5. Ms. Brown's flight left at 9:20 A.M. Her plane landed 1 hour and 23 minutes later. What time did her plane land?

____

Name ______________________

Lesson 86

COMMON CORE STANDARD CC.4.MD.2

Lesson Objective: Solve problems involving mixed measures.

Mixed Measures

Gabrielle's puppy weighs 2 pounds 7 ounces. What is the weight of the puppy in ounces?

Step 1 Think of 2 pounds 7 ounces as 2 pounds + 7 ounces.

Step 2 Change the pounds to ounces.

Think: 1 pound = 16 ounces

So, 2 pounds = 2 × 16 ounces, or 32 ounces.

Step 3 Add like units to find the answer.

  32 ounces
+ 7 ounces
  39 ounces

So, Gabrielle's puppy weighs 39 ounces.

Gabrielle played with her puppy for 2 hours 10 minutes yesterday and 1 hour 25 minutes today. How much longer did she play with the puppy yesterday than today?

Step 1 Subtract the mixed measures. Write the subtraction with like units lined up.

Think: 25 minutes is greater than 10 minutes.

  2 hr 10 min
− 1 hr 25 min

Step 2 Rename 2 hours 10 minutes to subtract.

1 hour = 60 minutes

So, 2 hr 10 min = 1 hr + 60 min + 10 min, or 1 hr 70 min.

  1 70
  ~~2~~ hr ~~10~~ min
− 1 hr 25 min
  0 hr 45 min

Step 3 Subtract like units.

1 hr − 1 hr = 0 hr; 70 min − 25 min = 45 min

So, she played with the puppy 45 minutes longer yesterday than today.

Complete.

1. 4 yd 2 ft = ______ ft

2. 1 hr 20 min = ______ min

3. 4 qt 1 pt = ______ pt

Add or subtract.

4. 2 gal 1 qt + 3 gal 2 qt

5. 3 lb 12 oz − 1 lb 8 oz

6. 4 yr 9 mo − 1 yr 10 mo

Name ______________________________

Mixed Measures

Complete.

1. 8 pounds 4 ounces = <u>132</u> ounces

Think: 8 pounds = 8 × 16 ounces, or 128 ounces.
128 ounces + 4 ounces = 132 ounces

2. 5 weeks 3 days = ________ days

3. 4 minutes 45 seconds = ________ seconds

4. 4 hours 30 minutes = ________ minutes

5. 3 tons 600 pounds = ________ pounds

6. 6 pints 1 cup = ________ cups

7. 7 pounds 12 ounces = ________ ounces

Add or subtract.

8. 9 gal 1 qt
+ 6 gal 1 qt

9. 12 lb 5 oz
− 7 lb 10 oz

10. 8 hr 3 min
+ 4 hr 12 min

Problem Solving REAL WORLD

11. Michael's basketball team practiced for 2 hours 40 minutes yesterday and 3 hours 15 minutes today. How much longer did the team practice today than yesterday?

____

12. Rhonda had a piece of ribbon that was 5 feet 3 inches long. She removed a 5-inch piece to use in her art project. What is the length of the piece of ribbon now?

____

Name ____________________

Perimeter

Lesson 87

COMMON CORE STANDARD CC.4.MD.3

Lesson Objective: Use a formula to find the perimeter of a rectangle.

Perimeter is the distance around a shape. You can use grid paper to count the number of units around the outside of a rectangle to find its perimeter.

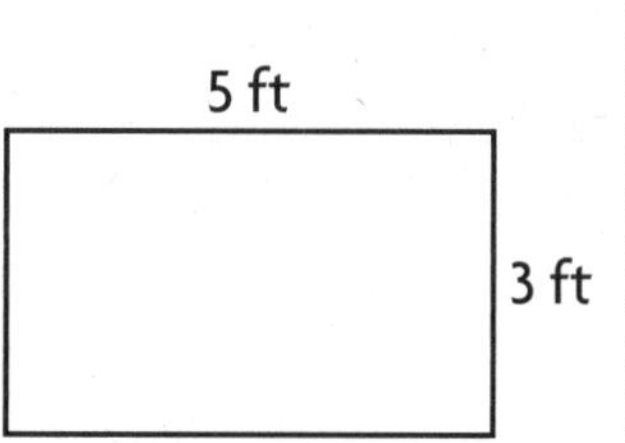

How many feet of ribbon are needed to go around the bulletin board?

Step 1 On grid paper, draw a rectangle that has a length of **5** units and a width of **3** units.

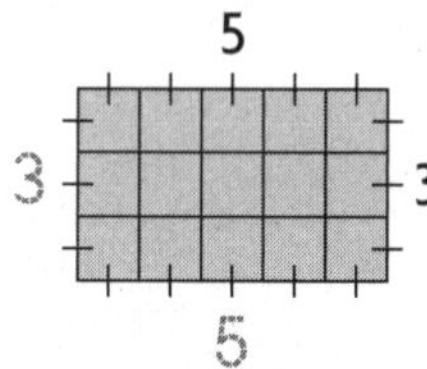

Step 2 Find the length of each side of the rectangle. Mark each unit of length as you count.

Step 3 Add the side lengths. **5 + 3 + 5 + 3 = 16**

The perimeter is __16__ feet.

So, __16 feet__ of ribbon are needed to go around the bulletin board.

1. What is the perimeter of this square?

___ + ___ + ___ + ___ = ___ centimeters

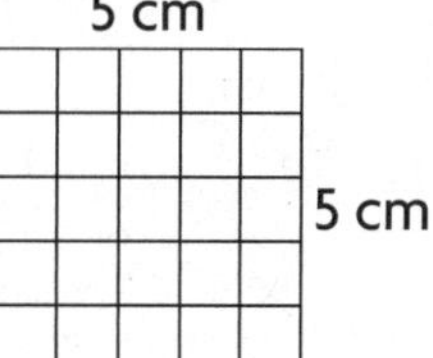

Find the perimeter of the rectangle or square.

2. 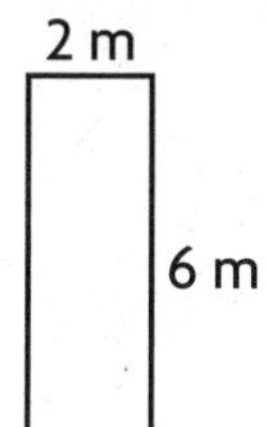

______ meters

3. 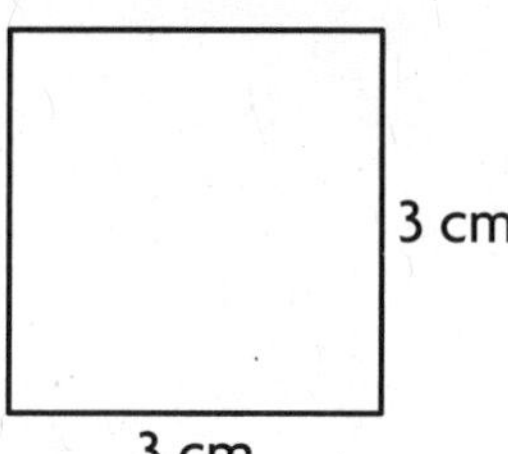

______ centimeters

4. 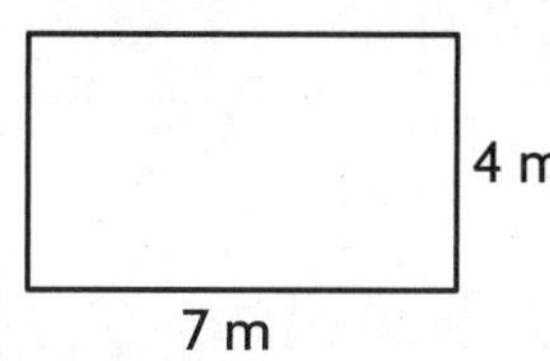

______ meters

Name ______________________

Lesson 87
CC.4.MD.3

Perimeter

Find the perimeter of the rectangle or square.

1. 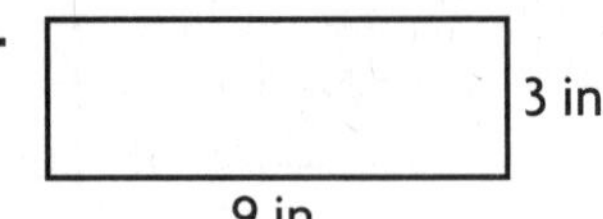

$9 + 3 + 9 + 3 = 24$

24 inches

2. 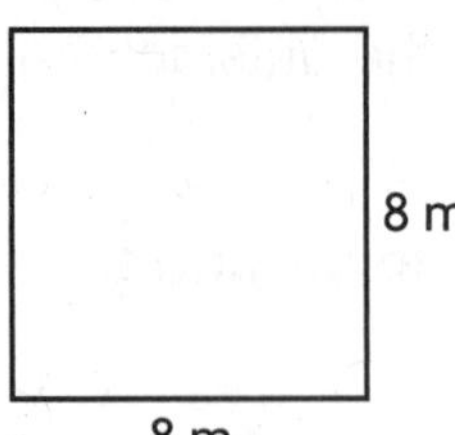

_____ meters

3. 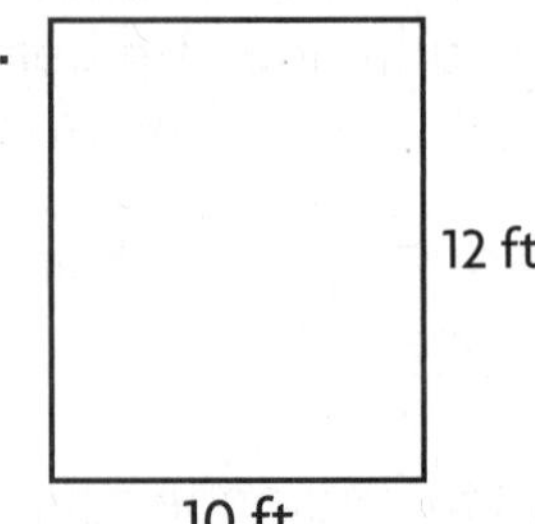

_____ feet

4. 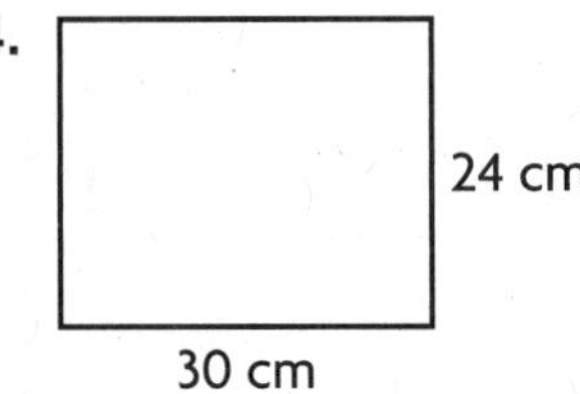

_____ centimeters

5. 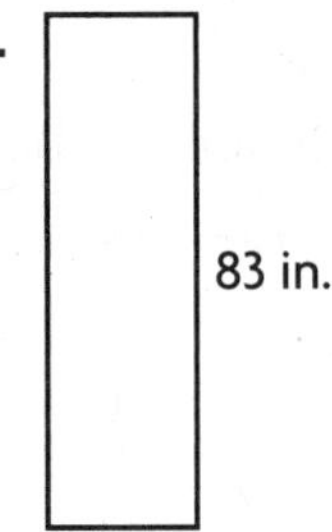

_____ inches

6. 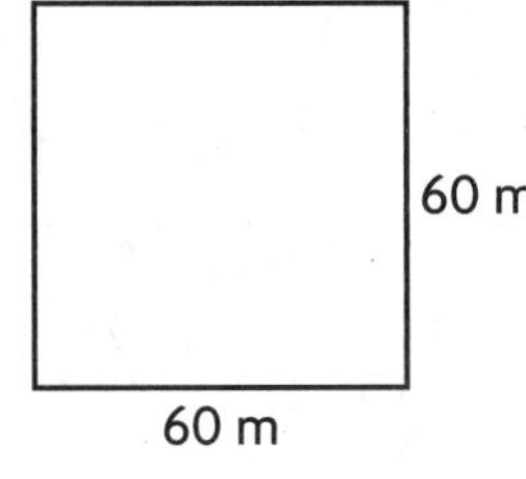

_____ meters

Problem Solving REAL WORLD

7. Troy is making a flag shaped like a square. Each side measures 12 inches. He wants to add ribbon along the edges. He has 36 inches of ribbon. Does he have enough ribbon? **Explain.**

____

8. The width of the Ochoa Community Pool is 20 feet. The length is twice as long as its width. What is the perimeter of the pool?

____

Name ______________________________

COMMON CORE STANDARD CC.4.MD.3

Lesson Objective: Use a formula to find the area of a rectangle.

Area

Area is the number of **square units** needed to cover a flat surface.

Find the area of the rectangle at the right.

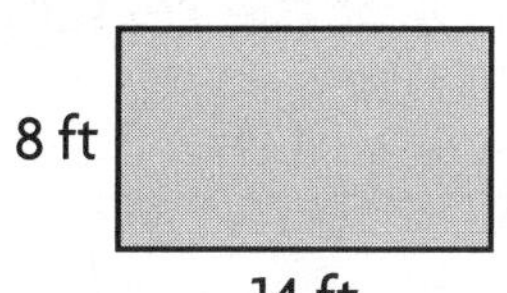

You can use the formula **Area = base × height**.

Step 1 Identify one side as the base.

The base is __14__ feet.

Step 2 Identify a perpendicular side as the height.

The height is __8__ feet.

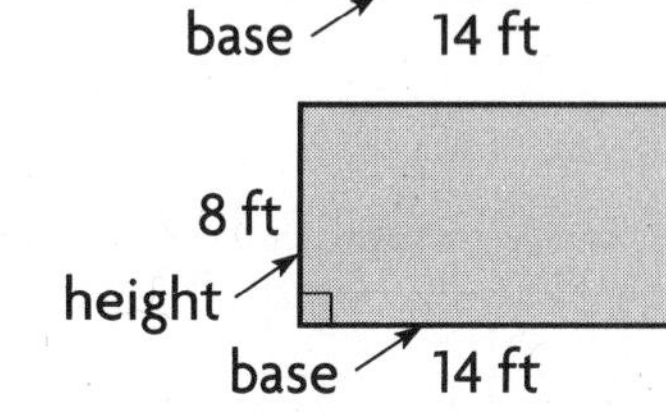

Step 3 Use the formula to find the area.

Area = base × height
= 14 × 8
= 112

So, the area of the rectangle is 112 square feet.

Find the area of the rectangle or square.

1.

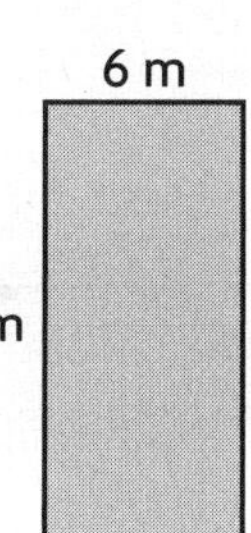

____

2.

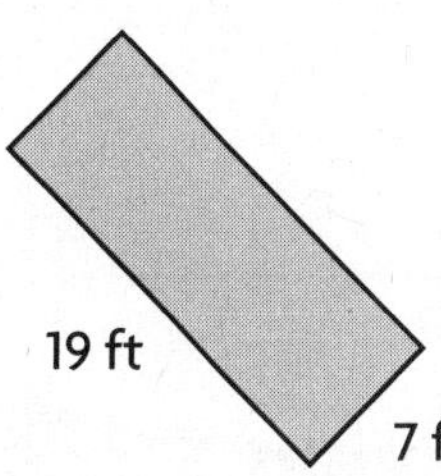

____

3.

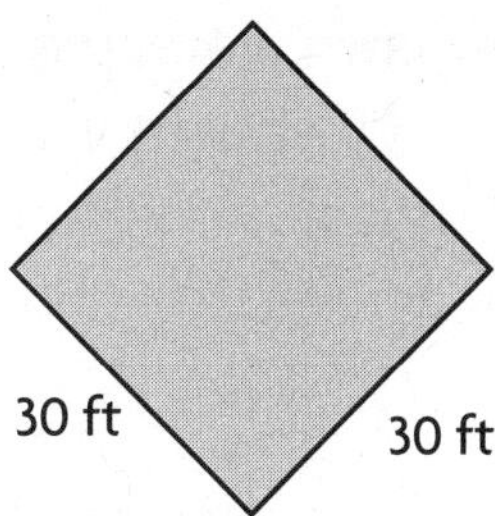

____

4.

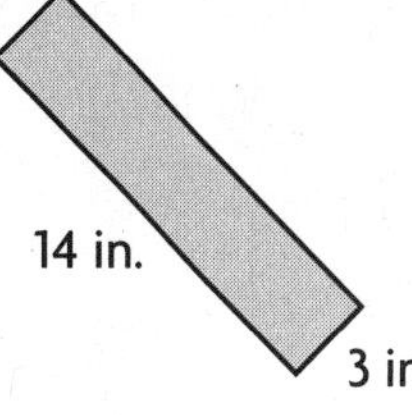

____

Name ______________________

Area

Lesson 88
CC.4.MD.3

Find the area of the rectangle or square.

1. 12 ft

9 ft

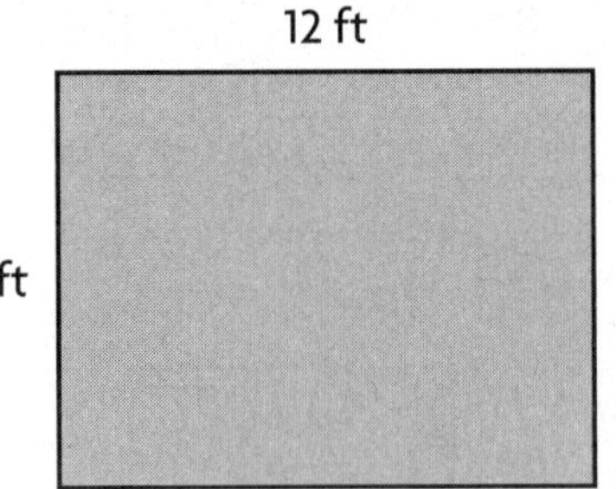

$A = b \times h$

$= 12 \times 9$

108 square feet

2. 8 yd

8 yd

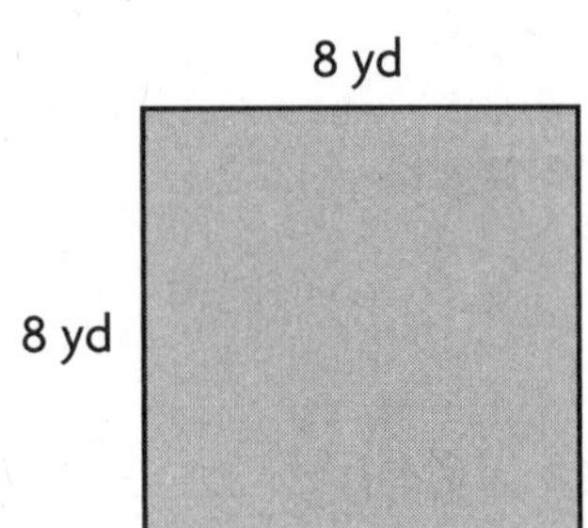

____

3. 15 m

3 m

____

4. 13 in.

6 in.

____

5. 30 cm

5 cm

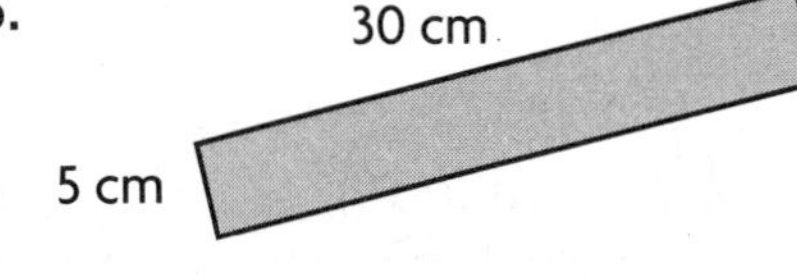

____

6. 14 ft

4 ft

____

Problem Solving REAL WORLD

7. Meghan is putting wallpaper on a wall that measures 8 feet by 12 feet. How much wallpaper does Meghan need to cover the wall?

____

8. Bryson is laying down sod in his yard to grow a new lawn. Each piece of sod is a 1-foot by 1-foot square. How many pieces of sod will Bryson need to cover his yard if his yard measures 30 feet by 14 feet?

____

Name ______________________________

Lesson 89

COMMON CORE STANDARD CC.4.MD.3

Lesson Objective: Find the area of combined rectangles.

Area of Combined Rectangles

Find the area of the combined rectangles.

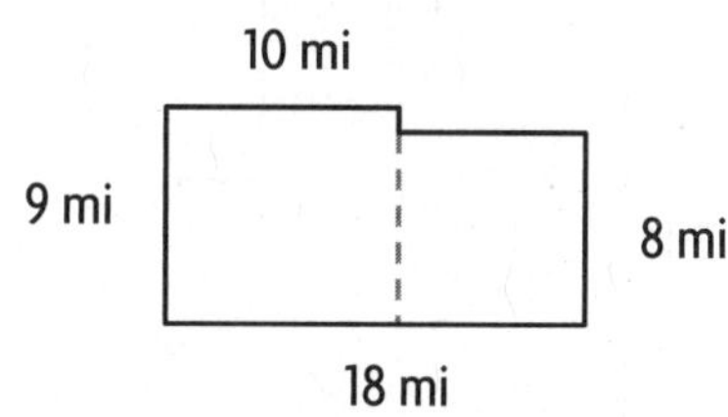

Step 1 First, find the area of each section of the shape.

LEFT	RIGHT	
$A = b \times h$	$A = b \times h$	
$= 10 \times 9$	$= 8 \times 8$	**Think:** $18 - 10 = 8$
$= 90$	$= 64$	

Step 2 Add the two areas. $90 + 64 = 154$

So, the total area is <u>154</u> square miles.

Find the area of the combined rectangles.

1.

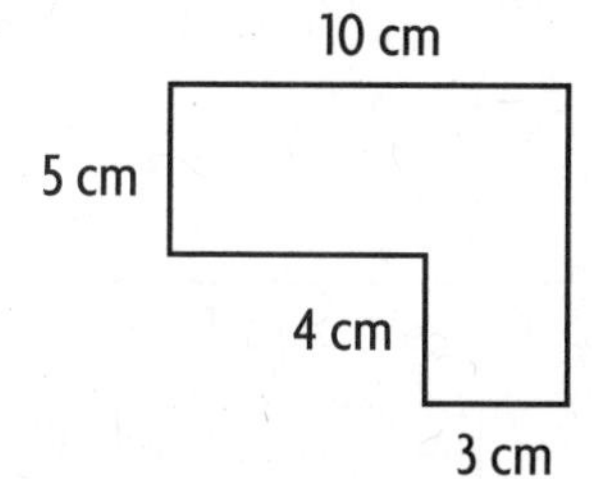

____

2.

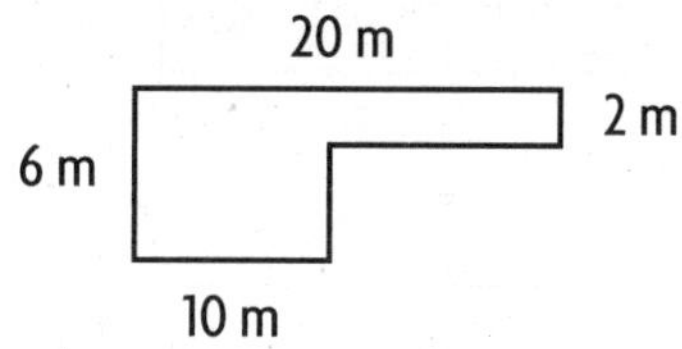

____

3.

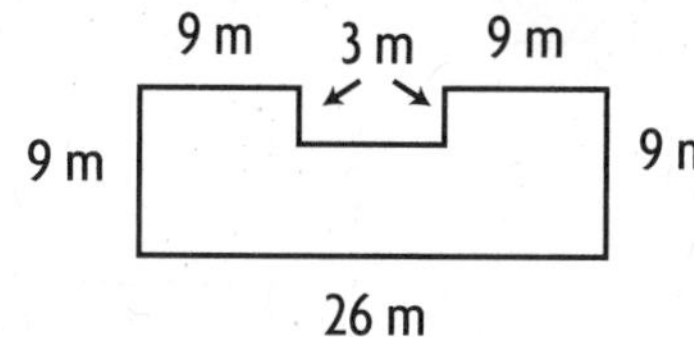

____

4.

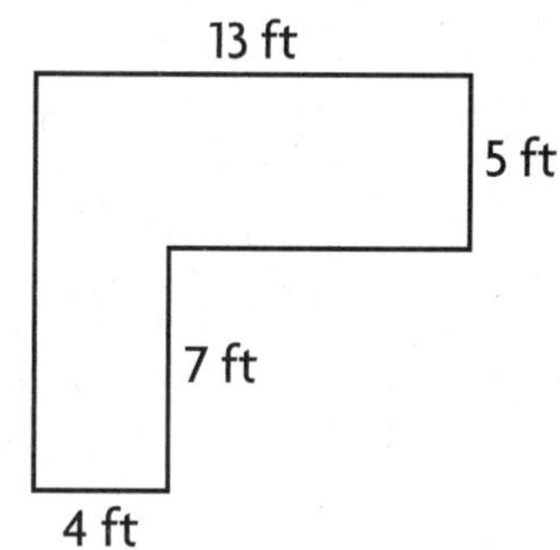

____

5.

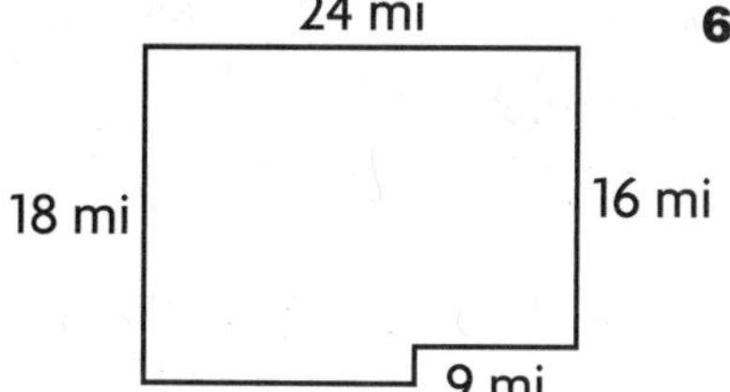

____

6.

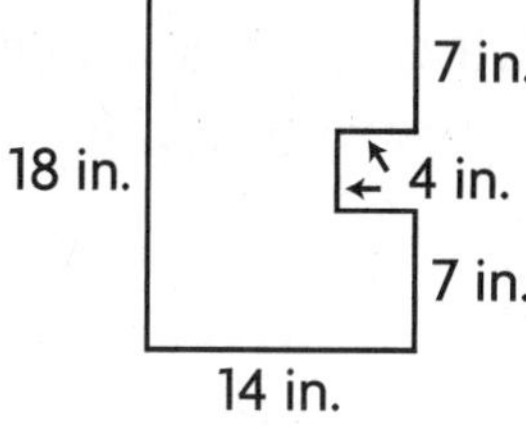

____

Name ______________________

Area of Combined Rectangles

Find the area of the combined rectangles.

1. 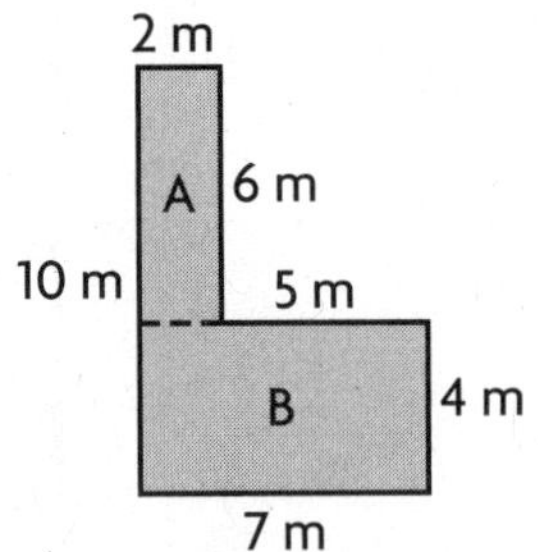

Area A = 2 × 6,
Area B = 7 × 4
12 + 28 = 40
40 square meters

2. 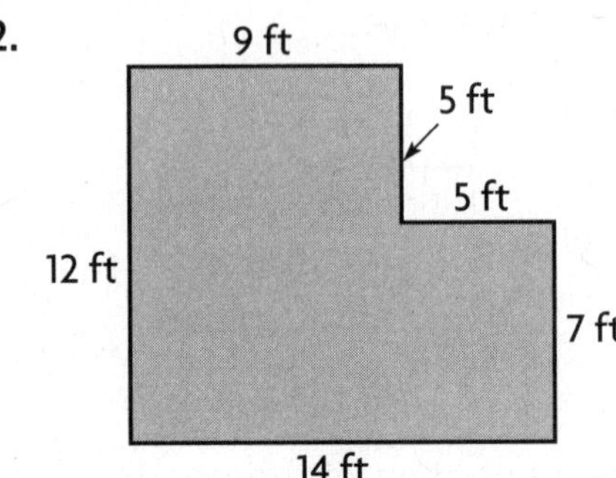

____

3. 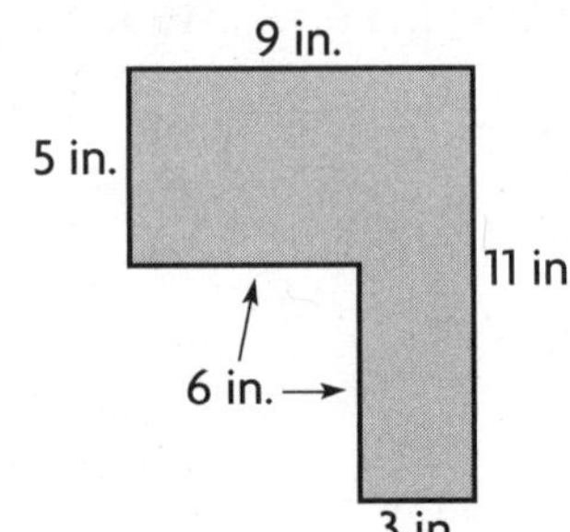

____

4. 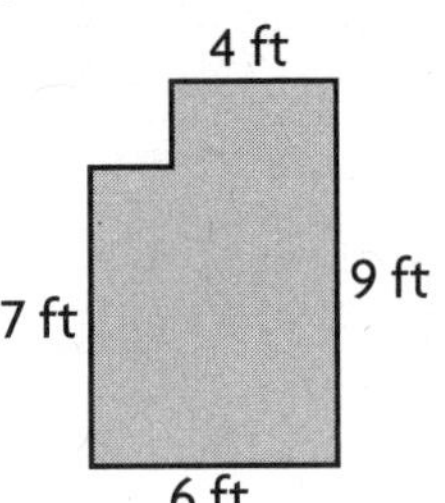

____

5. 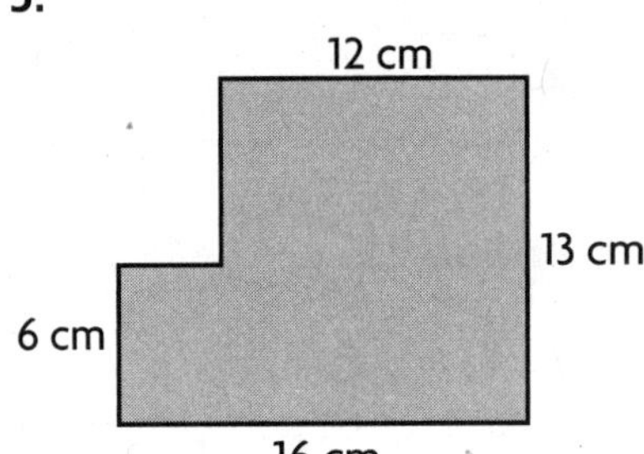

____

6. 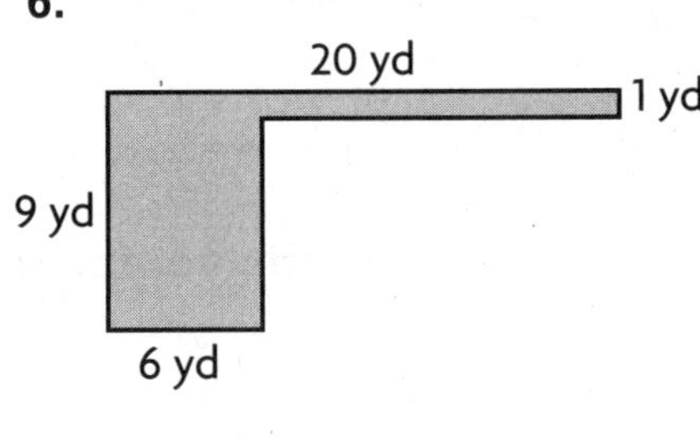

____

Problem Solving REAL WORLD

Use the diagram for 7–8.

Nadia makes the diagram below to represent the counter space she wants to build in her craft room.

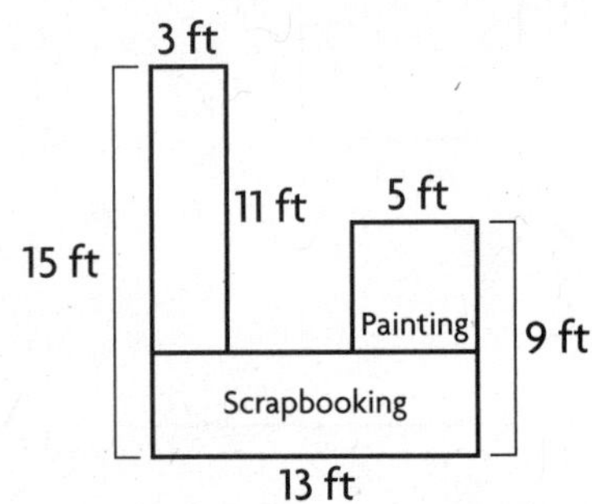

7. What is the area of the space that Nadia has shown for scrapbooking?

____

8. What is the area of the space she has shown for painting?

____

Name ________________________

Lesson 90
COMMON CORE STANDARD CC.4.MD.3
Lesson Objective: Given perimeter or area, find the unknown measure of a side of a rectangle.

Find Unknown Measures

Fred has 30 yards of fencing to enclose a rectangular vegetable garden. He wants it to be 6 yards wide. How long will his vegetable garden be?

?
6 yd

Step 1 Decide whether this problem involves area or perimeter.

Think: The fencing goes *around the outside* of the garden. This is a measure of perimeter.

Step 2 Use a formula for perimeter. The width is 6. The perimeter is 30. The length is unknown.

$$P = (2 \times l) + (2 \times w)$$
$$30 = (2 \times l) + (2 \times 6)$$
$$30 = 2 \times l + 12$$

Step 3 Find the value of l.

$18 = 2 \times l$, so the value of l is 9.

The length of Fred's garden will be 9 yards.

Carol has 120 square inches of wood. The piece of wood is rectangular and has a height of 10 inches. How long is the base?

Step 1 Decide whether this problem involves area or perimeter.

Think: *Square inches* is a measure of area.

Step 2 Use a formula for area. The height is 10. The area is 120. The length is unknown.

$$A = b \times h$$
$$120 = b \times 10$$

Step 3 Find the value of b.

Since $120 = 12 \times 10$, the value of b is 12.

The base of Carol's piece of wood is 12 inches.

Find the unknown measure.

1.

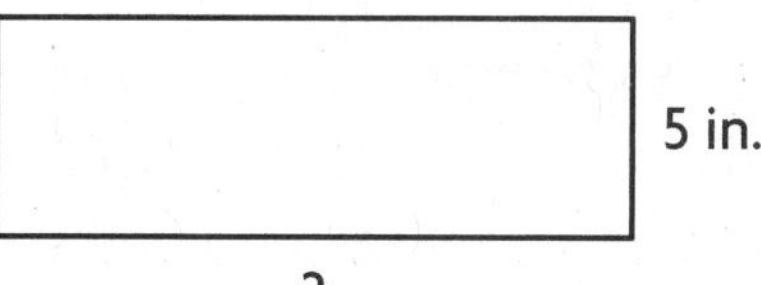

Perimeter = 40 inches

width = ________________________

2.

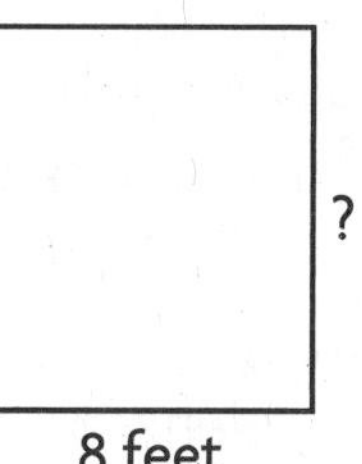

Area = 72 square feet

height = ________________________

Name ___________________________

Lesson 90

CC.4.MD.3

Find Unknown Measures

Find the unknown measure of the rectangle.

1.

?

20 ft

Perimeter = 54 feet

width = 7 feet

Think: $P = (2 \times l) + (2 \times w)$

$54 = (2 \times 20) + (2 \times w)$

$54 = 40 + (2 \times w)$

Since $54 = 40 + 14$, $2 \times w = 14$, and $w = 7$.

2.

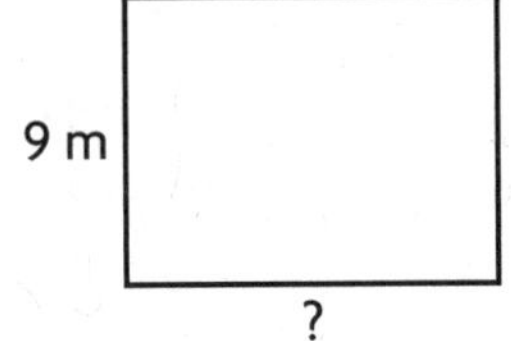

Perimeter = 42 meters

length = ___________

3.

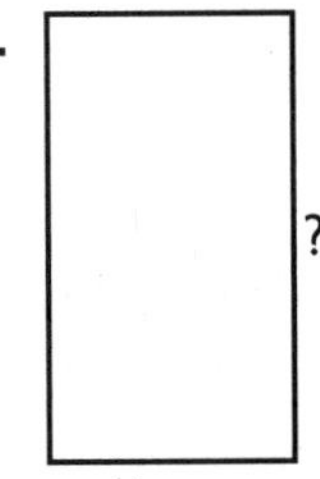

Area = 28 square centimeters

height = ___________

4.

25 in.

Area = 200 square inches

base = ___________

Problem Solving REAL WORLD

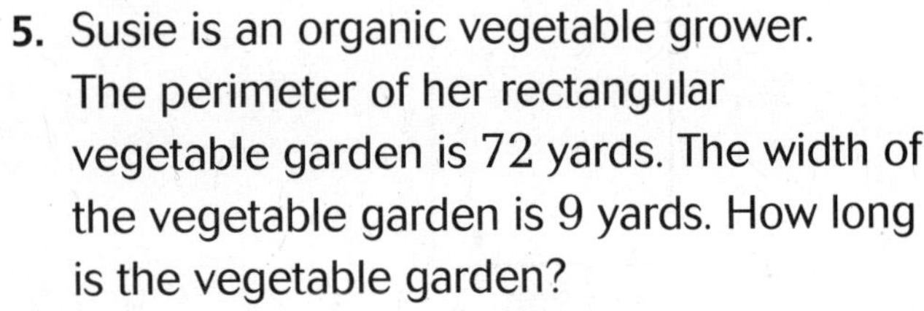

5. Susie is an organic vegetable grower. The perimeter of her rectangular vegetable garden is 72 yards. The width of the vegetable garden is 9 yards. How long is the vegetable garden?

____

6. An artist is creating a rectangular mural for the Northfield Community Center. The mural is 7 feet tall and has an area of 84 square feet. What is the length of the mural?

____

Name ______________________________

Lesson 11

COMMON CORE STANDARD CC.4.MD.3

Lesson Objective: Use the strategy *solve a simpler problem* to solve area problems.

Problem Solving • Find the Area

Use the strategy *solve a simpler problem*.

Marilyn is going to paint a wall in her bedroom. The wall is 15 feet long and 8 feet tall. The window takes up an area 6 feet long and 4 feet high. How many square feet of the wall will Marilyn have to paint?

Read the Problem	Solve the Problem
What do I need to find? I need to find how many square feet of the wall Marilyn will paint.	First, find the area of the wall. $A = b \times h$ $= 15 \times 8$ $= 120$ square feet
What information do I need to use? The paint will cover the wall. The paint will not cover the window. The base of the wall is 15 feet and the height is 8 feet. The base of the window is 6 feet and the height is 4 feet.	Next, find the area of the window. $A = b \times h$ $= 6 \times 4$ $= 24$ square feet Last, subtract the area of the window from the area of the wall.
How will I use the information? I can solve simpler problems. Find the area of the wall. Then, find the area of the window. Last, subtract the area of the window from the area of the wall.	120 − 24 96 square feet So, Marilyn will paint 96 square feet of her bedroom wall.

1. Ned wants to wallpaper the wall of his bedroom that has the door. The wall is 14 feet wide and 9 feet high. The door is 3 feet wide and 7 feet high. How many square feet of wallpaper will Ned need for the wall?

____

2. Nicole has a rectangular canvas that is 12 inches long and 10 inches wide. She paints a blue square in the center of the canvas. The square is 3 inches on each side. How much of the canvas is NOT painted blue?

____

Name ______________________________

Lesson 91
CC.4.MD.3

Problem Solving • Find the Area

Solve each problem.

1. A room has a wooden floor. There is a rug in the center of the floor. The diagram shows the room and the rug. How many square feet of the wood floor still shows?

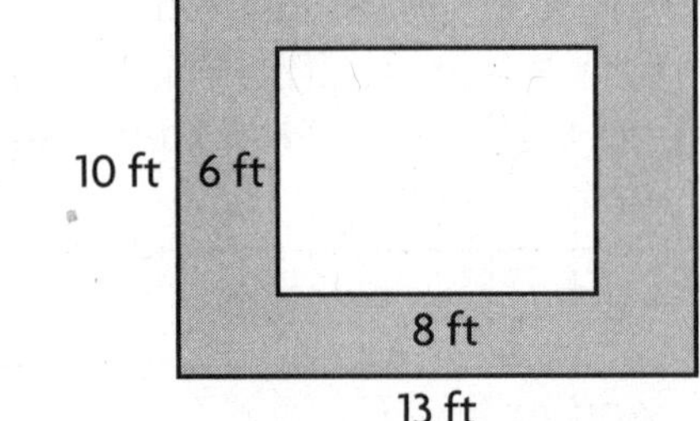

82 square feet

Area of the floor: $13 \times 10 = 130$ square feet
Area of the rug: $8 \times 6 = 48$ square feet
Subtract to find the area of the floor still showing: $130 - 48 = 82$ square feet

2. A rectangular wall has a square window, as shown in the diagram.

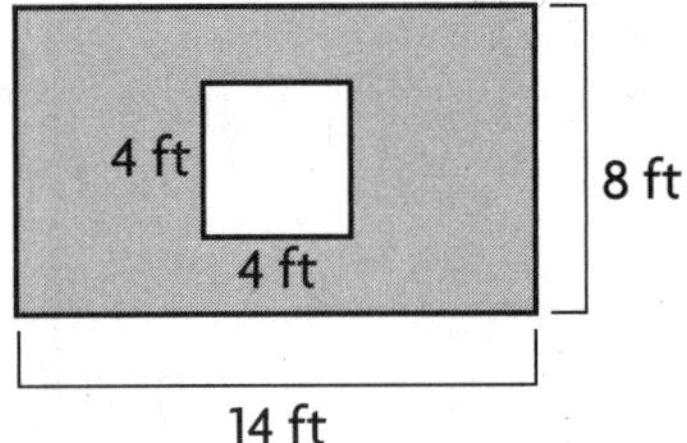

What is the area of the wall NOT including the window?

____

3. Bob wants to put down new sod in his backyard, except for the part set aside for his flower garden. The diagram shows Bob's backyard and the flower garden.

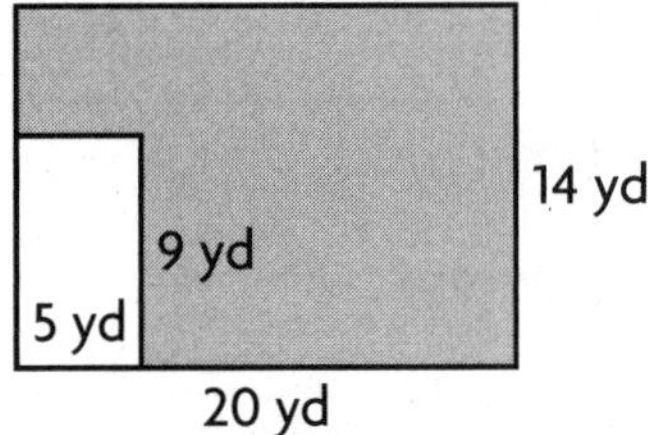

How much sod will Bob need?

____

4. A rectangular painting, including the frame, is 28 inches wide and 24 inches tall. The opening inside the frame is 24 inches wide and 20 inches tall. What is the area covered by the frame?

____

5. One wall in Jeanne's bedroom is 13 feet long and 8 feet tall. There is a door 3 feet wide and 6 feet tall. She has a poster on the wall that is 2 feet wide and 3 feet tall. How much of the wall is visible?

____

Name ______________________

Line Plots

Lesson 12

COMMON CORE STANDARD CC.4.MD.4

Lesson Objective: Make and interpret line plots with fractional data.

Howard gave a piece of paper with several survey questions to his friends. Then he made a list to show how long it took for his friends to answer the survey. Howard wants to know how many surveys took longer than $\frac{2}{12}$ hour.

Time for Survey Answers (in hours)						
$\frac{1}{12}$	$\frac{3}{12}$	$\frac{1}{12}$	$\frac{2}{12}$	$\frac{6}{12}$	$\frac{3}{12}$	$\frac{5}{12}$

Make a line plot to show the data.

Step 1 Order the data from least to greatest.

$\frac{1}{12}, \frac{1}{12}, \frac{2}{12}, \frac{3}{12}, \frac{3}{12}, \frac{5}{12}, \frac{6}{12}$

Step 2 Make a tally table of the data.

Survey	
Time (in hours)	**Tally**
$\frac{1}{12}$	||
$\frac{2}{12}$	|
$\frac{3}{12}$	||
$\frac{5}{12}$	|
$\frac{6}{12}$	|

Step 3 Label the fractions of an hour on the number line from least to greatest. Notice that $\frac{4}{12}$ is included even though it is not in the data.

Step 4 Plot an *X* above the number line for each piece of data. Write a title for the line plot.

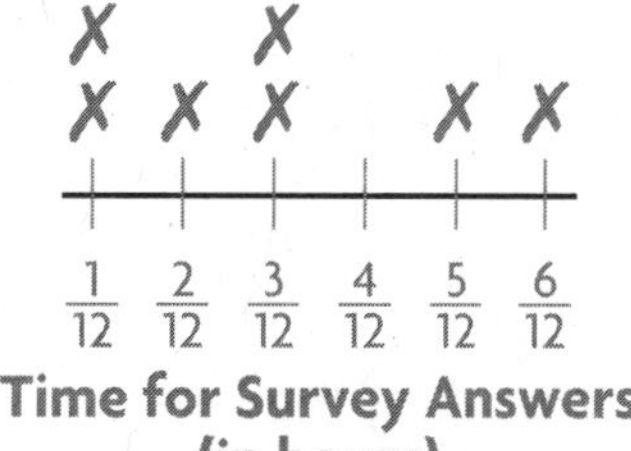

Time for Survey Answers (in hours)

Step 5 Count the number of *X*s that represent data points greater than $\frac{2}{12}$ hour.

There are __4__ data points greater than $\frac{2}{12}$ hour.

So, __4__ surveys took more than $\frac{2}{12}$ hour.

Use the line plot above for 1 and 2.

1. How many of the surveys that Howard gave to his friends were answered? ______________

2. What is the difference in hours between the longest time and the shortest time that it took Howard's friends to answer the survey?

____

Name ______________________________

Line Plots

Lesson 92
CC.4.MD.4

1. Some students compared the time they spend riding the school bus. Complete the tally table and line plot to show the data.

Time Spent on School Bus (in hours)
$\frac{1}{6}$, $\frac{3}{6}$, $\frac{4}{6}$, $\frac{2}{6}$, $\frac{3}{6}$, $\frac{1}{6}$, $\frac{3}{6}$, $\frac{3}{6}$

Time Spent on School Bus	
Time (in hours)	**Tally**
$\frac{1}{6}$	||
$\frac{2}{6}$	
$\frac{3}{6}$	
$\frac{4}{6}$	

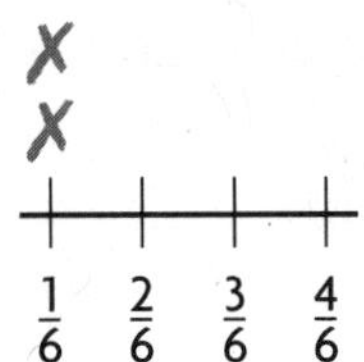

Time Spent on School Bus (in hours)

Use your line plot for 2 and 3.

2. How many students compared times? ____________

3. What is the difference between the longest time and shortest time students spent riding the bus? ____________

Problem Solving REAL WORLD

For 4–5, make a tally table on a separate sheet of paper. Make a line plot in the space below the problem.

4.

Milk Drunk at Lunch (in quarts)
$\frac{1}{8}$, $\frac{2}{8}$, $\frac{2}{8}$, $\frac{4}{8}$, $\frac{1}{8}$, $\frac{3}{8}$, $\frac{4}{8}$, $\frac{2}{8}$, $\frac{3}{8}$, $\frac{2}{8}$

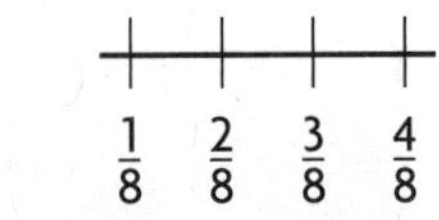

Milk Drunk at Lunch (in quarts)

5.

Distance Between Stops for a Rural Mail Carrier (in miles)
$\frac{3}{10}$, $\frac{4}{10}$, $\frac{5}{10}$, $\frac{1}{10}$, $\frac{5}{10}$, $\frac{4}{10}$, $\frac{4}{10}$, $\frac{3}{10}$

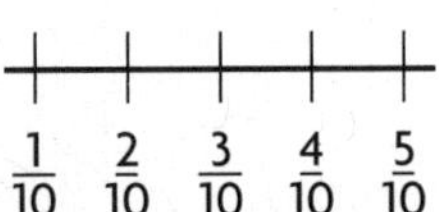

Distance Between Stops for a Rural Mail Carrier (in miles)

Name ____________________

Angles and Fractional Parts of a Circle

Lesson 93

COMMON CORE STANDARD CC.4.MD.5a

Lesson Objective: Relate angles and fractional parts of a circle.

Find how many $\frac{1}{6}$ turns make a complete circle.

Materials: fraction circles

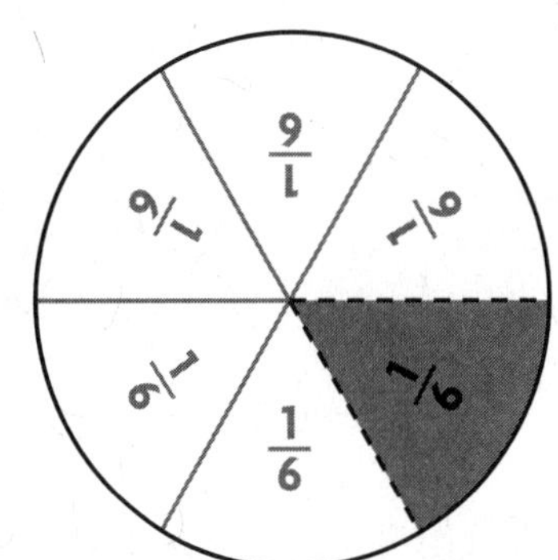

Step 1 Place a $\frac{1}{6}$ piece so the tip of the fraction piece is on the center of the circle. Trace the fraction piece by drawing along the dashed lines in the circle.

Step 2 Shade and label the angle formed by the $\frac{1}{6}$ piece.

Step 3 Place the $\frac{1}{6}$ piece on the shaded angle. Turn it clockwise (in the direction that the hands on a clock move). Turn the fraction piece to line up directly beside the shaded section.

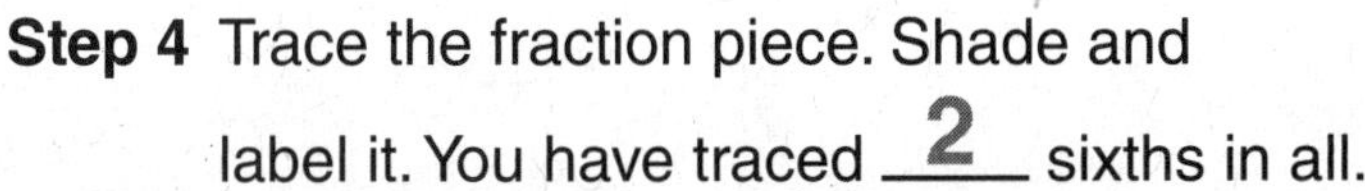

Step 4 Trace the fraction piece. Shade and label it. You have traced __2__ sixths in all.

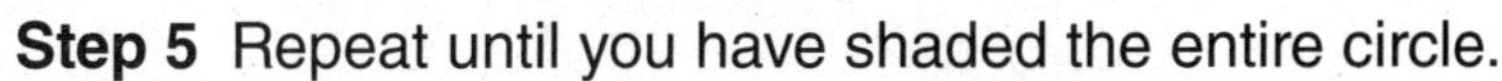

Step 5 Repeat until you have shaded the entire circle.

There are __six__ angles that come together in the center of the circle.

So, you need __six__ $\frac{1}{6}$ turns to make a circle.

Tell what fraction of the circle the shaded angle represents.

1.

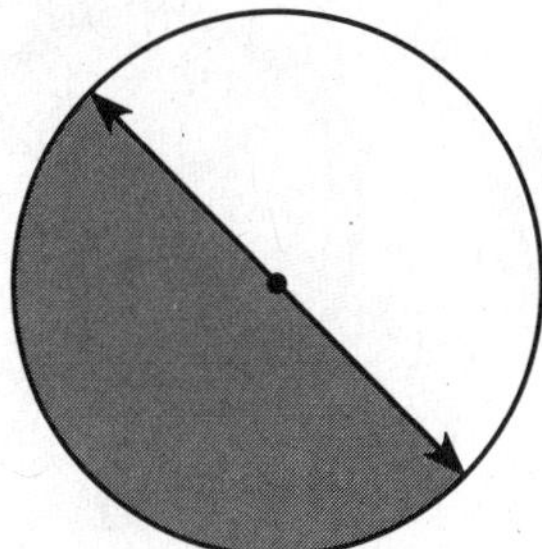

____

2.

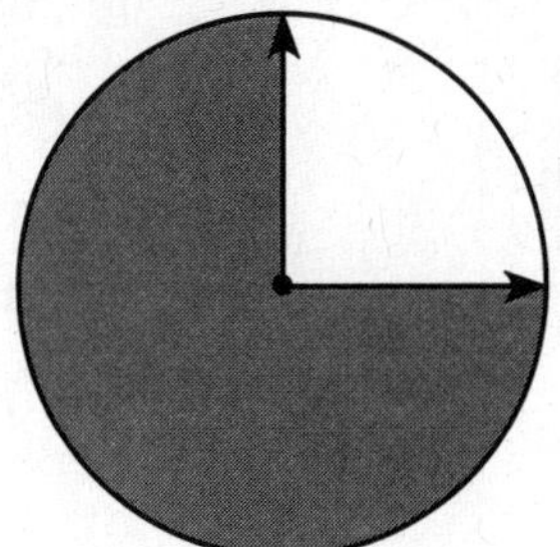

____

3.

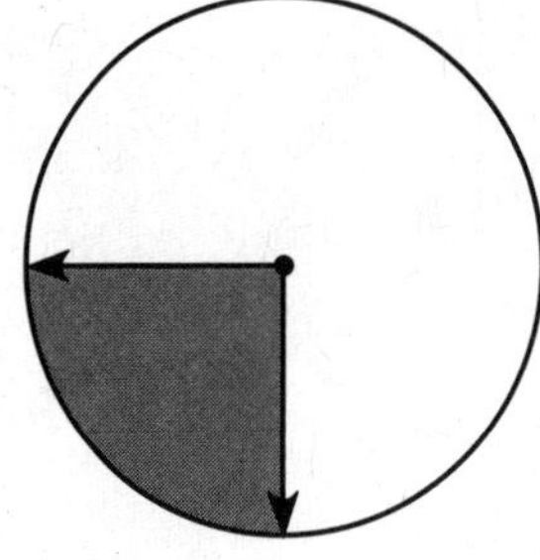

____

Name ____________________

Lesson 93
CC.4.MD.5a

Angles and Fractional Parts of a Circle

Tell what fraction of the circle the shaded angle represents.

1. 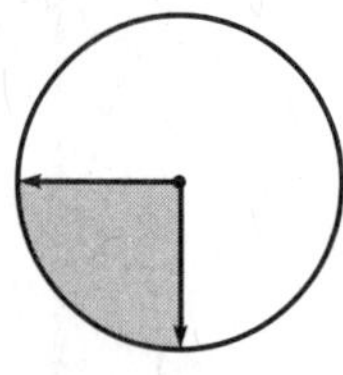

$\frac{1}{4}$

2. 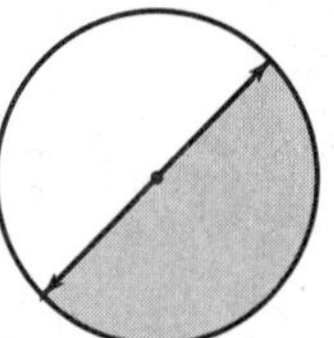

3. 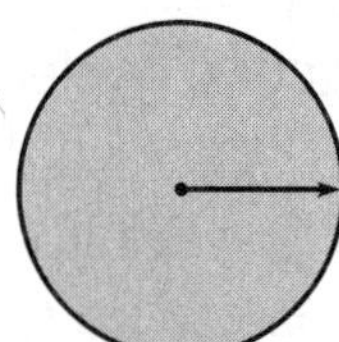

Tell whether the angle on the circle shows a $\frac{1}{4}$, $\frac{1}{2}$, $\frac{3}{4}$, or 1 full turn clockwise or counterclockwise.

4. 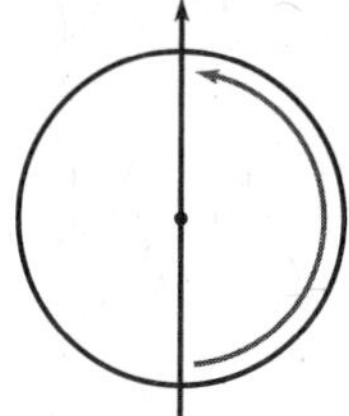

5. 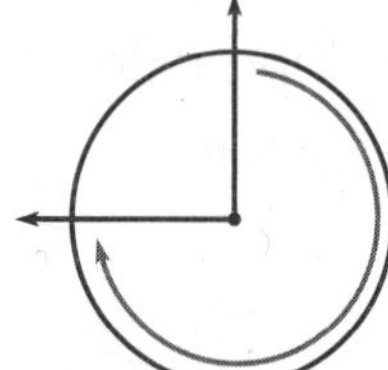

6. 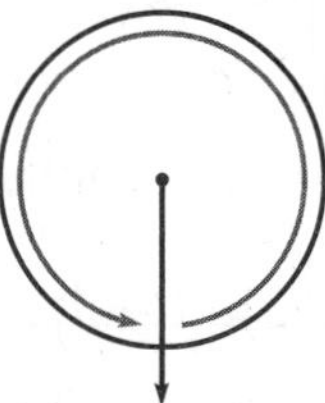

Problem Solving REAL WORLD

7. Shelley exercised for 15 minutes. Describe the turn the minute hand made.

Start

End

8. Mark took 30 minutes to finish lunch. Describe the turn the minute hand made.

Start

End

Name ______________________

Lesson 94

COMMON CORE STANDARD CC.4.MD.5b

Lesson Objective: Relate degrees to fractional parts of a circle by understanding that an angle that measures 1° turns through $\frac{n}{360}$ of a circle.

Degrees

Angles are measured in units called **degrees.** The symbol for degrees is °. If a circle is divided into 360 equal parts, then an angle that turns through 1 part of the 360 measures 1°.

An angle that turns through $\frac{50}{360}$ of a circle measures 50°.

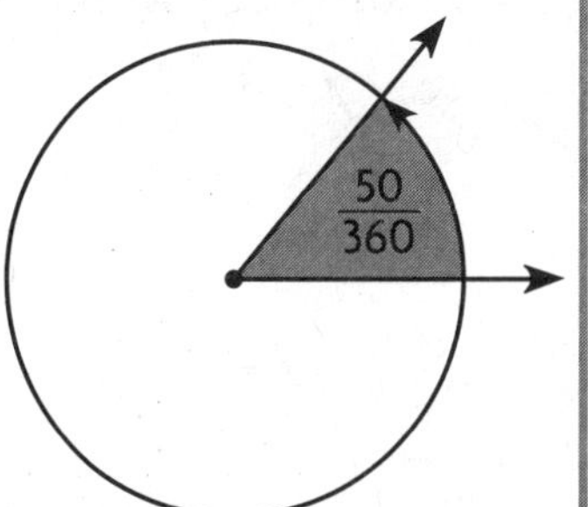

Find the measure of an angle that turns through $\frac{1}{6}$ of a circle.

Step 1 Find a fraction that is equivalent to $\frac{1}{6}$ with 360 in the denominator. **Think:** $6 \times 60 = 360$.

$$\frac{1}{6} = \frac{1 \times 60}{6 \times 60} = \frac{60}{360}$$

Step 2 Look at the numerator of $\frac{60}{360}$.

The numerator tells how many degrees are in $\frac{1}{6}$ of a circle.

So, an angle that turns through $\frac{1}{6}$ of a circle measures __60°__.

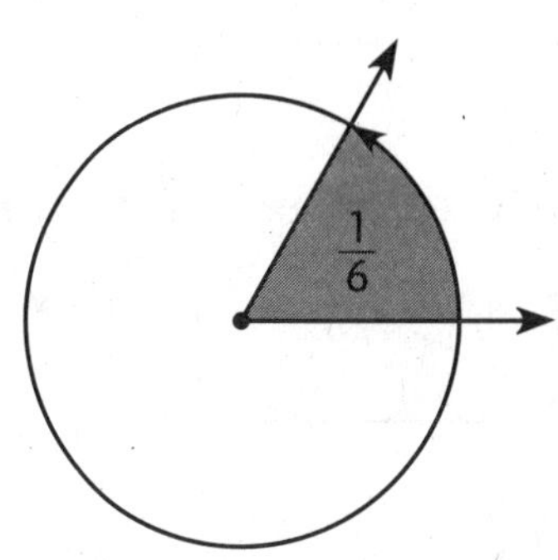

Tell the measure of the angle in degrees.

1.

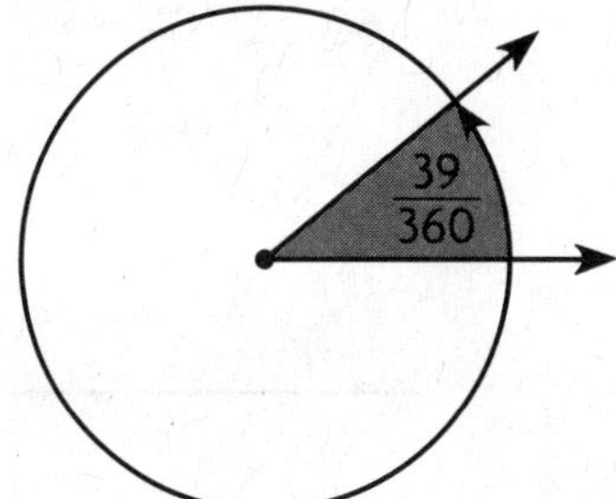

______

2.

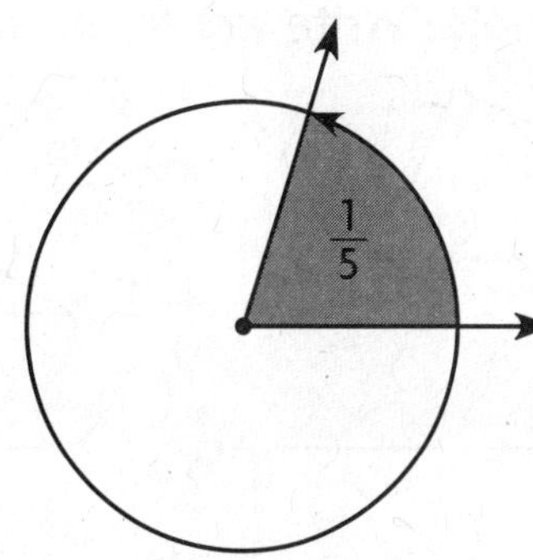

______

3.

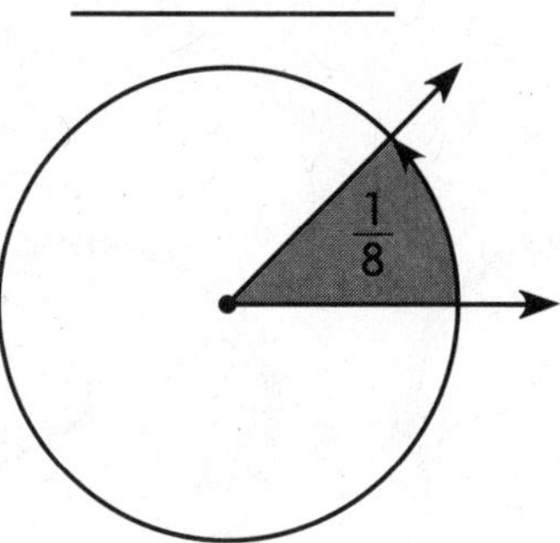

______

4.

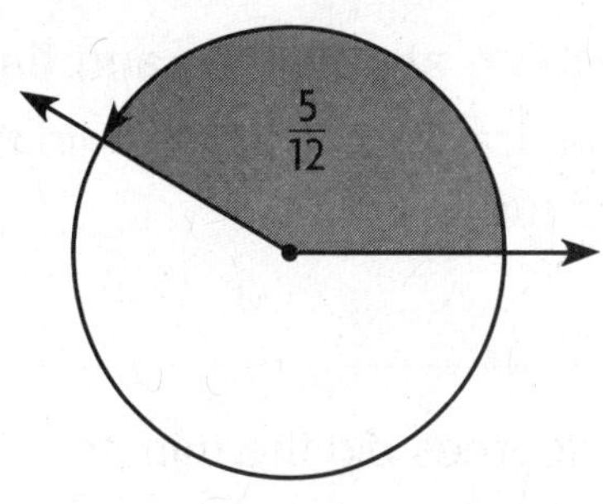

______

Name ______________________________

Degrees

Tell the measure of the angle in degrees.

1. 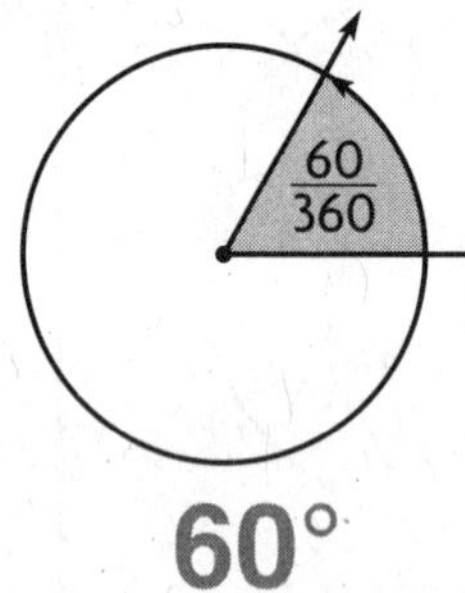

60°

2. 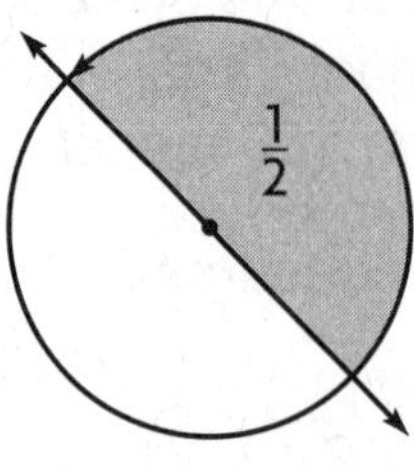

____

3. 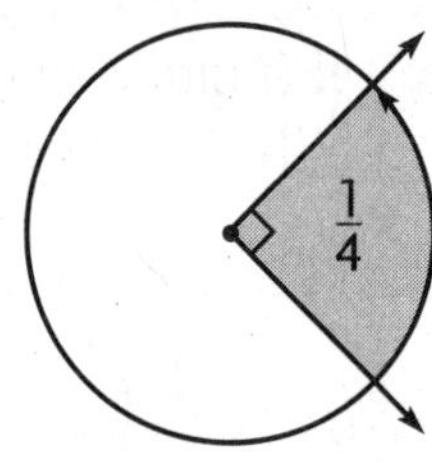

____

Classify the angle. Write *acute, obtuse, right,* or *straight.*

4. 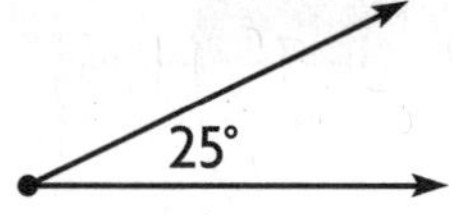

____

5. 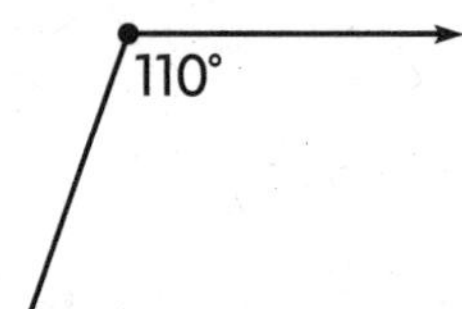

____

6. 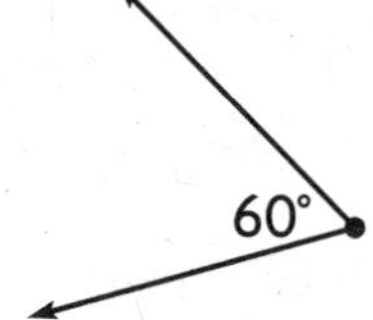

____

Classify the triangle. Write *acute, obtuse,* or *right.*

7. 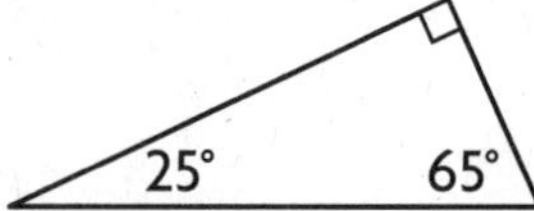

____

8. 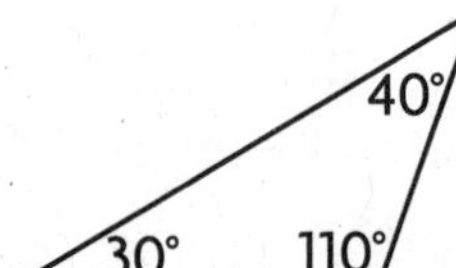

____

9. 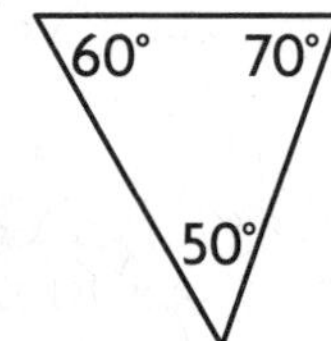

____

Problem Solving REAL WORLD

Ann started reading at 4:00 P.M. and finished at 4:20 P.M.

10. Through what fraction of a circle did the minute hand turn?

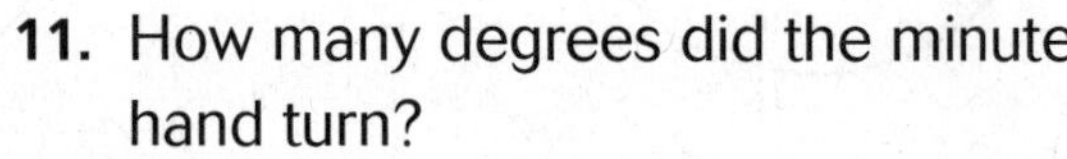

11. How many degrees did the minute hand turn?

____

Name ______________________________

Measure and Draw Angles

Lesson 95

COMMON CORE STANDARD CC.4.MD.6

Lesson Objective: Use a protractor to measure an angle and to draw an angle with a given measure.

A **protractor** is a tool for measuring the size of an angle.

Follow the steps below to measure ∠*ABC*.

Step 1 Place the center point of the protractor on vertex *B* of the angle.

Step 2 Align the 0° mark on the protractor with ray *BC*. Note that the 0° mark is on the outer scale or top scale.

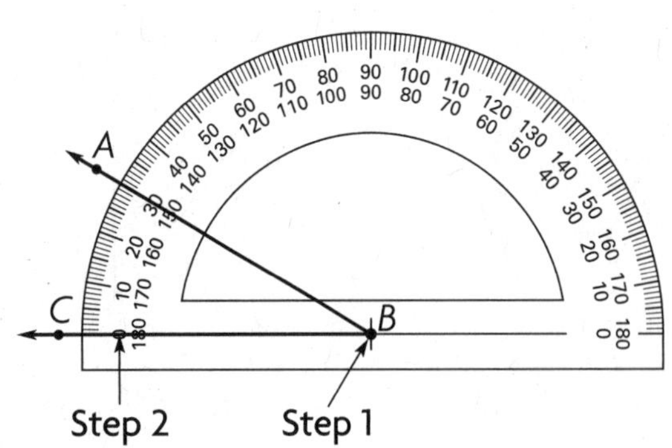

Step 3 Find where ray *BA* intersects the same scale.

Step 4 Read the angle measure on the scale.

The m∠*ABC* = 30°.

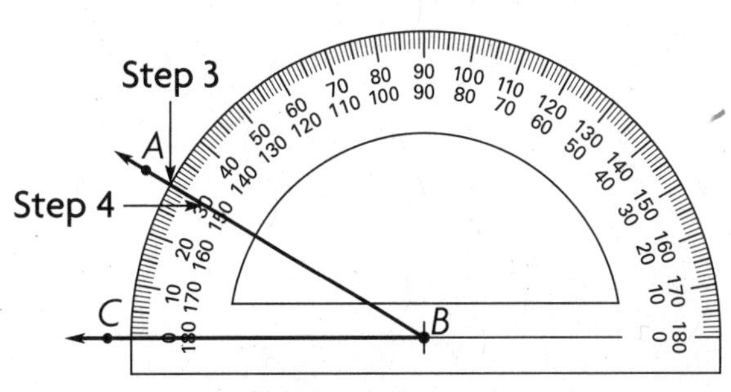

Use a protractor to find the angle measure.

1.

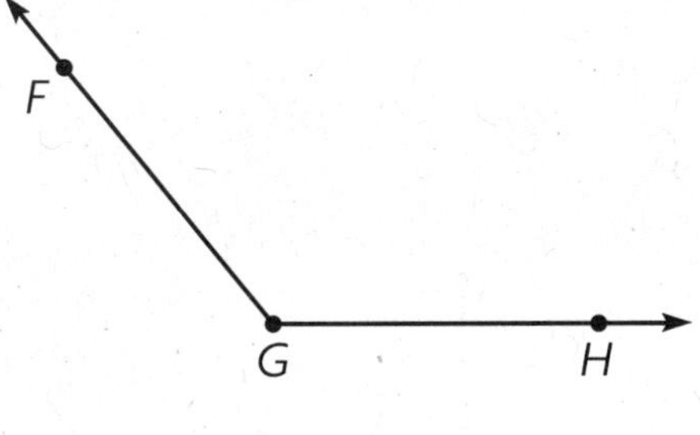

m∠*FGH* __________

2.

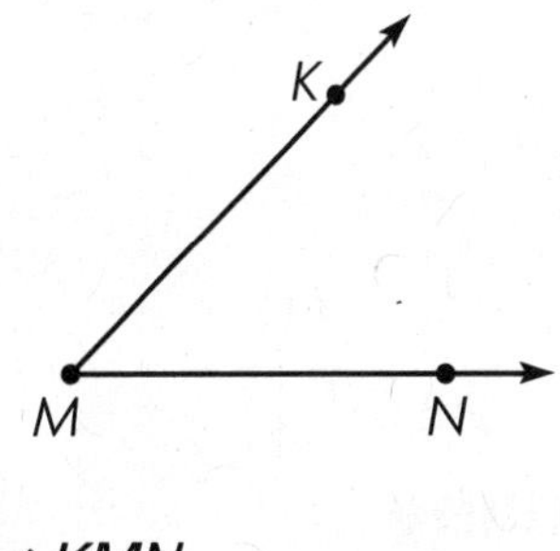

m∠*KMN* __________

Use a protractor to draw the angle.

3. 110°

4. 55°

Name ___________________________

Measure and Draw Angles

Use a protractor to find the angle measure.

1. 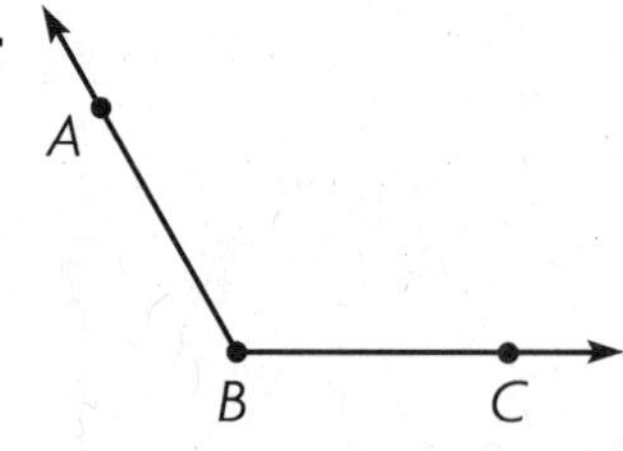

m∠ABC = 120°

2. 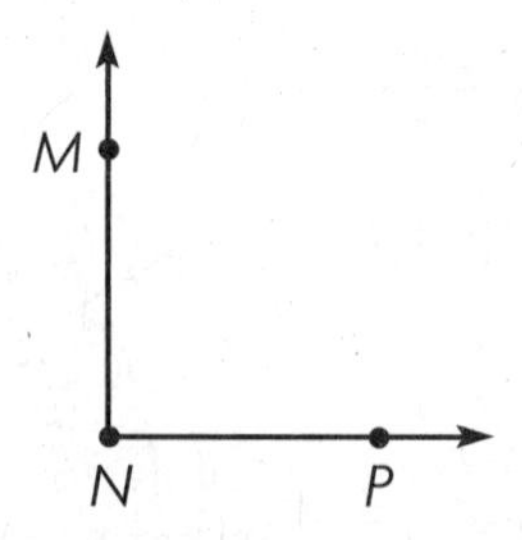

m∠MNP = __________

3. 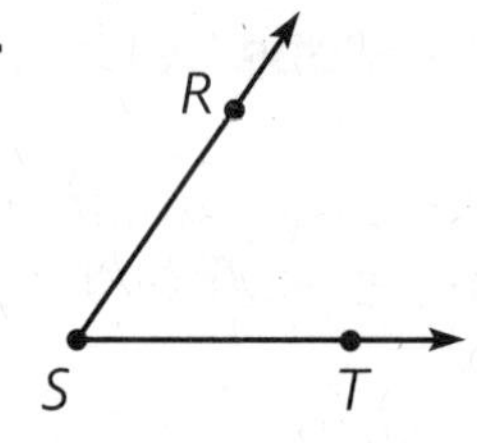

m∠RST = __________

Use a protractor to draw the angle.

4. 40°

5. 170°

Draw an example of each. Label the angle with its measure.

6. a right angle

7. an acute angle

Problem Solving REAL WORLD

The drawing shows the angles a stair tread makes with a support board along a wall. Use your protractor to measure the angles.

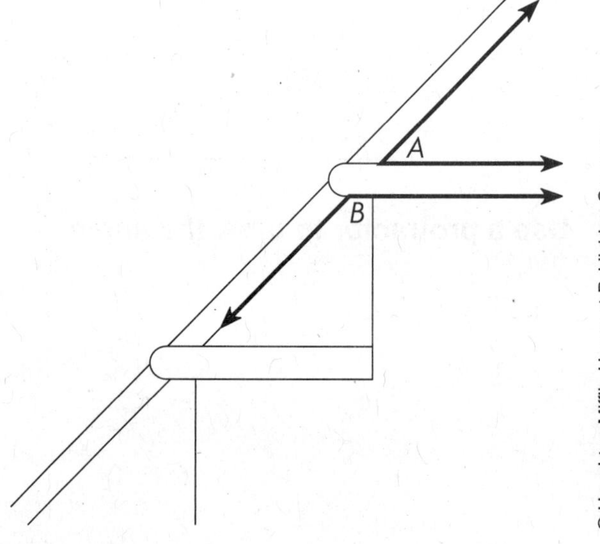

8. What is the measure of ∠A? __________

9. What is the measure of ∠B? __________

Name ______________________________

Lesson 96

COMMON CORE STANDARD CC.4.MD.7

Lesson Objective: Determine the measure of an angle separated into parts.

Join and Separate Angles

The measure of an angle equals the sum of the measures of its parts.

Use your protractor and the angles at the right.

Step 1 Measure $\angle ABC$ and $\angle CBD$. Record the measures.

$m\angle ABC$ = **35°**; $m\angle CBD$ = **40°**

Step 2 Find the sum of the measures.

35° + **40°** = **75°**

Step 3 Measure $\angle ABD$. Record the measure.

$m\angle ABD$ = **75°**

So, $m\angle ABC + m\angle CBD = m\angle ABD$.

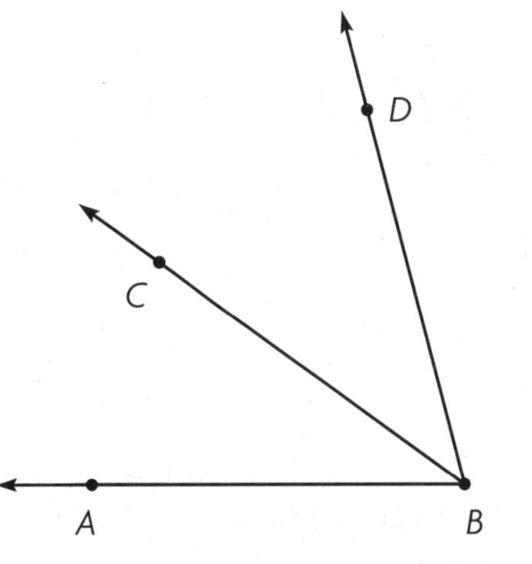

Add to find the measure of the angle. Write an equation to record your work.

1.

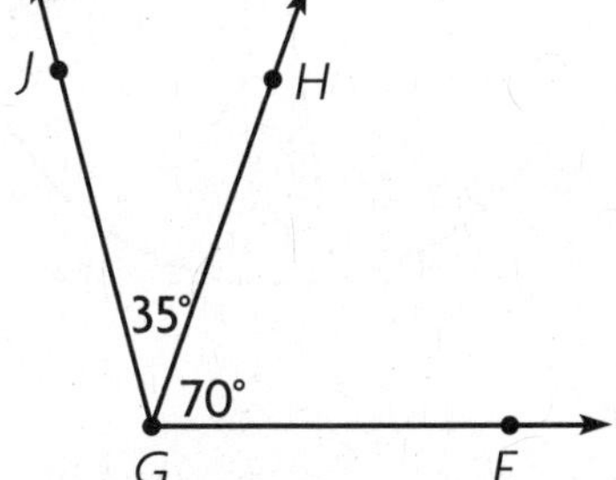

____

$m\angle EGJ$ = __________

2.

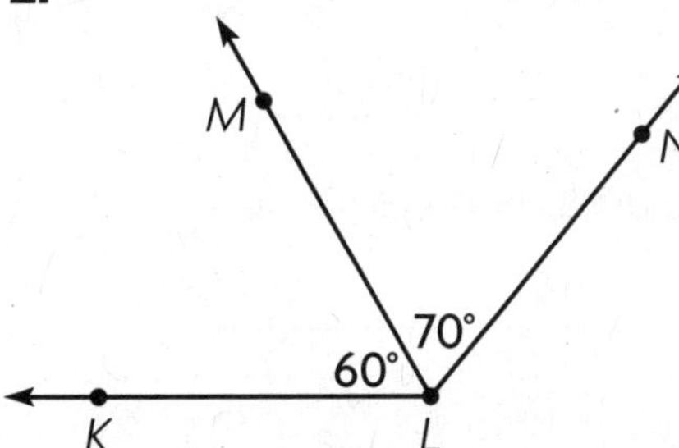

____

$m\angle KLN$ = __________

3.

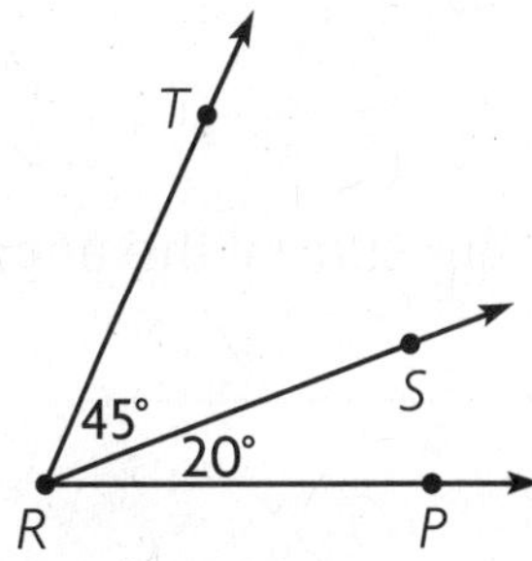

____

$m\angle PRT$ = __________

Use a protractor and the art at the right.

4. Find the measure of each angle. Label each angle with its measure.

5. Write the sum of the angle measures as an equation.

____

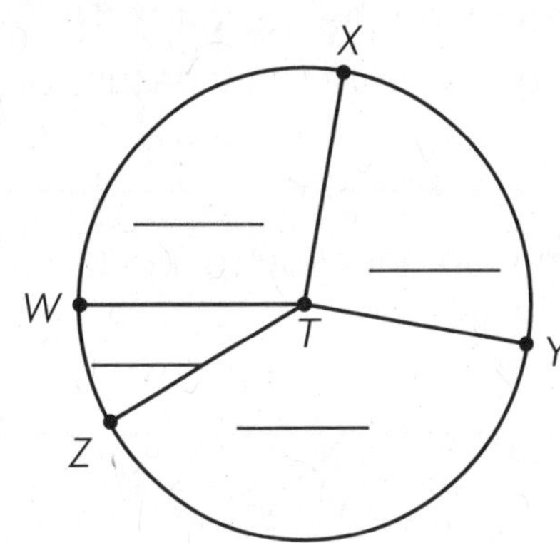

Name ______________________________

Join and Separate Angles

Add to find the measure of the angle. Write an equation to record your work.

1.

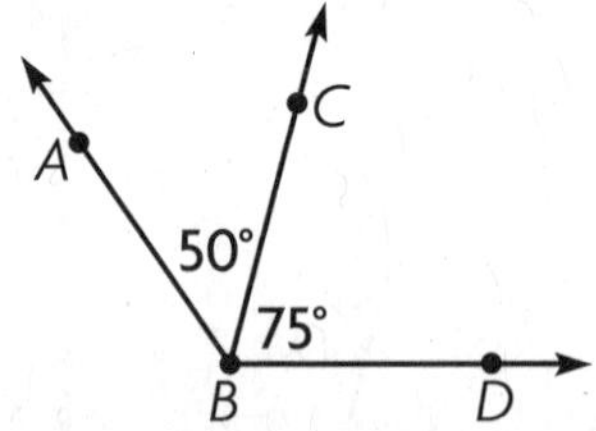

$50° + 75° = 125°$

m∠*ABD* = 125°

2.

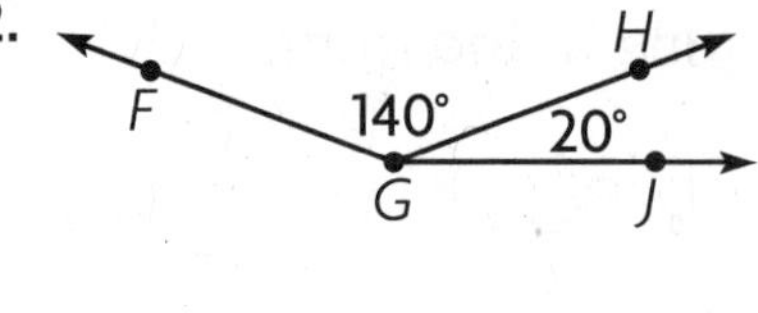

____

m∠*FGJ* = __________

3.

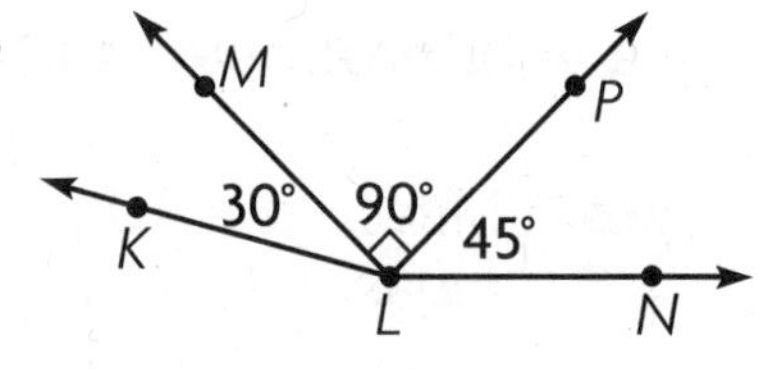

____

m∠*KLN* = __________

Use a protractor to find the measure of each angle in the circle.

4. m∠*ABC* = __________

5. m∠*DBE* = __________

6. m∠*CBD* = __________

7. m∠*EBA* = __________

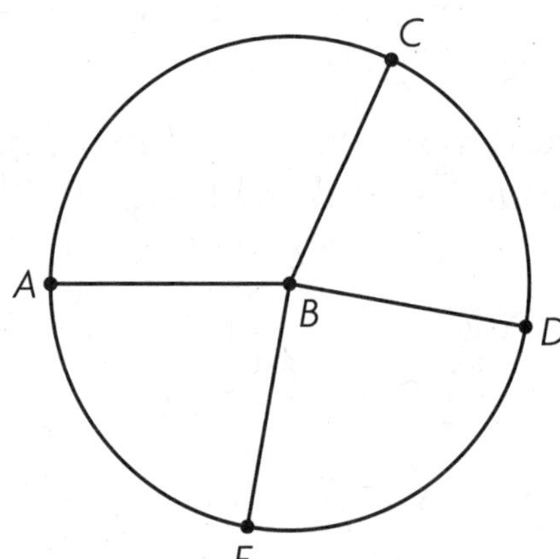

8. Write the sum of the angle measures as an equation.

____

Problem Solving REAL WORLD

9. Ned made the design at the right. Use a protractor. Find and write the measure of each of the 3 angles.

____

10. Write an equation to find the measure of the total angle.

____

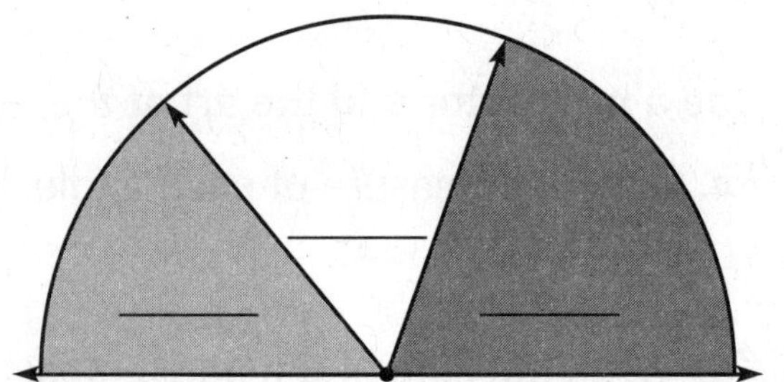

Name ______________________

Lesson 97

COMMON CORE STANDARD CC.4.MD.7

Lesson Objective: Use the strategy *draw a diagram* to solve angle measurement problems.

Problem Solving • Unknown Angle Measures

Use the strategy *draw a diagram.*

Mrs. Allen is cutting a piece of wood for a set for the school play. She needs a piece of wood with a 60° angle. After the cut, what is the angle measure of the part left over?

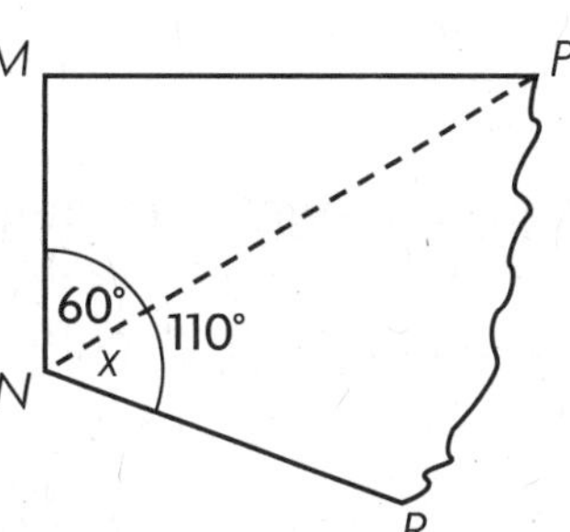

Read the Problem

What do I need to find?	What information do I need to use?	How will I use the information?
I need to find the angle measure of the part left over, or m∠*PNR*.	I can use the angle measures I know: m∠*MNP* = 60° and m∠*MNR* = 110°.	I can draw a bar model to find the unknown angle measure, or m∠*PNR*.

Solve the Problem

I can draw a bar model to represent the problem.

Then I can write an equation to solve the problem.

m∠*MNP* + m∠*PNR* = m∠*MNR*

60° + x = 110°

x = 110° − 60°, or 50°

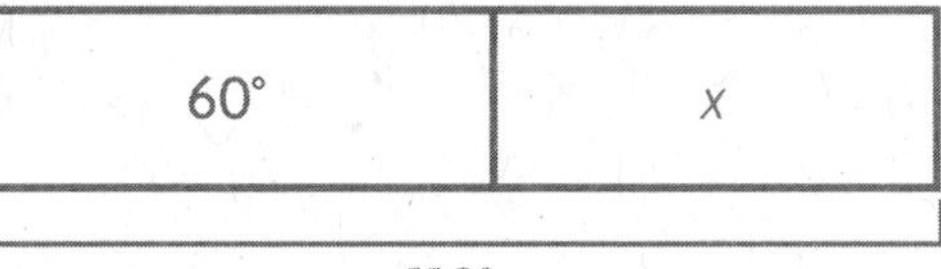

So, m∠*PNR* = 50°

The angle measure of the part left over is 50°.

1. Cal is cutting a rectangular board as shown. What is the angle measure of the part left over? ______

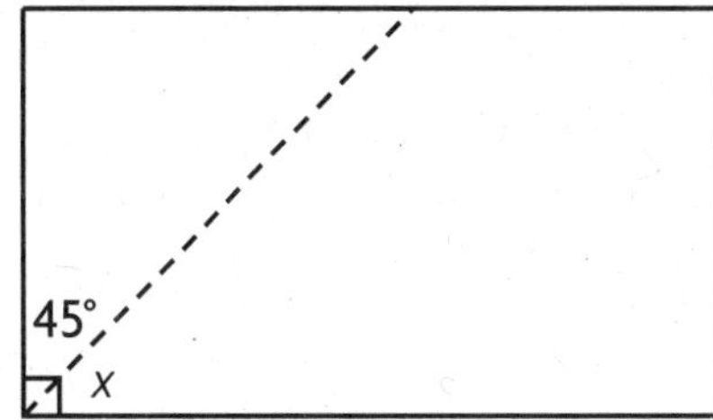

2. What equation did you use to solve?

____

Name ______________________

Problem Solving • Unknown Angle Measures

Lesson 97
CC.4.MD.7

Solve each problem. Draw a diagram to help.

1. Wayne is building a birdhouse. He is cutting a board as shown. What is the angle measure of the piece left over?

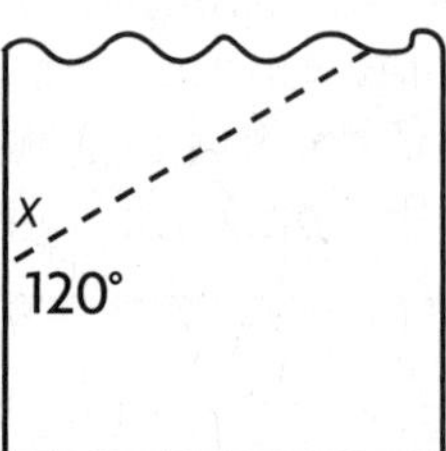

Draw a bar model to represent the problem.

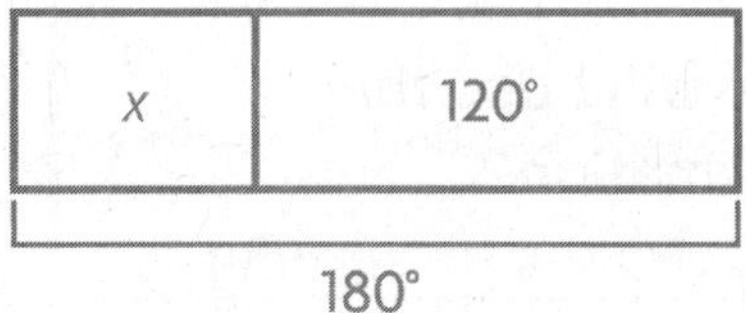

$x + 120° = 180°$

$x = 180° - 120°$

$x = 60°$

60°

2. An artist is cutting a piece of metal as shown. What is the angle measure of the piece left over?

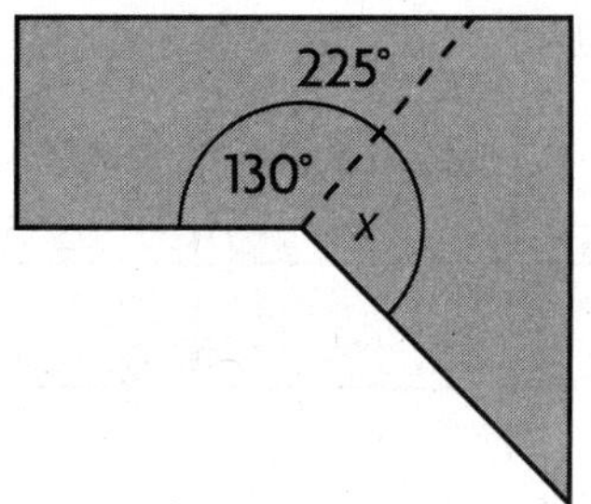

____

3. Joan has a piece of material for making a costume. She needs to cut it as shown. What is the angle measure of the piece left over?

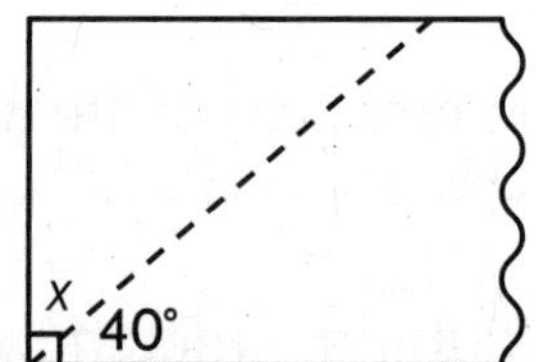

____

Name ______________________

COMMON CORE STANDARD CC.4.G.1

Lesson Objective: Identify and draw points, lines, line segments, rays, and angles.

Lines, Rays, and Angles

Name	What it looks like	Think
point *D*	*D* •	A **point** names a location in space.
line *AB*; $\overleftrightarrow{AB}$ line *BA*; $\overleftrightarrow{BA}$	*A* *B*	A **line** extends without end in opposite directions.
line segment *AB*; $\overline{AB}$ line segment *BA*; $\overline{BA}$	*A* *B*	"Segment" means part. A **line segment** is part of a line. It is named by its two endpoints.
ray *MN*; $\overrightarrow{MN}$ ray *NM*; $\overrightarrow{NM}$	*M* *N* *M* *N*	A **ray** has one endpoint and extends without end in one direction. A ray is named using two points. The endpoint is always named first.
angle *XYZ*; ∠*XYZ* angle *ZYX*; ∠*ZYX* angle *Y*; ∠*Y*	*X* *Y* *Z*	Two rays or line segments that share an endpoint form an angle. The shared point is the vertex of the angle.

A **right angle** forms a square corner.

An **acute angle** opens less than a right angle.

An **obtuse angle** opens more than a right angle and less than a straight angle.

A **straight angle** forms a line.

Draw and label an example of the figure.

1. $\overline{PQ}$

2. $\overrightarrow{KJ}$

3. obtuse ∠*FGH*

Name ______________________________

Lesson 98

CC.4.G.1

Lines, Rays, and Angles

Draw and label an example of the figure.

1. obtuse $\angle ABC$

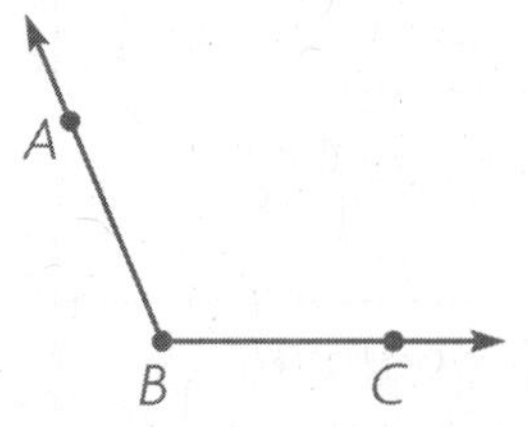

Think: An obtuse angle is greater than a right angle. The middle letter, B, names the vertex of the angle.

2. $\overrightarrow{GH}$

3. acute $\angle JKL$

4. $\overline{BC}$

Use the figure for 5–8.

5. Name a line segment. ______________________

6. Name a right angle. ______________________

7. Name an obtuse angle. ______________________

8. Name a ray. ______________________

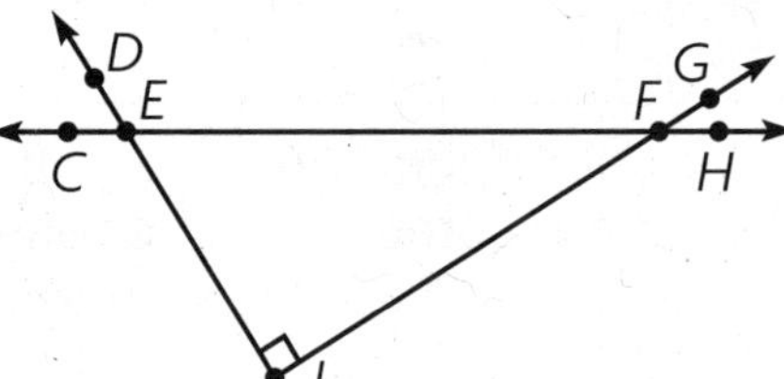

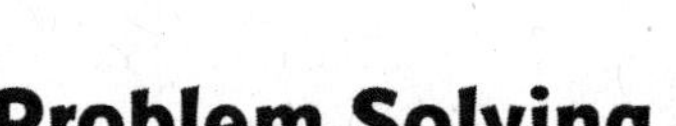

Problem Solving

Use the figure at the right for 9–11.

9. Classify $\angle AFD$. ______________________

10. Classify $\angle CFE$. ______________________

11. Name two acute angles.

____

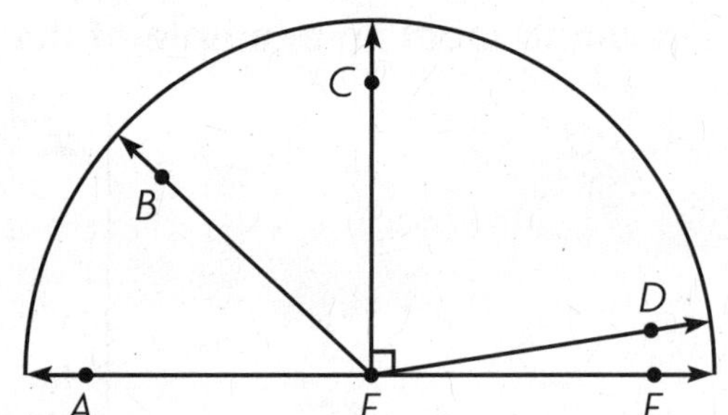

Name ____________________

COMMON CORE STANDARD CC.4.G.1

Lesson Objective: Identify and draw parallel lines and perpendicular lines.

Parallel Lines and Perpendicular Lines

Parallel lines are lines in a plane that are always the same distance apart. Parallel lines or line segments never meet.

In the figure, lines *AB* and *CD*, even if extended, will never meet.
The lines are parallel. Write $\overleftrightarrow{AB} \parallel \overleftrightarrow{CD}$.
Lines __AD__ and __BC__ are also parallel. So, $\overleftrightarrow{AD} \parallel \overleftrightarrow{BC}$.

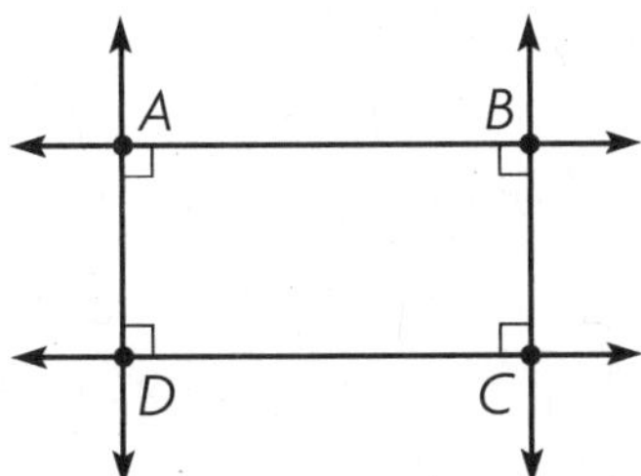

Intersecting lines cross at exactly one point. Intersecting lines that form right angles are **perpendicular.**

In the figure, lines __AD__ and __AB__ are perpendicular because they form right angles at vertex *A*. Write $\overleftrightarrow{AD} \perp \overleftrightarrow{AB}$.

Lines __BC__ and __CD__ are also perpendicular. So, $\overleftrightarrow{BC} \perp \overleftrightarrow{CD}$.

Use the figure for 1–3.

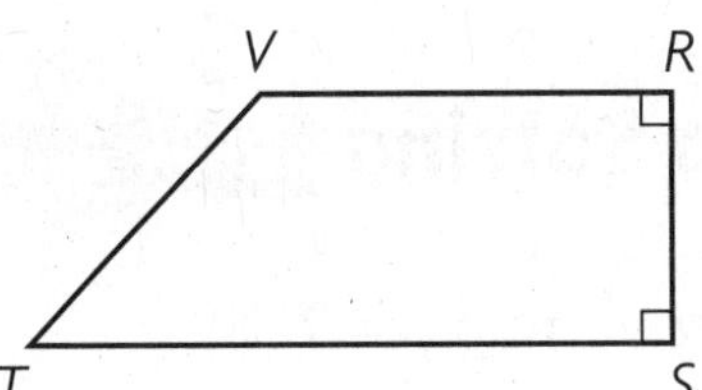

1. Name two sides that appear to be parallel.

   ____

2. Name two sides that appear to be perpendicular.

   ____

3. Name two sides that appear to be intersecting, but not perpendicular.

   ____

Name ________________________________

Parallel Lines and Perpendicular Lines

Use the figure for 1–3.

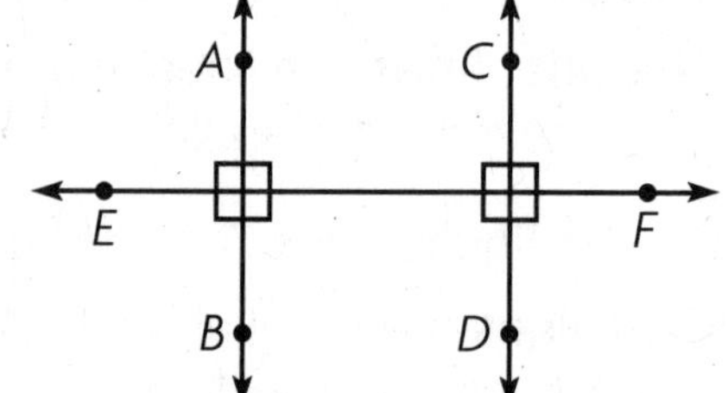

1. Name a pair of lines that appear to be perpendicular.

   Think: Perpendicular lines form right angles. $\overleftrightarrow{AB}$ and $\overleftrightarrow{EF}$ appear to form right angles.

   $\overleftrightarrow{AB}$ and $\overleftrightarrow{EF}$

2. Name a pair of lines that appear to be parallel.

   ____

3. *Name another pair of lines that appear to be perpendicular.*

   ____

Draw and label the figure described.

4. $\overleftrightarrow{MN}$ and $\overleftrightarrow{PQ}$ intersecting at point R

5. $\overleftrightarrow{WX} \parallel \overleftrightarrow{YZ}$

6. $\overleftrightarrow{FH} \perp \overleftrightarrow{JK}$

Problem Solving

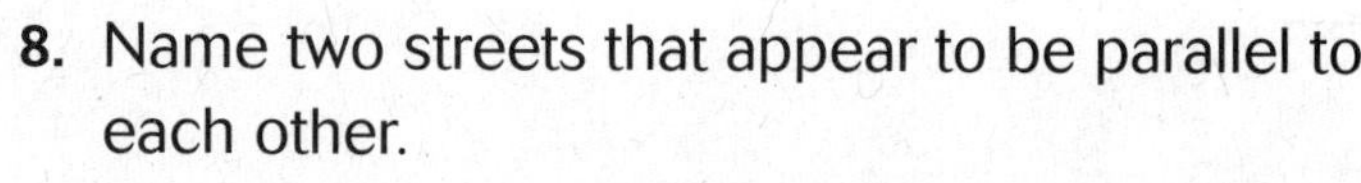

Use the street map for 7–8.

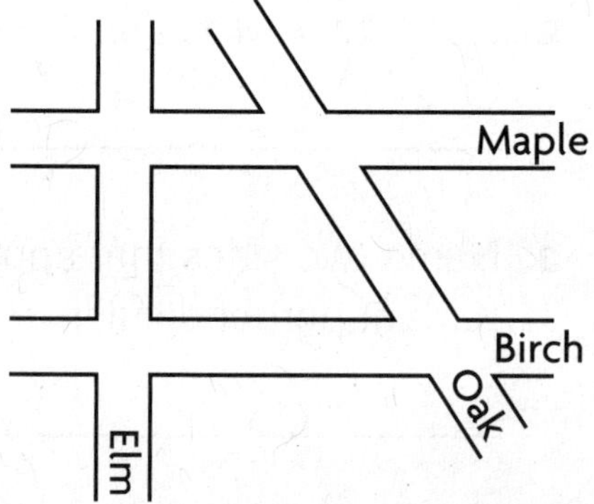

7. Name two streets that intersect but do not appear to be perpendicular.

   ____

   ____

8. Name two streets that appear to be parallel to each other.

   ____

Name ___________________________

Classify Triangles

COMMON CORE STANDARD CC.4.G.2

Lesson Objective: Classify triangles by the size of their angles.

A **triangle** is a polygon with __3__ sides and __3__ angles.
Each pair of sides joins at a vertex.

You can name a triangle by its vertices.

ΔPQR	ΔQRP	ΔRPQ
ΔPRQ	ΔQPR	ΔRQP

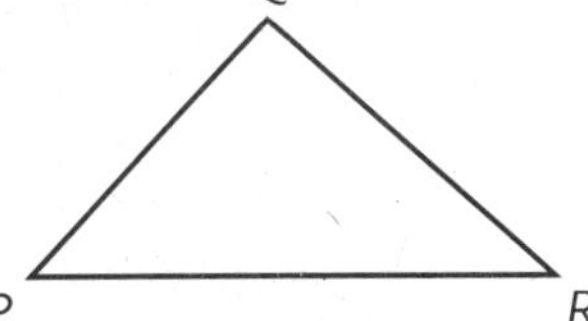

There are __3__ types of triangles. All triangles have at least __2__ acute angles.

Obtuse triangle
one obtuse angle

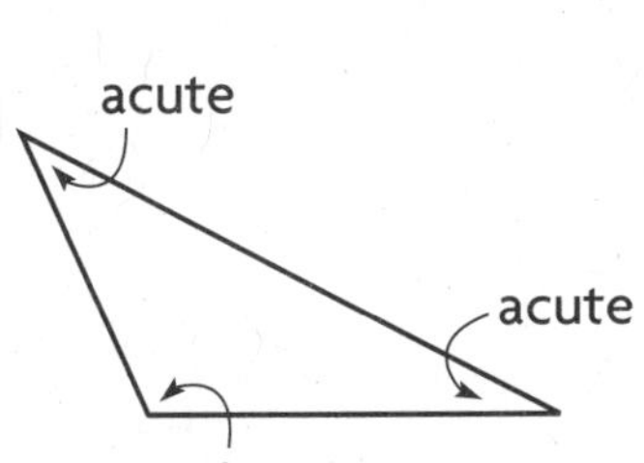

Right triangle
one right angle

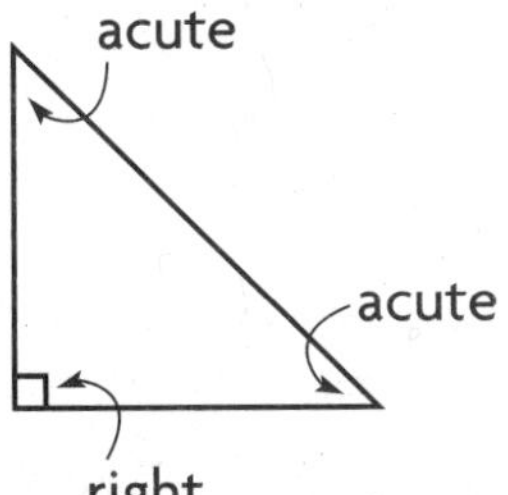

Acute triangle
three acute angles

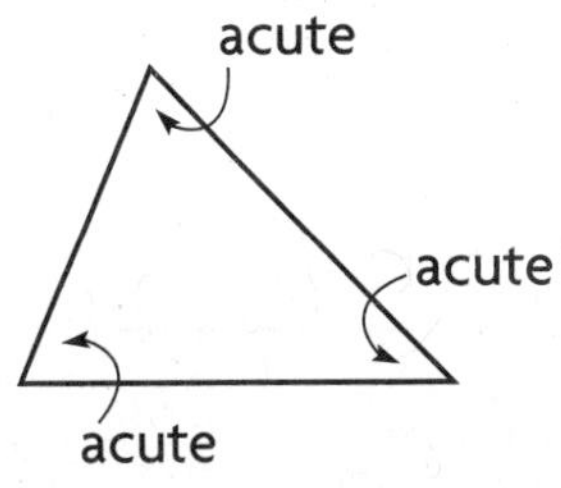

1. Name the triangle. Tell whether each angle is *acute*, *right*, or *obtuse*. A name for the triangle is ____________.

$\angle X$ is ____________.

$\angle Y$ is ____________.

$\angle Z$ is ____________.

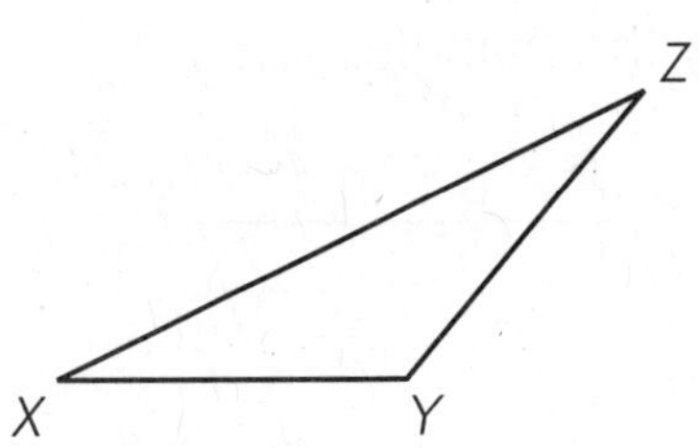

Classify each triangle. Write *acute*, *right*, or *obtuse*.

2.

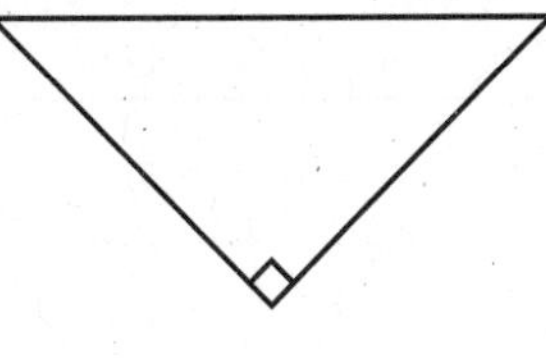

____

3.

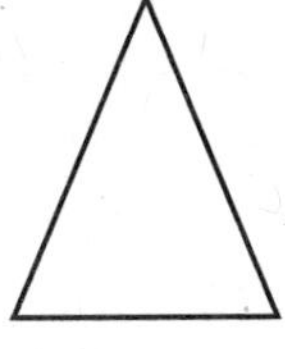

____

4.

____

Name ______________________

Classify Triangles

Classify each triangle. Write *acute, right,* or *obtuse.*

1. 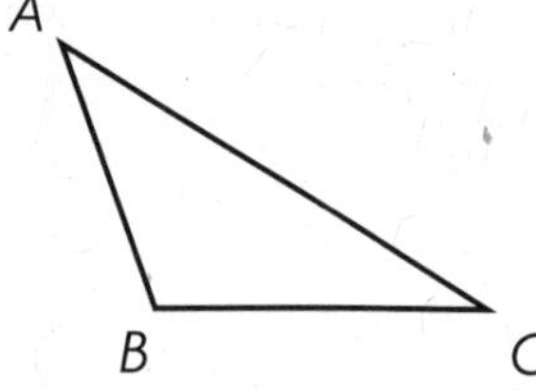

Think: Angles *A* and *C* are both acute.
Angle *B* is obtuse.

obtuse

2. 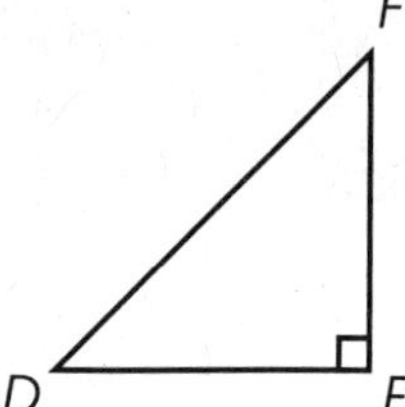

3. 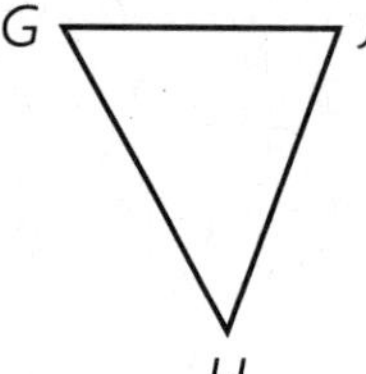

4. 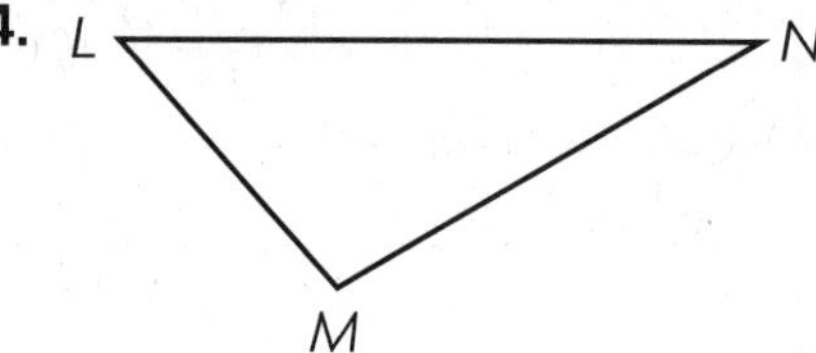

______________ ______________ ______________

Problem Solving REAL WORLD

5. Use figure *ABCD* below. Draw a line segment from point *B* to point *D*. Name and classify the triangles formed.

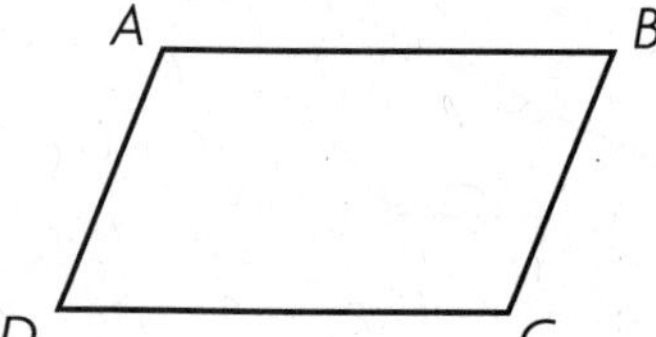

____
____
____

6. Use figure *ABCD* below. Draw a line segment from point *A* to point *C*. Name and classify the triangles formed.

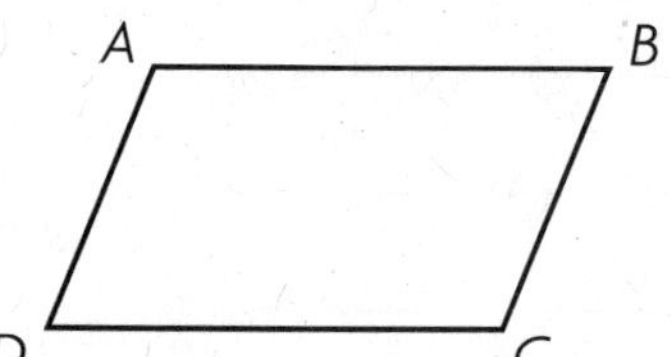

____
____
____

Name ______________________

COMMON CORE STANDARD CC.4.G.2

Lesson Objective: Sort and classify quadrilaterals.

Classify Quadrilaterals

A **quadrilateral** is a polygon with __4__ sides and __4__ angles.
Some quadrilaterals have special names:

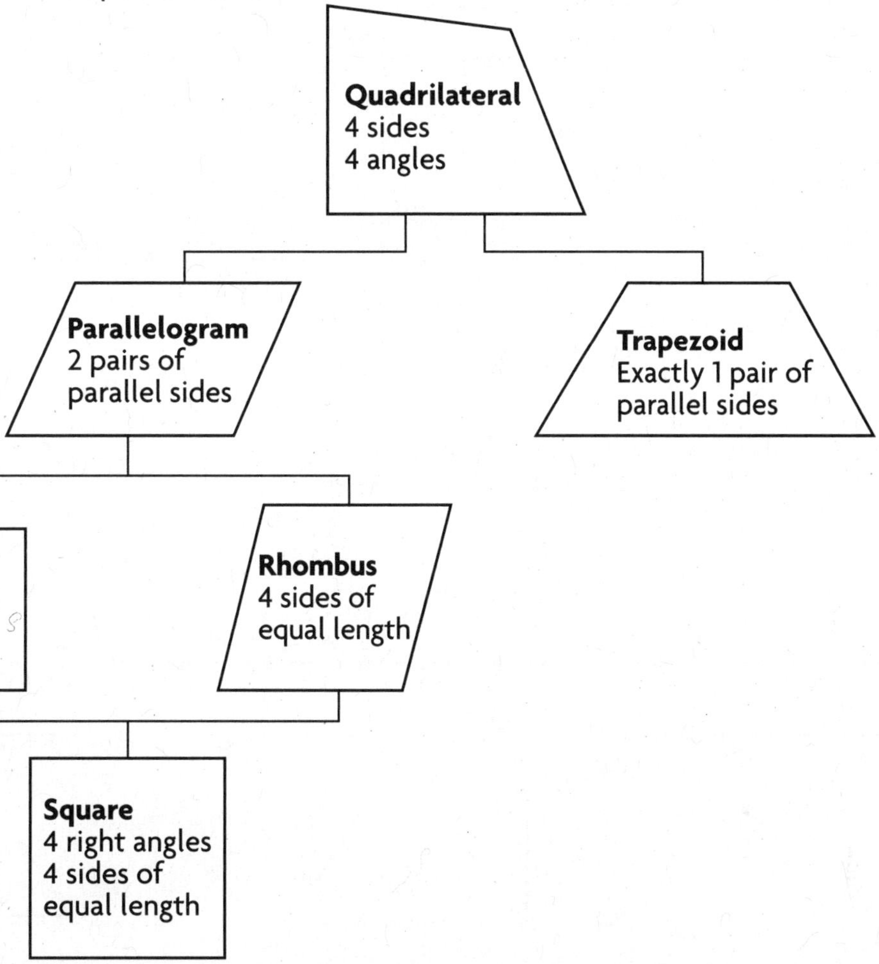

Quadrilateral
4 sides
4 angles

Parallelogram
2 pairs of parallel sides

Trapezoid
Exactly 1 pair of parallel sides

Rectangle
4 right angles
2 pairs of parallel sides

Rhombus
4 sides of equal length

Square
4 right angles
4 sides of equal length

Classify each figure as many ways as possible. Write *quadrilateral*, *trapezoid*, *parallelogram*, *rhombus*, *rectangle*, or *square*.

1.

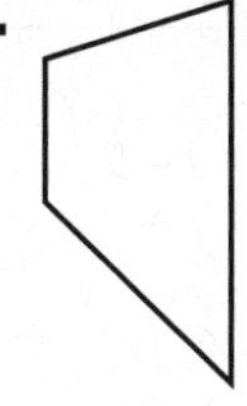

____
____
____
____

2.

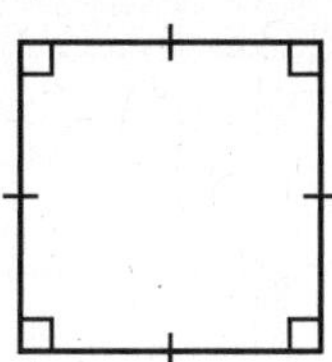

____
____
____
____

3.

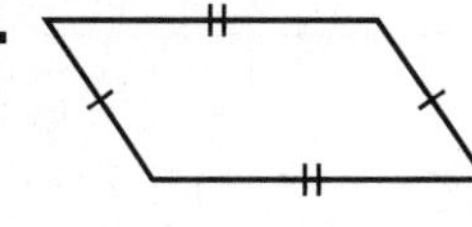

____
____
____
____

Name ______________________________

Lesson 101
CC.4.G.2

Classify Quadrilaterals

Classify each figure as many ways as possible. Write *quadrilateral, trapezoid, parallelogram, rhombus, rectangle, or square.*

1. 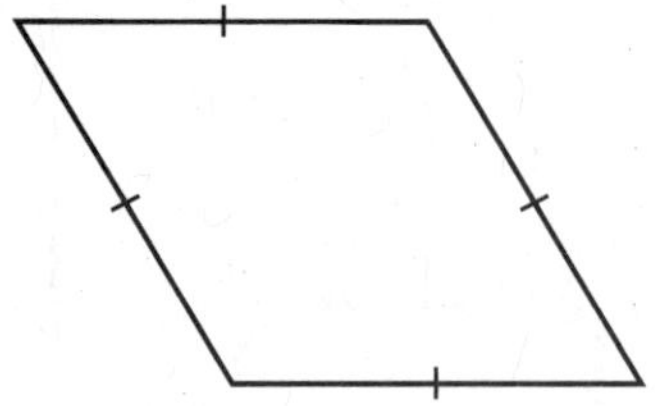

Think: 2 pairs of parallel sides
4 sides of equal length
0 right angles

quadrilateral, parallelogram, rhombus

2. 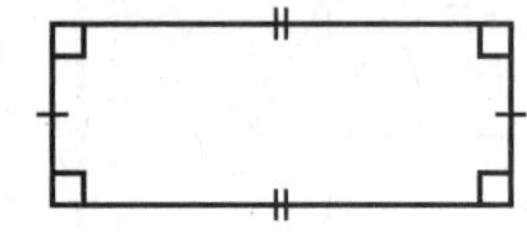

____

____

____

3. 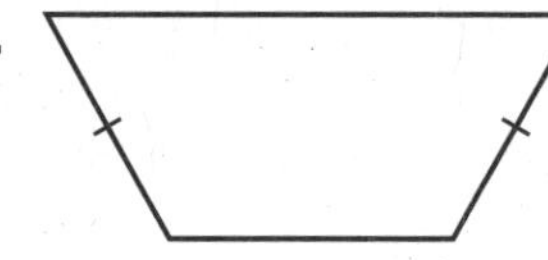

____

____

____

4. 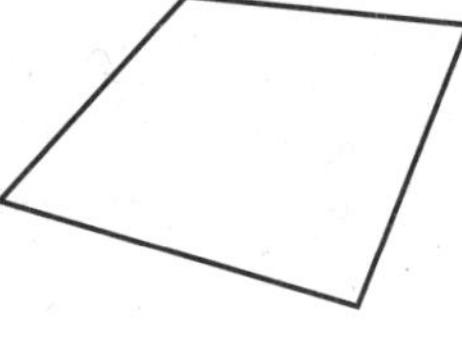

____

____

____

5. 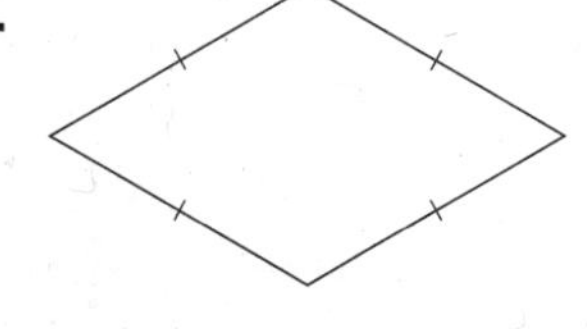

____

____

____

6. 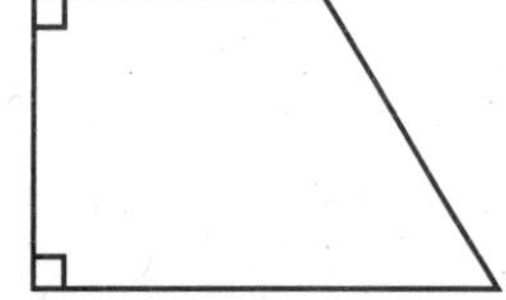

____

____

____

7. 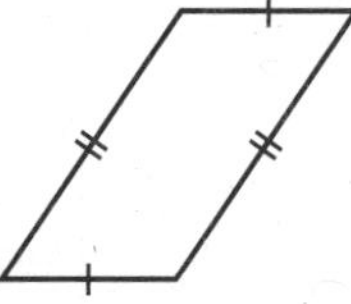

____

____

____

Problem Solving

8. Alan drew a polygon with four sides and four angles. All four sides are equal. None of the angles are right angles. What figure did Alan draw?

____

9. Teresa drew a quadrilateral with 2 pairs of parallel sides and 4 right angles. What quadrilateral could she have drawn?

____

Name ______________________________

COMMON CORE STANDARD CC.4.G.3

Lesson Objective: Determine whether a figure has a line of symmetry.

Line Symmetry

Tell whether the parts on each side of the line match. Is the line a line of symmetry?

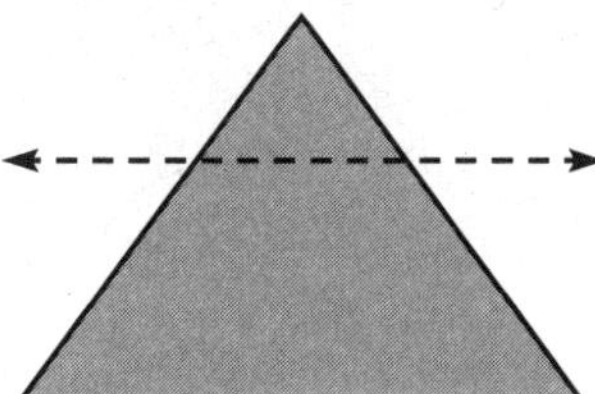

Step 1 Trace and cut out the shape.

Fold the shape along the dashed line.

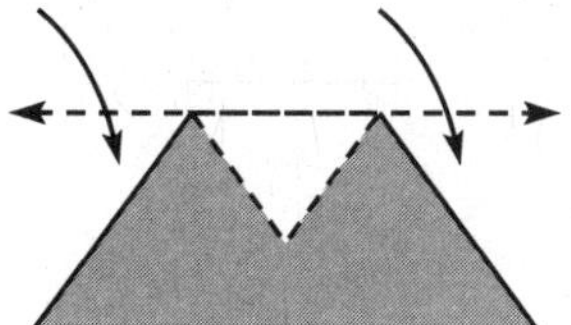

Step 2 Tell whether the parts on each side match.

Compare the parts on each side.

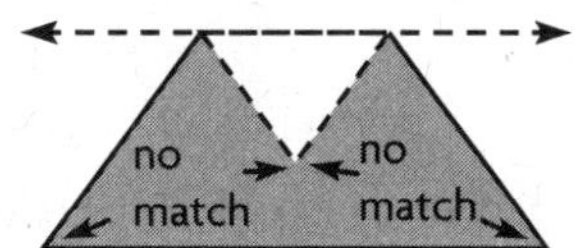

The parts do not match.

Step 3 Decide if the line is a line of symmetry.

The parts on each side of the line do not match.

So, the line **is not** a line of symmetry.

Tell if the line appears to be a line of symmetry. Write *yes* or *no*.

1.

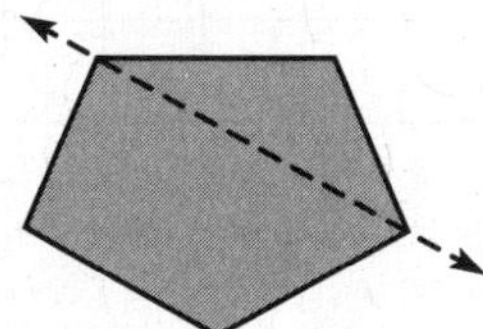

____

2.

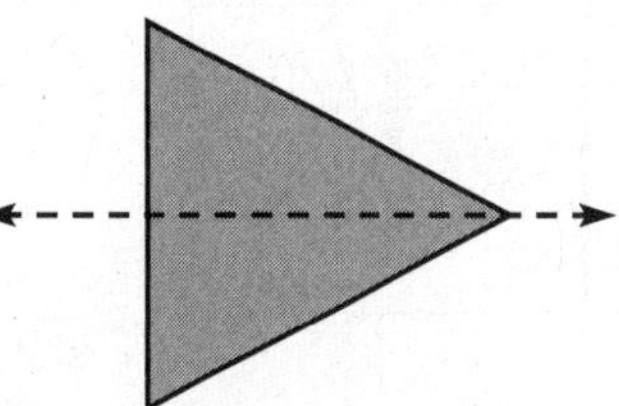

____

3.

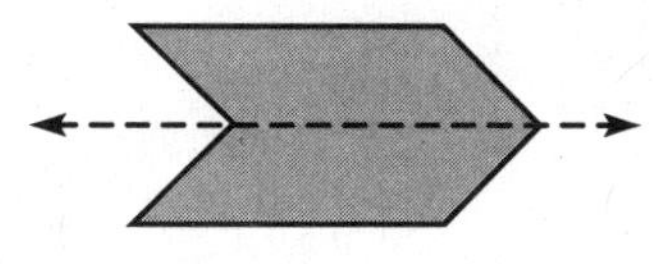

____

4.

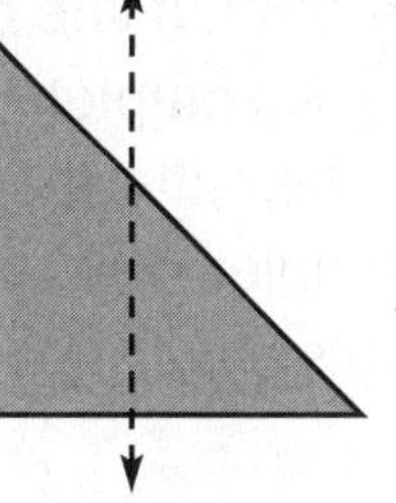

____

Name ___________________________

Lesson 102

CC.4.G.3

Line Symmetry

Tell if the dashed line appears to be a line of symmetry. Write *yes* or *no*.

1. 

yes

2. 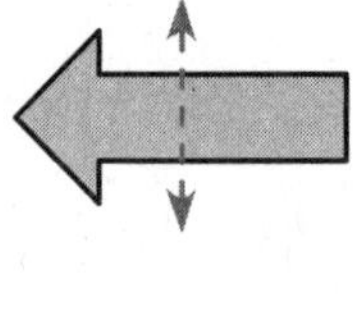

____

3. 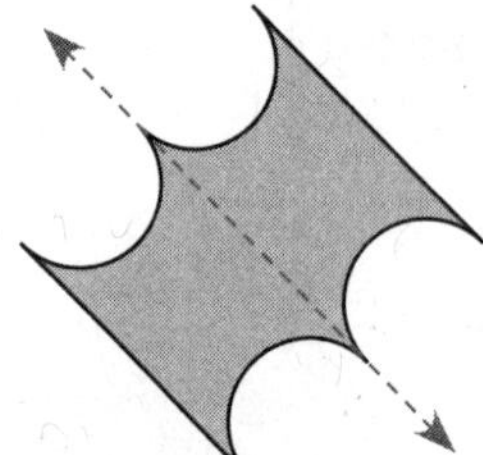

____

4. 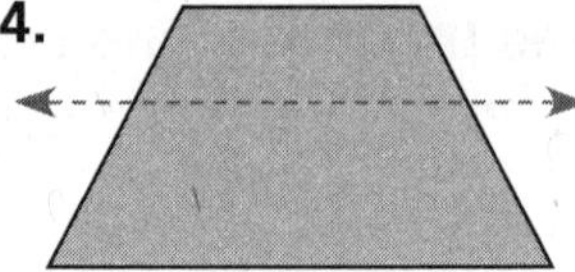

____

5. 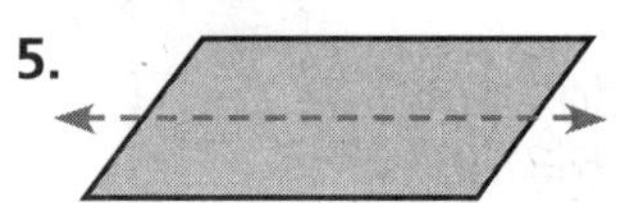

____

6. 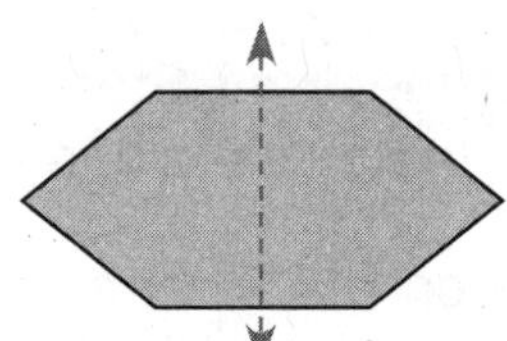

____

7. 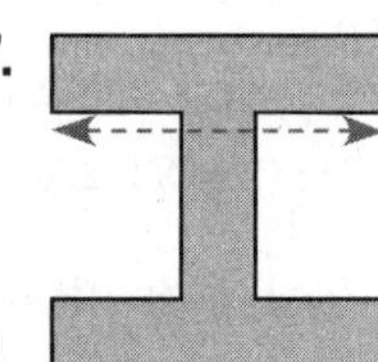

____

8. 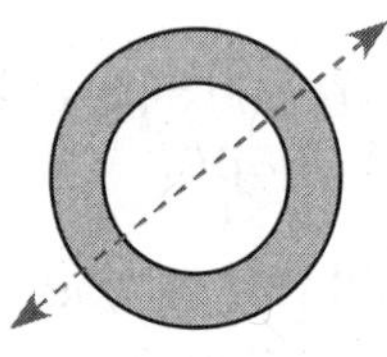

____

Complete the design by reflecting over the line of symmetry.

9. 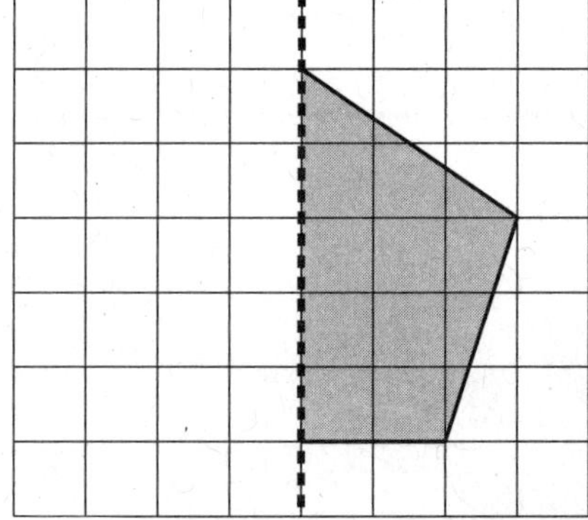

10. 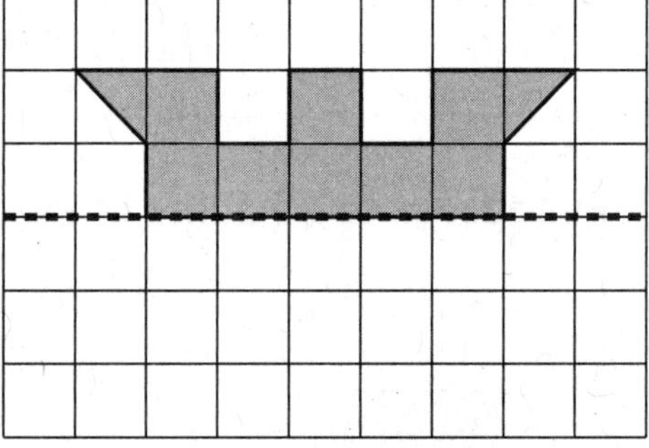

Problem Solving REAL WORLD

11. Kara uses the pattern at the right to make paper dolls. The dashed line represents a line of symmetry. A complete doll includes the reflection of the pattern over the line of symmetry. Complete the design to show what one of Kara's paper dolls looks like.

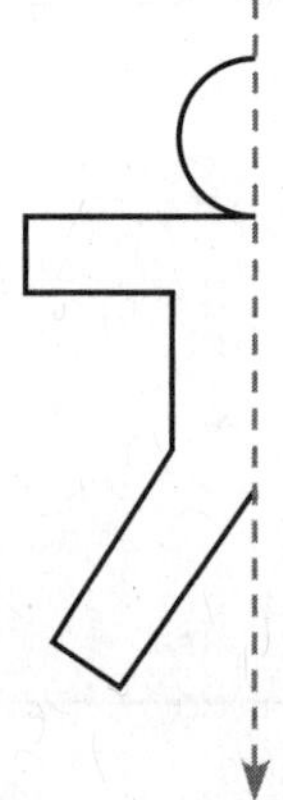

Name ____________________

COMMON CORE STANDARD CC.4.G.3

Lesson Objective: Identify and draw lines of symmetry in two-dimensional figures.

Find and Draw Lines of Symmetry

Tell whether the shape appears to have zero lines, 1 line, or more than 1 line of symmetry. Write *zero, 1,* or *more than 1*.

Step 1 Decide if the shape has a line of symmetry.

Trace and cut out the shape. Fold the shape along a vertical line.

Do the two parts match exactly? yes

Step 2 Decide if the shape has another line of symmetry.

Open the shape and fold it along a horizontal line.

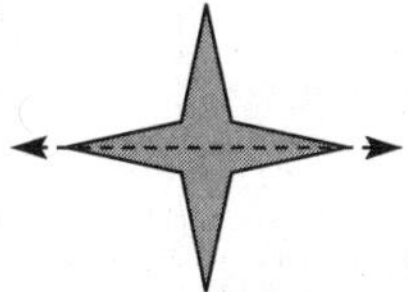

Do the two parts match exactly? yes

Step 3 Find any other lines of symmetry.

Think: Can I fold the shape in other ways so that the two parts match exactly?

I can fold the paper diagonally two different ways, and the parts match exactly.

So, the shape appears to have more than 1 line of symmetry.

Tell whether the shape appears to have zero lines, 1 line, or more than 1 line of symmetry. Write *zero, 1,* or *more than 1.*

1.

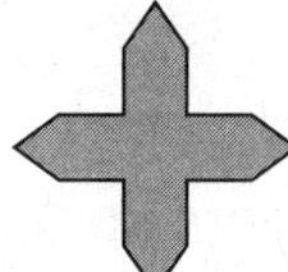

____

2.

____

3.

____

Name ______________________

Lesson 103
CC.4.G.3

Find and Draw Lines of Symmetry

Tell whether the shape appears to have zero lines, 1 line, or more than 1 line of symmetry. Write *zero, 1,* or *more than 1.*

1. 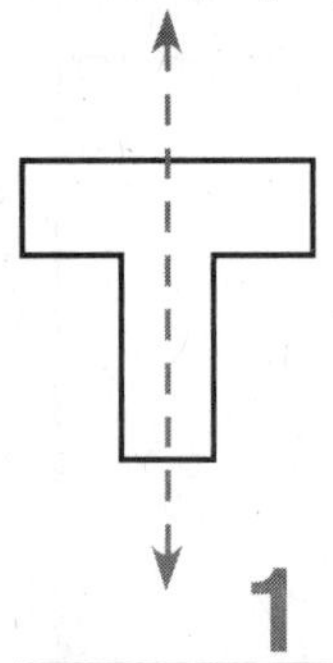
1

2. 
______

3. 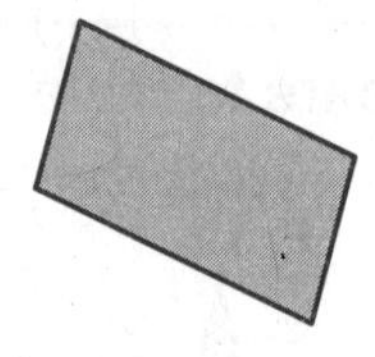
______

4. 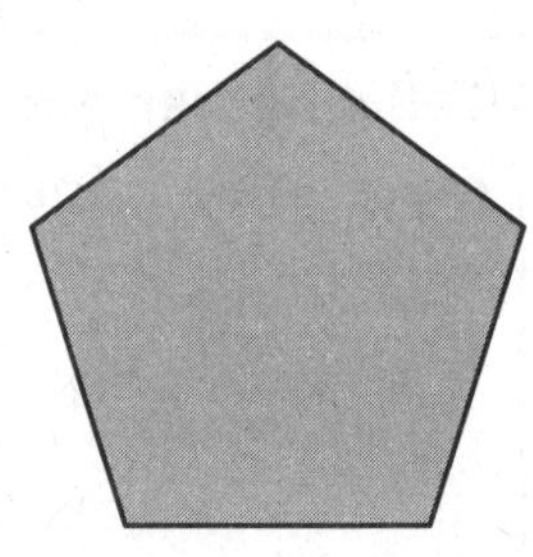
______

Does the design have line symmetry? Write *yes* or *no*. If your answer is yes, draw all lines of symmetry.

5. 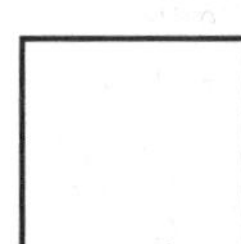
______

6. 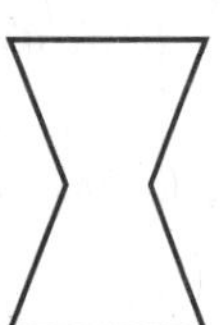
______

7. 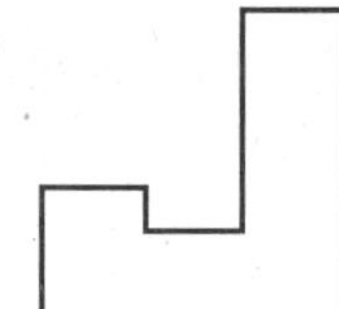
______

8. 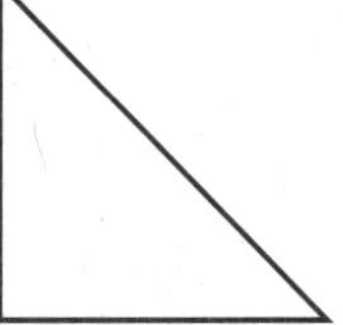
______

Draw a shape for the statement. Draw the line or lines of symmetry.

9. zero lines of symmetry

10. 1 line of symmetry

11. 2 lines of symmetry
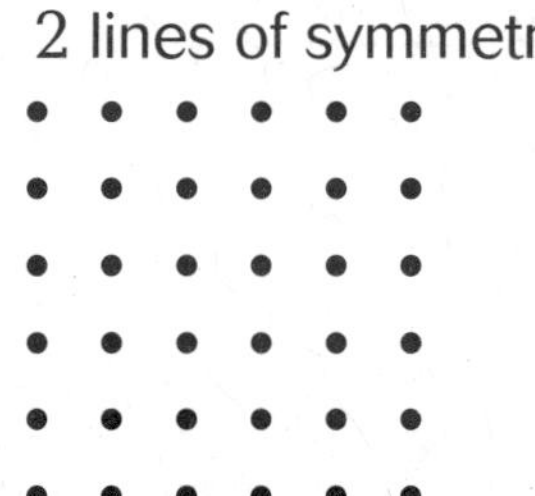

Problem Solving REAL WORLD

Use the chart for 12–13.

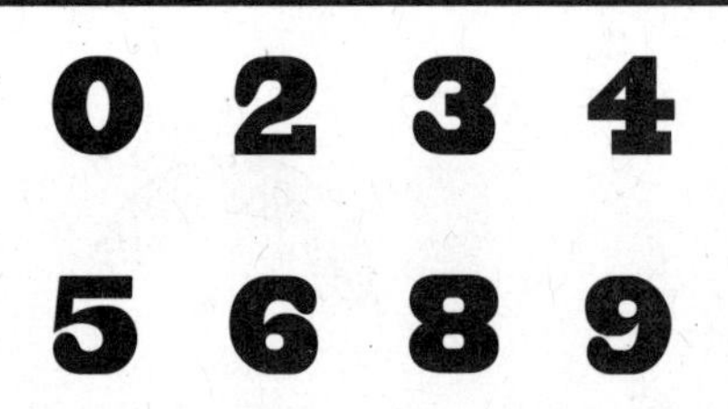

12. Which number or numbers appear to have only 1 line of symmetry?
______

13. Which number or numbers appear to have 2 lines of symmetry?
______